THE EXECUTION OF
OFFICER BECKER

THE EXECUTION OF OFFICER BECKER

The Murder of a Gambler, the Trial of a Cop, and the Birth of Organized Crime

STANLEY COHEN

CARROLL & GRAF PUBLISHERS
NEW YORK

THE EXECUTION OF OFFICER BECKER
The Murder of a Gambler, the Trial of a Cop, and the Birth of Organized Crime

Carroll & Graf Publishers
An Imprint of Avalon Publishing Group, Inc.
245 West 17th Street
11th Floor
New York, NY 10011

AVALON
publishing group incorporation

Library of Congress Cataloging-in-Publication Data is available.

ISBN-13: 978-0-78671-757-6
ISBN-10: 0-78671-757-2

9 8 7 6 5 4 3 2 1

DESIGNED BY PAULINE NEUWIRTH, NEUWIRTH AND ASSOCIATES, INC.

Printed in the United States of America
Distributed by Publishers Group West

CONTENTS

PROLOGUE

When Herman "Beansie" Rosenthal stepped out into the sweltering streets of downtown Manhattan that July night he had only a few hours left to live. It was nearing midnight, but the late hour offered no relief from the heat that had stifled the city for weeks during the summer of 1912. But Beansie was not much concerned with the weather. His mood was bright, and his step was easy. He had just left a late-night meeting with District Attorney Charles Whitman at the Criminal Courts building. They had discussed political graft and police corruption, and these were subjects Beansie knew a lot about. Illegal gambling houses in the Tenderloin District of midtown Manhattan, later known as Times Square, were doing business as openly as grocery stores. They were kept running by a mechanism of bribes and pay-offs that operated so smoothly it was referred to, quite simply, as the System. The police department appeared to be running the city government while the underworld ran the police department. That the System existed would come as no surprise to the district attorney. It was the most loosely kept secret in town, but no one was reckless enough to talk about it on the record; no one, that is, until Beansie Rosenthal.

Rosenthal was a small-time operator with big-time ambitions and a taste for the bright lights. He had begun his career as a bookmaker at local race tracks, then opened a succession of nondescript gambling houses on the Lower

East Side, only to have each of them shut down. He fared no better with a casino in Far Rockaway on Long Island. Finally, he decided to try his luck on Broadway, in the heart of the Tenderloin. Early in 1912, he opened the Hesper Club at 104 West Forty-fifth Street and prepared to compete with an array of other casinos in the area. On opening night, he was visited by an officer in New York City's police department, a Lieutenant Charles Becker, who explained how the System worked and what was expected of him. The two men were not strangers, and Rosenthal could not have been altogether surprised about what he heard. But it did not take long for his patience to wear thin. He resented having the police as managing partners in his casino. He had some political connections at Tammany Hall, which had run the city government for decades, and he thought they might afford him protection. But Beansie had taken his case to the wrong end of the power chain; Tammany was the engine that made the System run, and it would not soon interfere with how cops earned their living.

Finding no relief in political precincts, Rosenthal decided to up the ante. He told his story to the press, and from that point on there was no turning back. There were more than a dozen daily newspapers in New York at the time, and the competition among them was fierce. But the one that was ready to place the bet on the word of an underworld figure with an axe to grind was Joseph Pulitzer's *New York World*, where an aggressive young reporter by the name of Herbert Bayard Swope was more than eager to kick down any door that might show the way to the head of the pack.

On July 13, the *World* carried a long interview with Rosenthal in which he accused highly placed police officials of being on the take. A day later, he became more specific. The Sunday front page of the *World* carried verbatim an affidavit charging that Lieutenant Becker was the force that propelled the System. It said he was averaging $10,000 a month in payoffs and suggested that men even "higher up" were also riding the gravy train. The sworn statement earned Rosenthal a private meeting with the D.A. the following night. A man with ambitions of his own, Whitman listened carefully and told Rosenthal he would convene a grand jury to hear the case. Of course, Whitman was not the only interested party to take note of the published affidavit. Word spread quickly through the Tenderloin that Rosenthal was a man with a price on his head and a target on his back.

Beansie alone seemed to be unaware that he was walking into a future whose prospects were bleak. Thirty-eight years old, Rosenthal was a chunky, round-faced man who groomed himself carefully and dressed to catch the eye. His cuff links, tie pin, and belt buckle were made of gold with the initials H.R. prominently displayed. He was rather pleased with himself when he left the D.A.'s office that night. He walked down the long flight of stairs of the Criminal Courts building on Centre Street and began looking for a taxi. Even near midnight, it was too hot to walk. He removed his suit jacket and draped it over his arm. His collar was unbuttoned, and his necktie hung loose. His pink dress shirt was soaked with perspiration and billowed out above his belt. He hailed a cab at Pearl Street and directed the driver to take him uptown to Forty-second Street and Broadway. The cab moved through the night, and with the windows open wide the breeze felt good against the dampness of his shirt. Still, he was a bit edgy. He looked back occasionally to see if he was being followed, but after a few blocks he began to relax. When he exited the taxi, it was a short walk to the Metropole Café on Forty-third Street, just east of Broadway. The cafe was located off the lobby of a narrow, six-story hotel building of the same name. Owned by Big Tim Sullivan, a state senator also known as the King of the Tenderloin, in partnership with the Considine brothers—Jim and George—the Metropole had a license to stay open all night, and it was at its liveliest when most of the city's population was asleep.

Rosenthal was feeling really good about himself now; he had finally broken through. He had the district attorney on his side and the press following his every move, and he was confident that he was beyond harm's reach. He would have been surprised to know that not long after midnight a stranger had called the *World*'s city room and asked a reporter, "Has Rosenthal been killed yet?" When the reporter replied that he had heard nothing, the caller warned, "Watch out, you might hear of it at any moment."

The Metropole was a hangout frequented chiefly by Tenderloin insiders—gamblers, hustlers, political hacks, prizefighters and their hangers-on. Rosenthal was a familiar face there, so no one paid particular note when he sashayed in that night. The doors that opened into the lobby as well as those that led out onto the street were wedged open in a vain attempt to catch a stray breeze, but the only air that moved inside was driven by two huge electric fans just inside the doors. Rosenthal settled in at a back table, joining three other small-time gamblers named Boob Walker, Fat Moe Brown, and Butch Kitte. He ordered a glass of ginger ale and a king-size Cuban cigar and began making small talk. At about one-thirty, he left the table, walked across the lobby and returned with the early editions of the morning papers under his arm. He was pleased to see himself featured on the front pages. Best of all was the headline in the World: "GAMBLER CHARGES POLICE LIEUTENANT WAS HIS PARTNER." He bought six extra copies and showed it around, but he found that the mood in the lounge seemed to have shifted. The piano player had stopped grinding out his ragtime tunes. Conversation was hushed. The room had become unnaturally quiet. It was as if all the air had been sucked out of the place. His table companions were no longer where he had left them. Others too had begun to leave. Everyone knew but Beansie. He sat by himself, reading the papers, speaking to no one.

At about 1:40 A.M., a Metropole regular by the name of Bridgey Webber came through the room, paused briefly at Rosenthal's table and said, "Hello, Herman." "Hello, Bridgey," Rosenthal said. It was more than a casual exchange of greetings. Webber was taking attendance. He left the hotel immediately. Within ten minutes the street outside, usually bustling even at that early hour, was quiet enough to hear one's own pulse beat. Taxicabs that lined up outside the hotel were sent off into the night. Pedestrians were told to keep moving. The street was kept clear until shortly before two when a seven-passenger 1909 Packard touring car turned into Forty-third Street and Sixth Avenue. It slowed to a stop about one hundred feet east of the hotel. Inside the car were four men with names that belonged to the folklore of street crime—Gyp the Blood, Lefty Louie, Whitey Lewis, and Dago Frank— and they had one thing in common: they were all killers.

Rosenthal was still sitting alone, reading about himself in the morning papers when a thin, young man approached his table and said, "Can you come outside a minute, Beansie? Someone out here wants to see you." Rosenthal dropped a dollar on the table to cover an eighty-cent tab. Still smoking his cigar, he folded his paper and walked outside. The bright lights of the Tenderloin blinded him for a moment, but he saw the shape of a man step from the shadows, touch the brim of his hat, and quickly disappear. Then he heard a voice call out, "Over here, Beansie." In the darkness to his left, he could make out the figures of four men, but it was too late to react. Five shots were fired quickly at close range. One lodged in the door frame of the hotel. The others all found their mark. One struck Rosenthal in the neck, another in the nose, and two in the side of his face. He fell to the sidewalk on his back. Lefty Louie had a final statement to make. He leaned over the fallen body and said, "Hello, Herman," then fired one more shot that blew his skull apart and said, "Goodbye, Herman."

The four shooters piled into the Packard which was waiting across the street, a driver at the wheel, and sped away at the then-breakneck speed of thirty-five miles an hour. An off-duty policeman in the back of the Metropole dining room heard the shots and ran to the entrance. He tripped over the body on the way out and saw the car pull away. Two other officers, walking their beat, hurried to the scene. The three cops flagged down a cab and gave chase down Sixth Avenue, but they could not overtake the Packard. It was, according to legend, the first time in American history that a getaway car was used in a killing.

Back at the Metropole, a crowd had gathered, clogging the street. The owner of the hotel covered the bloody body with a tablecloth until a doctor arrived and pronounced the man dead. A patrol wagon took the corpse to the West Forty-seventh Street station house. Entered into the police blotter was: "Sudden death . . . Herman Rosenthal, aged 38, white, U.S., 104 West 45th Street, Gambler."

Reporters from all the papers were quick to respond but none quicker than Swope. He was at the scene fifteen minutes after the shooting, and he wasted no time in placing a call to Whitman. Over the past year or more, the pair had developed a mutually satisfactory relationship. Swope seized every opportunity to beat the drums for the prosecutor's relentless pursuit of justice in a city fairly oozing with corruption. In return, he often got the details of a story just enough ahead of the competition for it to make a difference. Now, Swope was on the phone to Whitman, telling him to get to the scene as quickly as possible. The D.A., his voice filled with sleep, thought it could wait until morning. Swope knew better. He took a cab to Whitman's apartment on Madison Square and hauled him to the station house. Swope understood that the future for both men was drawing nearer. This was more than a routine murder case. Before it was done, the city would be stripped, layer by layer, of the veneer that masked its corruption, and there was no telling what might be found at its center. It was the beginning of a saga that could lead a big-city district attorney to the governor's mansion, maybe even the White House.

Whitman was a man who was open to every opportunity. Though fundamentally a moralist, his devotion to rectitude was matched, some might even have said exceeded, by his ambition to climb the ladder of his profession. It was a wish he did not hide, but he did not display it openly either. In a cut-and-slash political world, Whitman's most valuable assets were a reputation for unquestioned probity and a disposition to take things step by step; his first bite was invariably a small one. In 1907, he was elected president of the Board of Magistrates as a compromise candidate, and fortune found him two years later when he was elected district attorney. That same year, 1909, Swope became a reporter for the *World*. It was an ironic turn of chance that would later seem to have about it an air of inevitability. In most respects, the two men made the oddest of couples, but circumstance, and shared ambition, had brought them together, and the slaying of Rosenthal forged their alliance.

Rosenthal's execution had taken place just hours after he had met with Whitman and with the ink barely dry on the *World*'s front-page exclusive. So it came as no surprise that the name of Charles Becker, whom Rosenthal had branded the force that drove the System, came first to mind when news of the murder began to circulate. It did not soften suspicions that Becker was found to be asleep at home when a reporter for the *Sun* called him that night. No one could have thought that he did the job himself. There were, after all, as many strata of authority in the System as there were in the military, and Becker had both rank and muscle at his disposal.

Becker had joined the New York City Police Department in 1893, and it was not long before he made his presence felt. He quickly built a reputation as being street-tough, but it was a quality that did not always serve him well. He was summoned to departmental trials several times on charges of brutality and false arrest, transgressions that were often treated with benign indifference at the time. In Becker's case, they were ascribed to excessive zeal and did not prevent him from climbing the ladder. He was transferred to the Sixteenth Precinct in the Tenderloin and soon promoted to sergeant. It was a position that opened many doors, not the least of which made him bagman for the precinct captain. He regularly picked up the cash payments from the casino operators, the pimps, and the prostitutes and received ten percent of the cut. In his very first year that was worth eight thousand dollars, a princely sum in the early 1900s. But even better times lay ahead.

His good work earned him a commission as lieutenant in 1911, and Police Commissioner Rhinelander Waldo named him to head one of his Special Squads, recently formed to help break up the street gangs in Lower Manhattan and clean out the gambling casinos. It was an assignment that was made to order for Becker. The Special Squads soon became known as strong-arm squads, and none was stronger than Becker's. He pocketed his take from the casino owners and made certain that payments were made on time. It was taken as catechism that his men were serious about business and could be very persuasive. Rosenthal apparently did not get the message.

Becker made no attempt to hide his distaste for Rosenthal, and no one on the inside thought Beansie had much of a future. In the weeks leading up to the shooting, Becker was variously quoted as saying, "There is no danger to anybody that has a hand in the murder of Rosenthal." It would be a good thing if someone "did Rosenthal up." "The feeling over at police headquarters is so strong that the man or men that croak him would have a medal pinned on them."

But despite Becker's ready-made status as principal suspect, there was no hard evidence that served to implicate him. What there was, was perhaps equally compelling. A great many people—from hoods to government officials—stood to profit from his arrest and conviction. And that, in the end, would be his undoing.

The Crime:

Corruption

and Murder

Anyone who was in New York during the summer of 1912 would tell you it had never been that hot before. The heat clogged the streets and held on like a dull ache. It had been that way for more than a week. In most of the city's newspapers, it was front-page news, on occasion claiming lead-story status in the right-hand column. People were sleeping on fire escapes or with their doors open, trying to catch a stray breeze. In public places, electric fans whirred nonstop, pushing the stale air from one side of the room to the other. Heat-stricken horses fell prostrate on the cobblestoned streets. It went on like that day after day, and it had begun to wear on the nerves. The murder rate was rising as fast as the temperature. More than thirty homicides were recorded in the month of July, though the heat could not be blamed for most of them.

Gangland killings had been a fact of life in New York for nearly half a century. They had begun mostly as turf wars, driven by the primitive instinct to protect one's space. But as the century approached its turn, gangs began to form as instruments of economic survival. The 1890s had brought with it what was then the worst depression in the country's history. It was a time when robber barons were building monuments of wealth whose trimmings might have shamed the royal houses of Europe, while the forces of labor went hungry and homeless. With jobs difficult to come by and wages meager at best, crime was often looked upon as an alternate means of employment for a population that was increasingly foreign born.

New York was a work in progress as it approached the start of the twentieth century. It was a city whose face was being transformed by a tidal wave of immigrants who had heard it said that the streets were paved with gold here and that each man was free to mine his own. So they continued to come, hundreds of thousands, landing at Ellis Island and settling in on the Lower East Side in unforgiving tenements that cut right to the bone. By 1900, more than one and a half million people, almost all of them recent immigrants, were living in slums throughout the city. A one-year record number of 1,285,349 arrived in 1907. A one-day high of 11,745 was recorded on April 17, 1911. The Lower East Side had become the most densely populated area in the world, more crowded than Bombay, with about seven hundred people per acre. By 1912, more than twenty-five percent of the population of the United States was foreign born. In New York City, the percentage was much higher. There were more Italians in New York than in Naples; more Irish than in Dublin. On the Lower East Side, one was hard-pressed to find a native-born American.

Too soon, the immigrant population discovered that there was no gold in the streets. Those who arrived with particular skills found work as tailors, bakers, or shopkeepers. Others were funneled into menial jobs where a day's wages was measured in small change. Many could find no work at all. The working poor and the unemployed were the two fastest growing classes in the city. With jobs scarce and their situations growing desperate, some looked for other ways to put bread on the table. Lone hoods found it helped to band together in street gangs, and the gangs soon evolved into more intricate underworld combines. Crime was becoming part of the fabric of life in New York City, and everyone knew it.

Gambling and prostitution had long been the meat and potatoes of organized crime. They were endeavors that thrived in good times and bad, and neither was in short supply in early 1900s New York. On the West Side of Manhattan alone, there were scores (some said hundreds) of gambling casinos and thousands (some said tens of thousands) of prostitutes offering their services at a wide range of prices. And since both were illegal, they depended for survival on the cooperation of those whose job it was to put them out of business. Tammany Hall politicians and highly placed police officers were more than ready to oblige.

Tammany Hall had been the operative arm of the Democratic Party in New York since its creation in 1828. Named for an early Delaware Indian chief known for his wisdom, it was formed mainly to provide aid and comfort to the flood of Irish immigrants who came to America during a potato famine that left many of them hungry and destitute. They were among the first massive infusion of immigrants who came to the New World with hopes high, only to find ethnic discrimination at every turn. Advertisements of job openings were often accompanied by the caveat, "Irish Need Not Apply." Tammany officials provided the new arrivals with a variety of services. They helped them get naturalization papers, supplied a lawyer if one was needed, got them licenses to operate saloons, and somehow managed to arrange things so that city officials cooperated wherever possible and viewed minor infractions with a wink and a nod. If jobs in private industry were few, the city was able to find openings in many of its agencies, particularly in the police department. Hundreds of Irish immigrants joined the force, and subsequent generations followed in their footsteps.

Tammany Hall had become a lifeline for the Irish, and those it had helped responded with proper gratitude and devotion, backing the Democratic Party in every election. For more than a century, Tammany grew in size and influence until it controlled nearly every nuance of city life. It became a notable illustration of Lord Acton's adage about power and corruption. No city permits could be obtained without Tammany's sanction. No business opened without its blessing. No new buildings would rise unless money was passed to the right hands. Graft had become part of the city's bureaucratic structure, and gambling and prostitution continued to be its backbone. At one point, the *New York Times* reported that a Tammany Commission had been formed, consisting of a city official, two state senators, and the head of a poolroom syndicate. The commission, it said, grossed more than three million dollars a year. Few unions could have been more natural or more firmly bonded than the one between Tammany Hall politicians and the New York City Police Department. It was a marriage of both convenience and necessity, for each depended upon the other; the first saw to the production of the revenue, the second collected it and provided protection. Both relied for survival on what might be called the judicious administration of corruption. Everyone knew how it operated, and everyone got his piece of the pie.

As is true of most industries, gambling operations shifted this way and that until finally locating in a central district. The Lower East Side, where many casinos first opened their doors, had lost its appeal. Its streets were crammed with peddlers selling their wares from pushcarts, horse-drawn wagons offering fruits and vegetables, droves of children at play while their parents sat on the stoops of tenements looking for a hint of fresh air. Further up the East Side, the streets were easier to navigate, and there was more of a sense of seclusion, but it lacked panache, the tingle of excitement that nourishes the impulse to see money change hands quickly on the turn of a card or the roll of the dice. It was the West Side of Manhattan the area that became known as Times Square when the *New York Times* opened its new building there in 1904, that had the glow. This was the Crossroads of the World, the Great White Way of bright lights and movie marquees, legitimate theaters and top-end restaurants, dance halls and hotels, skyscrapers growing out of the ground. It was an area with a pulse of its own, and it attracted the kind of clientele that appreciated the enticements of quick pleasure and high-priced risk.

Before long, the highest concentration of the city's estimated five hundred gambling houses and a hefty percentage of its approximately thirty thousand prostitutes were located in that less-than-one-square-mile area on the West Side. It was the center of night life in what was becoming the most cosmopolitan city in the country. The gambling casinos ranged in style from super-elegant parlors, tastefully furnished, to last-chance dives offering a quick way out to those whose luck had long ago left them. The after-theater crowd often arrived in hansom cabs with closed carriages called broughams or in chauffeur-driven motor cars that were just beginning to make their appearance on streets that had yet to see their first traffic signal.

Since the latter part of the nineteenth century, the area had been popularly known as the Tenderloin. Fittingly, it was given its name by a high-ranking police officer who had a full appreciation for the opportunities afforded an ambitious member of New York's Finest. Inspector Alexander Williams, whose frequent use of his nightstick had earned him the nickname "Clubber," had been transferred from a staid precinct where the pickings were slim to what was then the Twenty-ninth Precinct. The Twenty-ninth covered an area from Twenty-third to Forty-second Streets between Fourth and Seventh Avenues, and Inspector Williams was a man who recognized a money tree when he saw one. "I've had nothing but chuck steak for a long time," he told a newspaperman. "Now I'm going to get me a little of the tenderloin." That was in 1893. By 1900, half of all the buildings in the area were said to cater to vice of one type or another. Religious reformers had taken to calling it "Satan's Circus." But there was little they could do to interfere with business as it was being conducted. Over the next few years, the Tenderloin moved slightly uptown, embracing the area from Forty-second Street to the mid-Fifties and from Fifth to Seventh Avenues. It was sometimes referred to as the New Tenderloin, but the meat was still well aged, as rare as ever, and a proper feast for a man who knew where to find the finest cuts.

Now and again, there comes on the scene a personality who appears to have been fashioned for a particular time and place. When Charles Becker joined the force in 1893, he might well have served as a poster boy for the tough New York City street cop, for he both looked the part and embraced the attitude. More than six feet tall and weighing in at two hundred fifteen pounds, Becker looked like a challenger for the heavyweight title just won by James J. Corbett. He was powerfully built, with broad shoulders and hands so large they looked like a pair of hams dangling from the end of his arms. It was said that he could kill a man with a punch, and his disposition often suggested that he might be inclined to do so. His jaw jutted forth like a block of granite. His eyes, gazing straight ahead, could dissolve a man's will. Yet there was also something alluringly charming in his aspect. He had an engaging smile that produced a deep dimple in his left cheek and lent a boyish quality to a very harsh façade.

The son of Bavarian immigrants, Becker grew up in Callicoon Center, a farming community with a population measured in the hundreds, located at the foot of the Catskill Mountains in Sullivan County, New York. There was something about him that hinted at trouble right from the start. He was restless, easily provoked, and ill at ease in the face of authority. He quickly grew weary of life on the farm, and at age eighteen left home and moved to New York City. He worked for a while as a baker's assistant before finding a more congenial setting at a German beer garden just off the Bowery where he worked as a bouncer. He was ideally suited for that line of work and, with a temper to match his physique, he soon earned a reputation as a fearsome street fighter who was not to be trifled with.

It was in that position that he made the acquaintance of Edward "Monk" Eastman, a meeting that would set the course for the rest of his life. If there were a street crime hall of fame, Monk Eastman would have a niche all his own. He was more than just a killer, more than the leader of an army of some twelve hundred thugs. Eastman was a pioneer in labor racketeering and is credited with ushering organized gang life into the twentieth century. He had the look of a small-time club fighter who had stopped too many punches with his face. His nose was broken, his ears cauliflowered, his neck thick and buried deep in his shoulders. Though adept with a gun, his favored weapon was a sawed-off baseball bat that he used to crack the skull of an adversary. But even unarmed, he was life-threatening. He often boasted that he could break a man's back with his bare hands, and he was reputed to have demonstrated that skill with little persuasion. Not surprisingly, Eastman took an immediate liking to Becker. He admired his style, his swagger, the projection of raw power and the aura of impending doom that seemed to flow from him. Through Eastman, Becker met a number of well-connected people, and none better connected than Big Tim Sullivan.

Timothy D. Sullivan, leader of Tammany Hall, a member of the state senate, and the undisputed King of the Tenderloin, was the prototype of the big-city Irish politico who knew where all the bones were buried, the precise location of every link that wired authority to power, and who had the unerring sense to know which button to push and when to push it. Slightly over six feet and well proportioned, he could light up a room with his smile, and at a time when good fortune was in short supply, his twinkling blue eyes seemed to hold out the promise of better days ahead. He had, after all, known hard times himself.

Born in a Lower East Side tenement in 1863, he grew up on Clinton Street, poor and fatherless, and from the very start he learned how to scrape to get by. At the age of seven, he was selling newspapers on the street for pennies. When he was ten, a charitable grade-school teacher taught him a lesson that helped shape his career. He had come to school without shoes one day, and the teacher saw fit to buy him a pair. It was a gesture he never forgot, and he instinctively understood that generosity was a gift that paid back many times over. When he became head of Tammany, he would annually donate eight thousand pair of shoes to the needy along with free Christmas dinners and buckets of coal to heat cold-water flats. It was a practice he continued for thirty years.

Sullivan's relations with Tammany Hall began in the early eighties when he opened a saloon on Christie Street in a section of Lower Manhattan known at the time as the Five Points. Saloons were more numerous than food stores in the Five Points, but Sullivan's seemed to have a special appeal. It became the hangout of the Whyos, one of the toughest of the many Irish street gangs that waged war openly in the latter part of the nineteenth century. Before long, Sullivan put the Whyos to use in the service of Tammany Hall. There was no one better at getting out the vote. They ushered Democrats to the polls, often more than once, while Republicans were discouraged, sometimes forcefully, from casting their ballots. With the blessings of Tammany, Sullivan soon entered politics himself. In 1886, just twenty-three, he was elected a state assemblyman; four years later, he became a state senator. But these were little more than titles. Sullivan's true heft derived from his position as Tammany's most powerful district leader, reigning as he did in the city's most populous district. It was a population whose ethnic makeup had been changing dramatically, but Big Tim, as he had become known, was nothing if not adaptable. He welcomed the profusion of Jewish immigrants from Eastern Europe with a few words of Yiddish, and was a regular at Saturday Bar Mitzvahs, wearing a yarmulke and dancing the hora. When Italians began moving in, he changed steps and did the tarantella with no less gusto.

As his influence grew and his business interests multiplied, Sullivan moved north, into the Tenderloin, where the action was quicker and the stakes higher. He soon was overseeing all graft and bribery in Manhattan. By the early nineties, he chaired a committee that presided over all gambling operations in the borough. There were two other members: one from the gambling industry, the other a high-ranking police official. Police graft was the oil that kept the machine running. The network of payoffs, collection, and distribution ran to the very highest echelons of the department, with the notable exception of Commissioner Waldo who, forever trusting, seemed oblivious to the whole operation. The System relied on cops who were tough, reliable, and ambitious. These were qualities that Becker had in abundance, and Sullivan noticed them immediately. In 1893, shortly after meeting him, he offered Becker a place on the police force. Tammany usually charged a fee for such services; in Becker's case the fee was waived. Sullivan had an eye for talent.

Authority was nutrient for a man of Becker's disposition, and the uniform of New York's Finest fit him well in all respects. It consisted of a long blue coat with two rows of nine brass buttons, a hard gray helmet, a leather scabbard that held a nightstick adorned with a fancy blue tassel, and a service revolver. So outfitted, given his youth, his muscular frame and rugged good looks, Becker could have played the part of a legionnaire in the Praetorian Guard.

In just a few years, he began making news, not all of it good. In September 1896, he made front-page headlines with a story describing the fatal shooting of a burglar who was trying to make his getaway. He and his partner were patrolling their beat in the early dawn when they spotted a man climbing out the side window of a tobacco shop on Washington Street. They called for the man to halt, but he continued racing down the street and was outdistancing the policemen. Becker and his partner again shouted for the man to stop. When he didn't, they emptied their revolvers. The shots all missed their intended target, but one of the bullets struck a passerby who had just stepped from a building into the line of fire. The bullet pierced his heart and the man fell dead. Becker's official account of the shooting said the dead man was a known burglar by the name of John O'Brien. The two patrolmen were celebrated as heroes, Becker's photo appearing prominently in the next day's papers. Their celebrity lasted just two days, however, for it was then that the victim was identified by his family as a plumber's helper by the name of John Fay, a man with no criminal record, who had been killed accidentally. After a departmental hearing, Becker, who had filed the report, was suspended for a month.

It was the start of a bad season for the ambitious young officer. A month later, he again found himself in deep waters. In the early hours of an October morning, Becker arrested a young woman for prostitution outside a music hall on Thirty-second Street. No one questioned that the woman, Dora Clark, earned her living in the world's oldest profession. What was in question was whether she was actually caught in the act. Becker said he had seen her soliciting two men. Dora Clark said she had done nothing of the sort. What's more, she had a witness who was more than ready to corroborate her story. Ordinarily, the incident would have drawn little notice. But Dora's supporter was no ordinary witness. He was Stephen Crane, the young author who a year earlier was ushered into the literary elite with his Civil War novel, *The Red Badge of Courage.*

Crane, who had something of an affinity for the underside of big-city life, was at the dance hall, the Broadway Gardens, on assignment for the *New York Journal.* He was preparing a series of articles on some of the colorful characters who gave spice to the Tenderloin. He had left the hall in the company of two young women who were later joined by Dora Clark. Without cause or reason, Crane later said, Patrolman Becker took Clark into custody and had her booked on trumped-up charges. At her trial, Dora testified that she had been the victim of police harassment since she rebuffed the advances of a member of Becker's precinct. Unaware that there were no blacks on the force at the time, she said she had taken the dark-complexioned cop, whose name was Rosenberg, for a Negro and told him she did not go out with colored men. That, she said, had earned her an unusually intense degree of attention from the local constabulary. Largely on Crane's testimony, the charges against Dora Clark were dismissed.

Crane would have done well to let matters rest there, but he took things a step further, and it did no one any good. Crane had met the newly appointed police commissioner, Teddy Roosevelt, socially and had previously written to him complaining about police strong-arm tactics. Now he again contacted the commissioner, urging a departmental trial for Becker. It was a grave mistake. Becker's disciplinary hearing, on the charge of fabricating evidence, was the longest in the department's history, running from one day into the early hours of the next. It was attended by every off-duty cop in his precinct, and a casual observer would have thought it was Crane, rather than Becker, who was on trial. Becker's attorney prodded Crane with a series of questions implying that he was an opium addict and a pimp whose interest in the case was driven by his desire to protect one of his girls. The panel's conclusion was that Becker, though perhaps a bit overzealous, had made an honest mistake. Commissioner Roosevelt appeared at the station house to congratulate him on his exoneration and praise his overall record. As for Crane, it appeared that every policeman in the precinct had placed him in their sights. He was stalked and badgered at every turn until life in the city became intolerable. He traded in his New York beat for the life of a war correspondent, first in Cuba, then in Crete, where he covered the Greco-Turkish war. He died of tuberculosis three years later at the age of twenty-nine.

Becker's run-ins with the public continued; departmental hearings were being conducted with ritualistic regularity. At the end of 1896, he arrested the wife of a New Jersey textile manufacturer on charges of soliciting, saying, "I know a whore when I see one." She threatened to sue the department for false arrest and, despite an apology from the chief of police, it took the intervention of Big Tim Sullivan to persuade the woman and her husband to drop the charges. A few months later, a teenage boy accused Becker of pummeling him in the lobby of a movie house.

Even when the news he made was good, everything Becker did seemed in some way tainted. In the summer of 1898, he was walking along a Hudson River pier when he saw a man plummet into the water. Apparently unable to swim, the man was thrashing about, gasping for air. After diving in and hauling him to safety, Becker was acclaimed a hero and awarded the police department's medal for heroism. But the man, an unemployed clerk by the name of James Butler, later called the incident a setup. He said Becker had promised to pay him fifteen dollars to stage the rescue and had never given him the money. Butler later recanted and said Becker had actually saved his life, but the recantation was reported less prominently than the accusation, and the real truth of the incident was never determined.

All the same, Becker was clearly a force to be reckoned with. He had an instinct for the moment, a way of putting himself at the center of things. He was the type of cop who could be counted on to make things happen. The department recognized his special talent. In 1901, he was transferred to the Forty-seventh Street station, just off Broadway, in the heart of the Tenderloin. It was the perfect concurrence of a man to a time and a place. Becker, thirty-one years old, eight years on the force, had found his destiny.

The fusion of authority and power is always dangerous, and no one embodies it more than policemen walking the streets of a big city. On foot or in squad cars, they are all too visible, and even when their presence comforts, it is never without a suggestion of intimidation. It is no surprise then that big-city cops stir conflicting emotions more than any other public figures. They are embraced by a community that craves protection, but the prospect that some might abuse their power—might even be corrupt—introduces an element of suspicion as well. Police corruption is a moving target that, from time to time, falls within the sights of city government. Investigative panels are appointed to conduct probes, and the results are invariably the same—they find criminal mischief embedded in the system, make recommendations designed to clean things up, and pass measures that, in the long term, have no effect at all.

One of the earliest such investigations in New York City was conducted in 1894, driven by the righteous admonitions of a crusading clergyman, the Reverend Charles H. Parkhurst. Parkhurst was pastor of the Madison Square Presbyterian Church, which was located at the southern end of the Tenderloin, and he did not like what he saw. Doubling as head of the Society for the Prevention of Crime, he preached Sunday after Sunday about the dens of depravity and sin—particularly the brothels—he found flourishing throughout the area. Like most good soldiers in the legions of virtue,

Parkhurst had no difficulty identifying the chief cause of the problem. It was the sin-ravaged leaders of Tammany Hall. Parkhurst used the pulpit to denounce the Tammany leaders as "a lying, perjured, rum-soaked, and libidinous lot . . . that, under the pretense of governing this city, are feeding day and night on its quivering vitals."

When the Republicans took control of the state legislature in 1894, a thorough investigation of police corruption was prescribed. The investigative committee was putatively headed by a state senator from Rockland County, Clarence Lexow, and became known as the Lexow Committee. But Lexow provided the probe with little more than his name. The investigation was propelled by the committee's chief counsel, John W. Goff, and his two assistants, William Travers Jerome and Frank Moss. Soon after the inquiry, Goff would be chosen chief judge of the Court of General Sessions. Jerome was appointed to the Court of Special Sessions and later elected district attorney. Moss became president of the Board of Police Commissioners and then an assistant district attorney. The three would come together again, in a far different relationship, nearly twenty years later when Becker went on trial for murder.

One of the Lexow Committee's most voluble witnesses was Captain Max Schmittberger, of the Tenderloin precinct. Schmittberger had much to tell the committee, for if the System's network of graft had been a corporation, Schmittberger would have been its chief operating officer. He knew how it worked and could track the precise channel through which the money flowed. He was at first a reluctant witness, but when he was formally charged with accepting graft, he chose to make his separate peace with the committee and serve his own interests. In exchange for a grant of immunity, Schmittberger offered up a smorgasbord of testimony implicating, among others, Clubber Williams, his former boss, who had presided over the Tenderloin as inspector and, in fact, had given the district its name. Williams, for his part, was totally defiant, at one point even appearing to threaten Goff if the disagreement between the two became personal. Though not indicted, Clubber was retired from the force in 1895 by the newly appointed chairman of the Board of Police Commissioners, Theodore Roosevelt, who was charged with cleaning up the department. Schmittberger, in consideration of his testimony, was returned to his position as captain of the Sixteenth Precinct. It would be business as usual in the Tenderloin.

Schmittberger could not have welcomed Becker's arrival at his station house. The two men were natural adversaries. Becker, after all, had modeled himself on the style of Clubber Williams, and Schmittberger had effectively ended Clubber's career. He also had violated police force doctrine by selling out his fellow officers. It was not long before the new arrival crossed swords with the precinct captain. They clashed, initially, over Becker's cut of the graft money. The feud boiled over a few years later when Becker helped gather evidence that Schmittberger had not truly reformed but was still in charge of graft operations in the Tenderloin. Schmittberger was placed on departmental trial in 1906 and was acquitted. He and Becker never grew fond of one another, but their mutual hostility was trumped by their common interest. The money continued to flow into the precinct, and no one was better at collecting from reluctant club owners than Charles Becker.

In 1907, the newly appointed police commissioner, Theodore Bingham, elevated Becker to the rank of sergeant, skipping over several other candidates for promotion. Bingham had championed the losing case against Schmittberger and appreciated the help Becker had offered. Becker's new position was grease for the System's machinery. As sergeant, he was the number-one bagman for collections throughout the precinct. He was so effective that his ten percent cut was soon doubled. The eight thousand dollars he netted in his first year was a nice bonus for a man earning fifteen hundred a year, but it was just a suggestion of what lay ahead. Life was good for Becker and would soon get even better.

His promotion came not long after he had married Helen Lynch, a delicate wisp of a schoolteacher who, by all accounts, was unlike her husband in every way. Helen was soft-spoken, gently charming, and pretty in a manner that soothed, rather than excited, the senses. Becker had been married twice before, and both unions had ended badly. His first wife, Mary Mahoney, was the daughter of a storekeeper on Becker's beat. She was just eighteen when they married, in 1895, and within eight months she had died of tuberculosis. His second venture into wedlock, three years later, proved to be less tragic but more turbulent. Two years after they had wed, the couple had a son, but the marriage held little promise of long life. Becker's wife, Letitia, claimed that she had caught him in a hotel room with another woman and obtained a divorce on the grounds of adultery. She then married Charles's younger brother, Paul, and they moved west and took the child with them. But when it came to marriage, three was indeed the charm for Becker.

While it is unclear how they met, it is safe to say that Becker and Helen clicked immediately. He was in the midst of divorce proceedings when he began courting her, and they were married shortly after the divorce came through. She was teaching at P.S. 90, in the northwest reaches of Manhattan, and Becker often waited for her outside the school building until she ended her day. Helen taught what in those days were called "ungraded" classes, children of various ages who, in one way or another, were handicapped—often mentally retarded. Her compassion for these children seemed to rub off on Becker. It might even be said that Helen had, in Huck Finn's term, a "civilizing" effect on her husband, whom she affectionately called "Charley-boy." From the start of their relationship until its premature end, Becker turned toward her a side of his nature that had previously been well hidden. It was as if every trace of tenderness that he possessed had been saved through the years for their meeting; he squandered none of it on anyone else. They lived in an apartment on 159th Street and Edgecomb Avenue, not far from her school, and Helen had all she could ask for and more than she expected.

Tammany at the time, though still a power to be reckoned with, was hardly thriving. As the 1909 election approached, there was increasing talk of reform. The Tammany boss of the moment, Charles F. Murphy, sensed the shift in the public's mood and thought it best to find a mayoral candidate whose credentials were solid but who had a reputation for independence and incorruptibility; someone, in short, with no ties to the club. Such a man might cost Tammany a bit of influence, but it would be far better than taking a chance on losing City Hall. It was a bow to the time-tested political wisdom that chose expediency over ideology when the stakes were high and the percentages not entirely in one's favor. The same philosophy was being played out on the national level where labor strikes were rampant and socialism was gaining favor among the working class. Progressives such as Teddy Roosevelt found that measures of reform, distasteful as they might be, were the most effective way of maintaining the status quo. Give a little, keep a lot was the mantra, and the Tammany machine was nothing if not shrewd and practical.

The man chosen as the Democratic candidate for mayor was William Jay Gaynor, who came to the scene entirely unencumbered. A justice of the

Brooklyn supreme court for sixteen years, Gaynor had earned a reputation for being more than independent. He was, by turns, bombastic, engagingly eccentric, cantankerous, hard-scrabble tough, and relentlessly unyielding, all without ever losing the air of dignity that befit his distinguished demeanor. Trim and always elegantly turned out, he wore a graying Van Dyke beard that was offset by black eyebrows and crystal-clear blue eyes. Depending on mood and circumstance, he could appear forbidding at one moment and altogether charming the next.

Gaynor was a man who had traveled far and aged well. A scholarly type and well steeped in the classics, he had taught school, worked as a newspaper reporter, studied law, passed the bar, and set up a law office in the Flatbush section of Brooklyn. His law practice set the tone for the disposition he brought to the bench. The year he was first elected, 1893, marked the start of the economic depression that weighed on the country for the rest of the century. An Irishman whose heritage had made him familiar with the bruising consequences of poverty, Gaynor spent most of his time defending the downtrodden and oppressed—drunks, vagrants, and miscellaneous losers who had strayed on the wrong side of the law.

On the flip side, he had nothing but disdain for those who had power and abused it, particularly the police whose duty, as he saw it, was to "preserve the public peace and keep outward order and decency." In a judicial decision that many in authority viewed with dismay, Gaynor reversed a lower-court judgment by no less an eminence than Judge John W. Goff who had ruled against a police officer for failing to arrest the madam of a brothel. "The law," Judge Gaynor said, "does not commit the supreme folly of making [the police] the custodians or guardians of the private morals of the community.... So long as a house on my block is so decorous and orderly in the windows and on the stoops that I am not able to see a single thing wrong with it, I am willing to go by and leave it alone, and I want the police to do the same."

Given the general fall from public grace that Tammany had suffered, the election of the Democratic candidate was not the certainty it had been in the past. Gaynor was opposed by two candidates: Otto Bannard, a wealthy, colorless banker who ran as a Republican/fusion party nominee; and the formidable newspaper baron, William Randolph Hearst, who ran as an independent. Gaynor prevailed by a surprisingly wide margin with 43 percent of the vote;

it was a measure of Tammany's loss of favor that he was the only Democrat elected to office. Hearst finished a poor third, extending his streak as a political loser. He had failed in races for the presidency in 1904, mayor in 1905, and governor in 1906. Now, as the publisher of three New York dailies, Hearst would sustain the relentless attack he had mounted against Gaynor during the election campaign, perhaps still chafing from Gaynor's remark that "Hearst's face almost makes me want to puke."

For Tammany, Gaynor's election was one of those political victories that can make defeat seem inviting. Gaynor wasted no time rolling up his sleeves and trying to scrub the city clean. Tammany's claims on patronage were stricken from the books. The mayor's appointments were made without regard for political affiliation. If it was independence that was wanted, Gaynor would demonstrate what independence was. He eliminated agencies he considered superfluous. He slashed the city payroll and reduced its budget. He did all he could to put the brakes on the police, coming down hard on any hint of brutality and calling an end to warrantless raids, which had become routine. The public was encouraged to bring complaints against police directly to the mayor. The crackdown extended to off-duty hours as well. Police officers were barred from patronizing saloons and were no longer permitted to moonlight for private businesses as security agents during labor strikes.

It was clear from his first days in office that Gaynor's reputation as a liberal had been well earned and that his promise to act as a reformer was not made idly. He was the kind of mayor the public was quick to embrace regardless of the policies he might be promoting. It was his style—early twentieth-century New York—that captured the imagination, much as Fiorello LaGuardia and Ed Koch did decades later. Adorned with silk top hat, he walked across the Brooklyn Bridge on his way to work each morning, a trek of more than three miles, nodding to constituents who waved in greeting. His air of formality was somewhat tempered by his man-of-the-people manner, and the initial surge of his popularity caused some to regard him as presidential timber for the 1912 campaign. At the time, he was probably better known than Woodrow Wilson, the Democratic candidate who would win the presidency that year.

Less than a year into his term, Gaynor left on a summer vacation bound for

Europe aboard the transatlantic liner *Kaiser Wilhelm der Grosse*. With the ship still moored at the Hoboken Pier and Gaynor waving to well-wishers on shore, a disheveled little man came up behind him and shouted, "You have taken away my bread and butter," then pressed a pistol to the back of his neck, just below the right ear, and fired. The gunman, arrested immediately, was a disgruntled city employee, James J. Gallagher, who had recently been fired from his job as watchman for the New York City Department of Docks. In his pocket was a crumpled letter from Gaynor's secretary telling him that the mayor could not intervene in his behalf. Drenched in blood, Gaynor was treated by the ship's doctor, then rushed to St. Mary's Hospital in Hoboken where he remained for two weeks, his vacation abruptly ended. The bullet had passed beneath the base of his brain and lodged in his throat, and there it remained. His doctors decided it was best not to extract the bullet, and its presence plagued Gaynor for the rest of his life. His voice, always somewhat gruff, was now reduced to a hoarse whisper, and he was subject to prolonged fits of coughing. Worse, as time passed, his behavior became erratic. He would appear at City Hall at odd hours and sit in his office staring vacantly into space. He treated any disagreement as a personal betrayal and found enemies everywhere.

Gaynor's relationship with the police had always been uneasy. His time as a judge suggested an outlook that was at odds with the hard-edged demands of law enforcement. What appeared to others as a city increasingly open to gambling, prostitution, and police graft, seemed to him, at first flush, to be the fabrication of an activist and competitive press looking for attention-grabbing headlines. Carrying forth his judicial philosophy that the police should not be the custodians of private morality, he had insisted that they bypass establishments that presented no outward signs of disorder. It was a decision that was sweet to the taste of both the vice lords, who paid for protection, and the police, who provided it. But after a year in office, the view from City Hall proved to be a bit sobering. Gambling and prostitution appeared to be the lifeblood of the city, and it was police graft that kept them alive. Gaynor decided to do something about it.

He had replaced William F. Baker, the police commissioner he had inherited when he took office, and appointed a former colleague from the Brooklyn court system, Judge James C. Cropsey. But he and Cropsey were a poor fit. The new commissioner was as unbending as Gaynor, and they were often at cross purposes. In June 1911, Gaynor appointed his third police commissioner in less than a year. He was Rhinelander Waldo, who had been serving the mayor as fire commissioner. Waldo's resume was impressive, his roots venerable and sunk deep in the country's past. His given name derived from his mother's family, the Rhinelanders, whose origins ran back to the Dutch settlements in the seventeenth century. The Waldos also had their place among the city's bluebloods. Waldo, just thirty-four years old, struck a sharp contrast to the mayor, who was more than thirty years his elder. Where Gaynor projected the image of the highly esteemed elder statesman, Waldo had the youthful, fresh-faced look of an Eagle Scout who would never fail to say "sir" or "ma'am" when addressing an elder.

Despite his boyish appearance, however, Waldo came to the job with some macho credentials. After graduating from West Point in 1901, he had seen action in the Philippines during the Spanish-American War. When the war was over, he stayed on for several years as part of a militarized police force, earning the rank of captain. When he returned to New York, he found that Theodore Bingham, a retired army general he knew, was police commissioner, and in 1906 he was named Bingham's deputy. A year later, he moved on to become head of the police force for the Catskill water system before returning to New York as fire commissioner.

A student of police science, Waldo's apartment at the plush Ritz-Carlton Hotel was cluttered with leather-bound editions on the subject of law enforcement. The studiously academic approach he brought to the subject recommended itself to Gaynor, a bookish man in his own right. Waldo held the notion that the New York City police department could profit from emulating the style of the Metropolitan Police of London, better known as Scotland Yard. That, too, sounded good to the mayor. Gaynor believed he had found the man ideally suited to the task of bringing order to a city that had begun to spin out of control. They each had ideas on how to accomplish the job, and they seemed to be in total harmony. The problem was that theory was an inadequate tool when it came to making necessary adjustments. Waldo, by nature and training, was an idea man. He was poorly equipped to counter the forces that drove the System. In slightly more than a year, the police department would be a shambles. Waldo had become a popular subject of ridicule, and the value of the commissioner's office itself was being called to question.

The office of police commissioner was relatively new. Prior to 1901, the department was governed by a four-man board with a chairman at its head. The new system was intended to strengthen the hand of the department chief who was appointed to a five-year term and given wide statutory powers. He was authorized to name his own deputies, precinct captains, and borough commanders. He also could orchestrate the movement of any of his officers from precinct to precinct or beat to beat, like the pieces on a chess board. As enacted, the statute accorded the commissioner the kind of control that Teddy Roosevelt, who by then was president, had craved but never achieved. Once put into play, however, the new structure actually siphoned power from the commissioner's office to City Hall. Since the commissioner served at the mayor's pleasure, the mayor was able to respond to a rise in crime or any hint of wrongdoing within the police department by simply naming a replacement. The result was a succession of transient commissioners who served chiefly as office décor and whose presence was largely ceremonial. In precincts throughout the city, police brass had greeted the creation of the new office with the enthusiasm of a bank robber who had just been given the keys to the vault. As recorded by James Lardner and Thomas Reppetto in their book *NYPD: A City and Its Police,* a precinct captain, asked to describe the kind of commissioner he and his colleagues preferred, responded: "A nice, honest gentleman who does not know he is alive. He makes a good front . . . while the insiders do the business behind his back."

Enter Rhinelander Waldo. By the time he was appointed in 1911, Waldo was the eighth commissioner to serve in the position since its inception ten years earlier. He was widely depicted as being clueless, feckless, naïve, and unaware of what was going on around him. He was a favorite target of cartoonists, who often portrayed him in a Boy Scout uniform, certain that virtue would always triumph and that police corruption was an oxymoron. But even his most caustic critics did not deny that Waldo was also honest, eager, enthusiastic, and committed to crafting a police department that would cleanse the city of crime as completely as could be imagined.

An army veteran and disciple of its techniques, Waldo applied the military principle of assembling special units to perform special duties. He created strike squads to break up the street gangs in Lower Manhattan, then expanded their function to include cracking down on the gambling industry. These were the forebears of what later became known as vice squads. Waldo chose to form three squads rather than one in order to reduce the possibility of members of a single unit becoming too cozy with the entrepreneurs who ran the casinos.

Charles Becker was named to head one of the squads. Becker's record on the police force might have suggested the risks inherent in his appointment, but Waldo seemed not to notice. His early personnel decisions had already called his judgment to question. He had named Winfield Sheehan, formerly a reporter for the *New York World*, chief of staff to the commissioner, apparently unaware that Sheehan moonlighted as a member of Big Tim Sullivan's gambling commission. He also appointed George Dougherty deputy commissioner in charge of the Detective Bureau and Edward Hughes as inspector, both of whom were later charged with taking bribes. But none of those selections would have the impact of putting Becker, who had recently been promoted to lieutenant, in charge of a vice squad.

As commander of his own strike force, Becker grew to full size. He reported directly to the commissioner, and his operation was thus conducted beyond the watchful gaze of the precinct captain. His unit soon became known as a strong-arm squad, and word throughout the district spread quickly that it was not wise to mess with Becker or his men. To pacify

Waldo, several raids were made each week, but Becker was familiar with the terrain, and he knew his way around the turns. He shut down the less profitable casinos and boosted the payoff rates for the ones that prospered. He had become larger than the precinct captain, of greater influence than the commissioner. The casino operators in his area answered only to Becker, and Becker answered only to Sullivan. Between them, they had begun to give shape to what might be considered the incipient structure of organized crime. Becker, with a quick eye for the main chance, understood the elemental dictum of growing a business—a degree of authority had to be delegated; the grunt work should be left to others. He decided to contract out the routine work of collecting the payments.

The man he chose to head that part of the operation was Big Jack Zelig, a known killer and one of the most feared racketeers in the city. Zelig, whose real name was William Alberts, was a product of the Lower East Side, the son of rather conventional Jewish parents. He broke into the world of crime in his early teens as a pickpocket but soon began moving on to more noteworthy endeavors. He made his name one night in 1910 in a bar fight in Chinatown when he took on three of the area's most fearsome Italian gangsters and made short work of them in full view of a gaping crowd of neighborhood toughs. His newly burnished reputation made him heir to the leadership of Monk Eastman's gang when Monk was gunned down outside a local bar. Zelig was a natural selection for Becker. He had his own collection agency already in place—four battle-hardened deputies, trained by Eastman and ready to perform as instructed—Gyp the Blood, Lefty Louie, Whitey Lewis, and Dago Frank.

If Zelig was ideally suited to his role as enforcer, he would have been no one's first choice to supervise the venture. Becker needed a chief operating officer, and he settled upon a well-known Broadway type, a gambler, setup man, con artist, and all-around conniver by the name of Jacob Rosenzweig. Rosenzweig was better known on the streets as Bald Jack Rose, and not without reason. An early childhood disease had resulted in alopecia, total baldness, which left him without a hair on his body. The absence of eyebrows and eyelashes, together with a chalklike complexion, gave him a ghostly appearance which contrasted sharply with his careful grooming and impeccably precise manner of dress. He brushed his head with talcum powder to reduce the shine and on each hand sported a diamond ring much too large to go unnoticed. Rose received a healthy percent of the take, and by early accounts he was well worth it. During the first ten months of their collaboration, he collected $640,000 for Becker, the equal of roughly $10 million today.

By 1912, Becker had become one of the biggest men in town. He traveled in the fast lane, often in a chauffeured limousine provided by an associate. He liked the bright lights and thrived in the early hours of morning. He was a regular in the hottest nightspots on Broadway, making the scene regularly with his pal Bat Masterson, sports editor of the *Morning Telegraph* and former sheriff of Dodge City. He also retained the services of Charles Plitt, a bookmaker and one-time gossip columnist, to play the part of press agent and get Becker's name in the papers as often as possible. Before too long, Becker would not need a press agent to get his name in the papers.

The moments that turn a man's life can seldom be measured until long after the fact. A chance meeting, an inadvertent word dropped here or there, can at times have consequences far beyond their intent or expectation. Such a moment had come to Charles Becker on the last night of 1911 at a New Year's Eve party in the Elks' Club. He and his wife were, by no choice of their own, seated next to a low-level, East Side gambling house owner by the name of Herman Rosenthal. It was not an association in which Becker found comfort. Rosenthal had a reputation as a small-time operator who made more noise than his position warranted. His professional resume was a study in failure. After a brief spell as a bookmaker, he had run a succession of stuss houses (so named for a form of the card game faro which was played there) on the Lower East Side. One after another, they were shut down by the police to the shrill protests of the owner. He tried his luck with a casino in Far Rockaway on Long Island, but that one failed too.

To his great misfortune, Rosenthal and the police did not mix well. The word on the inside was that Rosenthal, who sported the nickname "Beansie," was not one to play by the rules. He was too quick to cry "foul" when police interfered with his operation, and such occasional interruptions, often in the form of cosmetic raids, were a part of the game. So it stood to reason that Becker did not wish to be seen in friendly discourse with a man who was shunned by the police, particularly since Deputy Commissioner Dougherty was part of the New Year's gathering. Rosenthal, for his part, was down on his luck, and might have reasoned that a cordial connection with Becker could improve his position. They did, after all, have something in common. They shared the good will and support of the biggest kahuna on the block, Big Tim Sullivan. As forceful a presence as he was, it did not stretch the imagination to think that Big Tim's influence might be enough to forge at least a casual, if somewhat reluctant, relationship between two of his protégés.

Sullivan had taken a liking to the young Rosenthal years earlier when Beansie was growing up on the Lower East Side. Rosenthal was five years old when he and his parents came to New York, in 1879, from one of the Baltic provinces of Russia. When he was fourteen, he left home and school and made his way selling newspapers and acting as a runner for a local poolroom operator. He found a home away from home at the Tammany district headquarters and spent as much time there as he could. Sullivan, himself a former newsboy, took Rosenthal under his wing. He looked after the youngster's interests, helped him along here and there, and offered a degree of protection when he thought it was needed. Rosenthal felt he could always count on Sullivan; he believed that the big man's partisanship offered him immunity from such inconveniences as police graft and corruption. It proved to be a fatal misjudgment.

In February 1912, Rosenthal received Sullivan's endorsement to open a gambling casino in the Tenderloin. At the time, he was operating a small room called the Hesper Club (probably named for the evening star, Hesperus) on Second Avenue between Fifth and Sixth Streets. A move to the Tenderloin would be of no small significance. The center of action had been moving uptown, from East Side to West, for a number of years, and it seemed ordained that Times Square, home of the Tenderloin, was the area that would forever define New York City. The Lower East Side was a welcoming venue to those who came seeking refuge, but they would labor hard and long in an effort to flee its cramped quarters for sections of the city that offered more space and better prospects. Though the Hesper Club was a mile or two north of the most congested areas of the East Side, the trip uptown was like seeing the world open up.

The avenues in Times Square were as wide as boulevards and studded with an array of restaurants, hotels, and entertainment centers that made it a magnet for visitors from all parts of the city and beyond. It was, as the song suggested, "where the underworld can meet the elite." At night, lit with theater marquees, the streets were brighter than anywhere else and streaming with more people than anywhere else, and there was room enough to accommodate them all. Women in fine furs and men in formal wear stepped from limousines into avenues they shared with blue-collar factory workers who might be looking at a motor car for the first time. Even the much narrower side streets, running from east to west, had begun to take on the look of the future. Equipped with new Otis elevators, buildings were growing taller (at twenty-six stories, the Pulitzer Building had eclipsed the Times Tower by one), giving the side streets the feel of long, gray canyons that served as counterpoint to the broad, glittering avenues.

It was on such a side street, in a brownstone at 104 West Forty-fifth Street, between Sixth Avenue and Broadway, that Rosenthal wished to open his casino. But while he had the blessings of the man who controlled the action in the area, he lacked the funds to finance the endeavor. He needed money, and he chose an unlikely source to provide it. Rosenthal was well aware that while Sullivan oversaw operations in the Tenderloin, Becker was the man whose hands were at the controls. He and the lieutenant had gotten together from time to time since their meeting on New Year's Eve, and now Rosenthal had a proposition to propose. He asked Becker to lend him $1,500 to open his casino. Becker agreed on the condition that he receive 20 percent of the profits. He also insisted that Rosenthal insure his investment by taking out a chattel mortgage on his household furniture. It was a deal. Becker and Rosenthal were now partners in a gambling casino; add to that that they were on opposite sides of the law and did not really like one another, and the ingredients were in place for an outcome that was beginning to appear foreordained.

Rosenthal opened early in March. As an economy measure, he and his family took residence in an apartment on the fourth floor, with the gaming rooms occupying the floors below. It was one of the more elegant establishments in the area. With space to spare, the roulette tables and faro stations were laid out to offer the players a degree of comfort not always available in the lower-end houses. Rosenthal was looking to attract a higher class of clientele. The Hesper Club would indeed be the evening star of the Tenderloin if Beansie had his say.

With Becker cast in dual roles as partner and payoff collector for the police precinct, Rosenthal was headed for trouble, and it came quickly. On opening night, Beansie balked when Becker told him he was not exempt from making regular payments to the department, the same as the other casino operators.

"No payoffs here," he said. "This is Big Tim's place. I answer to no one but Big Tim." Becker checked with Sullivan who told him to give Rosenthal some breathing room, to hold off for a while. Becker recalled that Sullivan had once referred to Rosenthal and another up-and-coming youngster as a couple of "smart Jew boys" who he expected would one day "go places." The other star-in-the-making was Arnold Rothstein.

Bald Jack Rose, who had been assigned by Becker to monitor operations at the Hesper Club, saw to it that Rosenthal would be afforded protection until things worked themselves out. But the room had barely started humming before the two men collided. When a local gambler by the name of John Freeman dropped $6,000, Rosenthal quickly siphoned off half of it to pay his personal debts before Rose got his cut. When Rose learned that he had been short-changed, the Hesper Club's protection seemed to evaporate.

Just a few days later, a police inspector by the name of Cornelius Hayes invited Beansie to meet him at a local restaurant. Hayes, whose district covered most of midtown Manhattan on the West Side, apparently accused him of running a "crooked wheel." Rosenthal took umbrage. "That's a lie," he responded. "I got straight faro tables and two honest wheels in my house." Rosenthal's protest was tantamount to a confession. He told the inspector, in effect, that he was breaking the law as honestly as he could. Hayes obtained a warrant and closed the Hesper Club less than a week after it had opened. As was the norm, it was soon allowed to reopen, but Rosenthal's real trouble was yet to come.

Big Tim Sullivan, whose influence had begun to wane after the 1909 elections, was ailing, and his days as power broker were now counted in small numbers. Sullivan was suffering from paresis, a disease of the brain that is most often associated with syphilis. His mind was slipping badly, and he would be of little help to Rosenthal or anyone else. Becker saw an opening and knew how to exploit it. He kept the pressure on, and Rosenthal, never a man to weigh the consequences of his actions too closely, provided all the help he needed.

The breaking point came in March 1912, just weeks after the new Hesper Club reopened, when Charles Plitt, Becker's informal press agent, was arrested for murder. Plitt apparently had been playing in an Uptown crap game when Becker's squad raided the place. During the course of the fray, one of the gamblers was fatally shot. A witness at the scene identified Plitt as the shooter. Becker, who was not present at the raid, felt it his duty to raise money for Plitt's defense. Every gambler in the precinct was assessed a sum commensurate with his earnings. Rosenthal's share was five hundred dollars, and he declined to pay it. Becker acted swiftly. He dispatched Big Jack Zelig to visit Rosenthal and collect not only the assessment but an additional five hundred, which would be the first of Beansie's monthly protection payments. Rosenthal again balked. Once more, he looked for help from Sullivan but found that Big Tim was no longer the man to see. Now completely in the grip of dementia, he had been replaced by his brother Florrie and Tom Foley, who had served as his first lieutenant. Florrie offered Rosenthal the best piece of advice he had received in some time. He told him to make his peace with Becker and try to cut a deal. But Rosenthal was determined to make his stand; he refused to make his payments.

Not to be trifled with, Becker pushed back hard. He stationed Rose inside the club to keep track of the receipts. It was a gesture that brought Rosenthal to a boil. The two men had developed a distaste for one another, and Rosenthal resented Bald Jack's ubiquitous presence. He also was beginning to sense that his partnership with Becker was too one-sided. He would soon learn just how one-sided it was.

For some time, Becker had been telling Rosenthal that Waldo was out to get him and it would serve his interest if he agreed to a sham raid being carried out on his club. He said it was standard procedure in the Tenderloin, and all the other casino owners went along with it. The police had to show the commissioner that they were cracking down on gambling establishments. Becker suggested that he rent some cheap wheels just for the raid so that his equipment would not be destroyed. There is no telling whether Rosenthal might have lived to a ripe old age if he had agreed to the plan, but he clearly courted trouble when he turned it down.

On April 13, Becker called Rosenthal and told him that "a certain party" wanted to see him. He said it was important and that he should be at a watering hole called Pabst's at Fifty-ninth Street and Broadway later that evening. Rosenthal showed up at the appointed hour, but there was no one to meet him. He soon grew uneasy and sensed that something was wrong. He hurried back to his home on Forty-fifth Street where he found the front door smashed and windows broken. A patrol wagon was waiting at the curb and several policemen were stationed outside the house. One of them advised Rosenthal to get away from the scene, telling him, "It's all right. Everything is all right. It's Charlie making the raid and it's all right."

It did not seem all right to Rosenthal. He waited across the street until the scene cleared, then went inside and found his place virtually demolished, his gambling equipment chopped to pieces. To aggravate matters, two young men—James Fleming and Herbert Hull—were arrested in the raid on gambling charges. Fleming, it turned out, was Mrs. Rosenthal's nephew. She told her husband that Becker had explained that the raid was made to mollify Waldo. He assured her that her nephew would be cleared in court and said that Rosenthal could consider his $1,500 debt paid in full; they were now even.

But as Beansie saw it, Becker was closer to even than he was. Since the raid, uniformed policemen had been stationed in his club round-the-clock, and they showed no signs of leaving. His nephew, who Becker had promised would be cleared of the gambling charge, was indicted by a grand jury a week later. Rosenthal saw no advantage in having Becker as a partner, and he was beginning to make some noise. He had long been known as a "holler guy"— in the argot of the trade, one who protested too much and too loudly—and it was a reputation that brought with it an element of risk.

As one veteran gambler explained to the *Evening Post:* "The trouble with Herman is that he don't know the rules. The rules are pay your license money . . . lay low, and play like gentlemen. When you get a hint, take it and close down. It's when fighting among the brotherhood is too noisy that the powers step in."

The brotherhood was growing more apprehensive of Rosenthal. If left to his own devices, it seemed likely that he would stir the waters and upset the delicate balance of powers that kept life humming in the Tenderloin. He had already squawked to high-ranking police officials, Tammany pols, and others in the gambling industry. He had petitioned the mayor for an audience, apparently oblivious to the impropriety of asking the mayor's help in conducting an illegal business. He had tried on several occasions to meet with District Attorney Charles Whitman, but he was not interested either. Rosenthal was a man with a story to tell, but no one was listening.

Finally, he decided to act on his own. On Friday, July 12, he filed a lawsuit against Inspector Hayes and Captain William Day, commander of the Sixteenth Precinct, charging that the patrolmen stationed at his club—which was also his home—constituted cruel and unjust treatment by the police. The police court magistrate told him to prepare an affidavit detailing the incidents of "oppression" he had suffered at the hands of the police.

Rosenthal was still hoping to take his case to the district attorney, but he was clearly running out of chances. He was entirely without an advocate; reviled by the police, scorned by politicians, distrusted by his colleagues who "played by the rules." There was only one possible outlet remaining and that was the press. But even the media were not eager to hear him out. Reporters for most papers were reluctant to take Rosenthal's testimony at face value. Stronger evidence than the word of an illegal gaming-house operator would be needed before they were ready to go on record with a tale of police corruption and oppression. There was at least one exception. The *World's* Herbert Bayard Swope, young, daring, and somewhat familiar with the twists and turns that led down the back alleys of the city's darker side, sensed that something big might be waiting if he had the nerve to follow this road to its end.

It is possible that Rosenthal's introduction to Swope came by way of Arnold Rothstein. Rothstein and Swope had much in common. They were both young, born just twelve days apart and not quite thirty when they met; they came from middle-class German-Jewish families, they shared more than just a taste for gambling, and both young men were aiming to see their names flashing in Broadway's brightest lights. Rothstein and Rosenthal, of course, were loosely linked through their association with Big Tim Sullivan. Rothstein, in fact, had advised Rosenthal that his going public would be in no one's best interest. But Beansie insisted that he was under Sullivan's protection and that he owed nothing to Becker. David Pietrusza, in his biography *Rothstein,* offers the following exchange between the two men:

"'The Big Feller [Sullivan] isn't here,' Rothstein shot back. 'And if he was, he'd tell you to keep your trap shut. All you can do is make trouble for a lot of people.'

"'I don't want to make trouble for anyone, only Becker,' Herman protested. 'They ask me about anybody else, I won't tell them. Only about Becker.'"

Rothstein didn't believe him.

"'They're smarter than you are,' A. R. responded. 'They're not interested in doing you any favors. Whitman is only interested in Whitman and the Republicans. He'll crucify the Big Feller.'"

Finally, Rothstein offered Rosenthal five hundred dollars to get out of town, but Beansie declined. "'I'm not leaving town,' he responded. 'That's what Becker wants me to do. I'm staying right here.' A few days later, Rosenthal had second thoughts. Shortly before he went to the *World* with his story, he visited Rothstein at his home. "'I've changed my mind,' he said. 'Give me the money and I'll get out of town.'

"Rothstein replied icily: 'You waited too long. . . . You're not worth five hundred to anyone any more, Beansie.'"

Rothstein's refusal was Swope's bonanza. It was the core of his talent to recognize opportunity when he saw it, and Swope offered Rosenthal the full range of his editorial services. But the editors at the *World* were understandably circumspect. They wanted some assurance that the D.A. was ready to act on Rosenthal's testimony. Here again, Swope had the angle on the most direct route to the D.A.'s office. He had established a connection with Whitman that fed their mutual ambitions. Whitman gave Swope the inside track on choice news stories, and Swope did his part by making certain that Whitman received the attention he craved in the best possible telling.

All the same, bringing Rosenthal and Whitman together was no simple matter. The D.A., who enjoyed some lofty connections of his own, was spending the brutally hot July weekend as the guest of some socialite friends in Newport, Rhode Island. Swope was undeterred. He made the trip to Newport and pried loose from Whitman the commitment to meet with Rosenthal when he returned. The D.A.'s word was good enough for the editors at the *World*.

On Saturday, July 13, the paper ran a lengthy interview in which Rosenthal made many charges but named few names. The real payoff came a day later. Swope helped Rosenthal prepare a long, detailed affidavit, with all the who's, where's, and when's. It occupied all of the front page of the Sunday edition and most of page two. A large headshot of Rosenthal, set in an oval frame, was directly beneath the headline that spanned the width of the page: GRAFT GOT TO HIGH OFFICIAL OF POLICE, MR. WHITMAN SAYS. Mr. Whitman also went on to say, in a large-type drop-head between the headline and the text: "I have a real use for Rosenthal, who, abused by the police, proposes to aid decency by revealing startling conditions." The "high official," of course, was Lieutenant Charles Becker, who was portrayed as the whole System of corruption that ran through the heart of the Tenderloin. Rosenthal and Becker were now joined forever in New York's gritty history of crime and corruption.

Rosenthal had a lot to say. He began at the beginning and omitted nothing. Detail for detail, he unwound a chronicle of events citing people and places with a precision that proclaimed either a memory of imposing dimension or a choreographed rehearsal that left nothing to chance. The central character of course was Lieutenant Charles Becker, and if Rosenthal's story could be trusted, there would be little room to wonder why Becker might not be the first to mourn his demise. But the issue turned on the question of how much of Rosenthal's tale was credible. Sorting fact from fiction was the challenge, and there were no guidelines to show the way. Complicating matters was the circumstance that Rosenthal would not long be available to respond to questions, for in less than two days he would be dead. Here, from the beginning is what his affidavit said:

"The first time I met Charles Becker, now a lieutenant of police in New York City, and who was holding the same office at the time of our first meeting, was at a ball given by the Order of the Elks on Forty-third street, near Sixth avenue, and we had a very good evening, drank very freely and we became very good friends. Our next meeting was by appointment on New Year's Eve, 1912 [sic; it was December 31, 1911], at the Elks' Club. . . .

"We drank a whole lot of champagne that night, and late in the morning we were all pretty well under the weather. He put his arms around me and kissed me. He said, 'Anything in the world for you, Herman. I'll get up at three o'clock in the morning to do you a favor. You can have anything I've got.' And then he called over his three men, James White, Charles Foy and Charles Steinhart, and he introduced me to the three of them, saying: 'This is my best pal, and do anything he wants you to do.' We went along and we met pretty often. Sometimes we would meet at the Lafayette Turkish bath, other times we would meet at the Elks' Club, and many nights we would take an automobile ride. And he told me then that he wished he could put in six months of this, he would be a rich man. He was getting hold of a lot of money. I told him then:

"'Don't you think you are taking a chance by me being seen with you so often?' And he told me: 'I don't have to fear. But when that guy down at Headquarters [meaning Waldo] puts it up to me about meeting you, I'll simply tell him that I am meeting you for a purpose—to get information from you.'

"He came to my house very often during the months of January and February and he used to tell me a lot of things about how much money he was making, and that he was making it awful fast. So I told him the latter part of February: 'I want to borrow $1,500 from you.' He says, 'You're on, on condition that you'll give me 20 percent of your place when you open.'

"So I told him that was satisfactory to me. So he said: 'Well, you go down to my lawyer in a week or so and he will give you what you want and you sign a chattel mortgage on your household furniture.'

"And he also said for me to bring my wife down with me, for her to sign. So I pleaded with him that I wouldn't do that.

"'I don't want her to feel as though you wouldn't trust me with $1,500 without signing over my home,' I said. He said, 'All right.' So I went down to see a lawyer he named at the St. Paul Building, and he says: 'Are you Mr. Rosenthal?' I said: 'Yes, I suppose you know what I am down here for.' He said: 'Why, call Charlie up. I just left him.' So he called up 300 Spring and he asked a man to connect him with the C. O. Squad and this conversation followed:

"He said, 'Charlie, that party is down here.' And the lawyer said, 'Yes, he has a brown hat and a brown tie.' He said, 'All right,' and with that he rang off. Now the lawyer told me: 'You have to sign this note and these papers,' and I did as he told me, signed the note for $1,500 to the order of J. Donohue.

I also signed some other papers. And I got the $1,500, and the lawyer said: 'It will cost you $50 now.' And I said, 'For what?' He said, 'For drawing up the papers.' So I asked him then: 'Will I tell Charlie about it?' So he said, 'I would rather not if I were you.' Well, I said, 'All right, I'll come and see you some time.'

"Well, I went along for a few weeks when finally Lieut. Becker met me by appointment and told me what a hard job he has got in stalling Waldo. That Waldo wanted him to 'get me.' 'I have told Waldo that I have got my men trying to get evidence. And by doing so I kept stalling him.' I met him three nights after that again. He told me that I must give him a raid. He said, 'You can fix it up any way you like. Get an old roulette wheel and I'll make a bluff and smash the windows. That will satisfy Waldo, I suppose.' I told him that I would not stand for it. That if he wanted to raid me he would have to get the evidence. That I would not stand for a 'frame-up.' 'Well, he said, I'll do the best I can to stall him.'

"Two nights afterward he called me on the wire at my home and he told me to go and see a certain party at half past ten in the evening at Fifty-ninth street and Broadway, at a place called 'Pabst's.' When I reached Pabst's there was nobody there to meet me. Then I suspected something was wrong. So when I came back to my home I found the windows broken, the doors smashed and the patrol wagon waiting outside. I wanted to go in when Policeman James White told me to get away, not to come. Everything is all right. It's Charlie making the raid and it's all right.

"So I stood across the street and waited until everything was over and went into my home, when my wife told me that Charlie said he had to make this raid to save himself. That it is all right, not to worry. 'And tell Herman to go down to the St. Paul Building tomorrow and get the papers from the lawyer. You tell him that I am standing the expenses of this raid, $1,500. You tell Herman that he and I are even, and I will see him to-morrow.'

"They arrested Jesse [sic] Fleming and Herbert Hull and charged them with being common gamblers. The next day in court Charlie told me to waive examination, that he wanted to make the raid look natural and that he would turn it out in the Grand Jury room. I said, 'Can I trust you?' He said, 'Why it is all right. You can.' So I had the case adjourned until the next day to think the matter over. So I waived examination the next day.

"I next met Lieut. Becker three or four nights later and hired a taxi-cab from Frawley's on Forty-fifth street and Sixth avenue and met him by appointment at Forty-sixth street and Sixth avenue. He jumped into the taxi with me. We rode downtown very slowly, talking over different things, and we finally had an argument. When we left we were on very bad terms.

"The last word I said to him that night, 'You know your promise.' 'Well,' he said, 'we'll see.' About a week later the Grand Jury handed in an indictment against James Fleming and Herbert Hull. I called Mr. Becker on the telephone that afternoon and I asked him what he meant by not living up to his promise. He told me, 'Aw, you talk too much. I don't want to talk to you at all.' I said: 'You had better consider. You know what you are doing.' 'Aw,' he said, 'you can go to hell.'

"I have never spoken to him since. But I tried to right this wrong and sent some people to Commissioner Waldo to explain things to him without any satisfaction. I went before District Attorney Charles Whitman and I laid the whole matter before him. It wasn't enough evidence for him to indict Becker. But he said, 'I'll investigate this matter thoroughly.'

"I have repeatedly sent persons to Becker to ask him to take the policeman out of my home and he told them to tell me that as long as he was in the Police Department he would see that the copper was not taken out. And he would also see that I would be driven from New York.

"I believe that the reason that Lieut. Becker wants to drive me out of New York is because I have not hesitated to tell anybody the truth regarding my own experience with Lieut. Becker, as representing the police."

Since no action could be taken on Rosenthal's charges without corroboration, he attached to his affidavit a list of gamblers, members of the police force, and city officials who he said were involved in the paying and taking of graft. Of course, none of them was likely to support Rosenthal's story unless he was subpoenaed to appear before a grand jury. It remained for Rosenthal to persuade the district attorney that a grand jury investigation was warranted.

The affidavit itself left much room for speculation. Elsewhere, Rosenthal had said he first met Becker the previous fall when he raided his place on the East Side, at 155 Second Avenue, which was far outside Becker's normal range of operation and months before the New Year's Eve meeting described in the affidavit. Many of the specifics sworn to in the statement appeared to be questionable on their face, and Becker, not surprisingly, denied almost all of them. There was room to dispute, for example, how the $1,500 loan was arranged and what was offered in exchange, but it was clear that a loan in that amount had been made and that Becker had received in return a financial interest in Rosenthal's establishment.

Regardless of the level of accuracy it achieved, the affidavit accomplished its purpose: It placed Becker at the center of the graft machine known as the System, and Rosenthal could no longer be ignored by the district attorney. With Swope's help, he had become a key player. He was somebody now, and so was Swope. The *World* was out front with the story of a major network of corruption that involved both the New York City Police Department and the core of municipal government. The other city papers picked it up in later editions, but the *World* was leading the way, and Swope was about to cross the threshold of a career that would be bigger than even he had dared to imagine.

Swope, whose family name was Schwab before they arrived in the United States, had come to New York from St. Louis in 1901. Not yet twenty, he took a job as a reporter with the *New York Herald*. Newspapers required little in the way of formal training at the time, and an aggressive young man with a pulse for events and a vision of glory could build a reputation quickly if circumstance fell in his favor. Swope, however, seemed to be more interested in being a part of the action than covering it. He learned about the dark side of life in New York at first hand; he made his gambling connections by frequenting the tables and developed a quick sense of who had their fingers on the levers of power. One of his closest friends was Arnold Rothstein who, when all the dust from the Becker case finally settled, would become the most influential player in New York's organized crime scene. Swope moved with equal ease and flair between the city's high-end social set and its underside, which had always shared a hostile allure for one another. By the time he moved to the *World,* in 1909, he had developed an unerring instinct for attaching himself to the people who could help him most. Whitman, he saw immediately, could be an invaluable asset to a newspaper reporter who was seeking a marginal advantage over his competitors.

Swope covered both a crime beat and local politics, and he was quick to note that the two were not unrelated. The year 1909 marked a shift in the New York political scene, with a weakening of Tammany's control and the election of Republicans to posts that traditionally had been Democratic. Among Republicans chosen for key offices was Charles Seymour Whitman, who was elected district attorney.

Whitman, whose father was the pastor of a church in Hanover, Connecticut, was raised in the climate of an unbending morality that offered no room for the escapades that came so naturally to Swope. As a youth, Whitman had little interest in the frivolous pursuits that engaged most teenagers and even less patience for those who gave the appearance of snipping at the edges of the virtuous life. He fit the mold of the pastor's son, and he looked the part as well. He was of slight build, with widely spaced hazel eyes, a shock of brown hair that he parted down the center, and unusually thin lips, which, when set tight, suggested a determination of purpose and a capacity for judgment that was not about to waver. In added contrast to Swope, whose high school diploma was awarded grudgingly and who spurned further education, Whitman was an eager and brilliant student. He earned honors in high school and was Phi Beta Kappa at Amherst College, where he prepared for the study of law. In need of funds for law school, he moved to New York and took a job teaching Latin and Greek at Adelphi Academy in Brooklyn while attending New York University Law School. He received his law degree and passed the bar in 1894 at the age of twenty-six.

Whitman set out in his own practice and found the going tough. He barely subsisted on small cases that came his way and spent his spare time at the Criminal Courts building, watching trials, looking for a niche he might make his own in the criminal justice system. What he found was a system that seemed to trample on the rights of the unfortunate, mostly immigrants, who had neither the know-how nor the money to navigate their way through the halls of justice. His religious sensibilities offended, Whitman began representing, pro bono, the detritus of the justice system—prostitutes, pickpockets, small-time operators—who were sometimes held for unconscionably long periods of time without being properly charged or arraigned. His persistent activities in their behalf were viewed as an unnecessary obstacle on the road to justice by the Tammany magistrates who ran the courts, but they earned Whitman a reputation as a man of principle, an advocate who could be trusted to apply the law evenly. It was a reputation that worked to his advantage, for a new mayor was about to take office, and he was looking to clean house.

Seth Low, former president of Columbia University, was elected mayor in 1899 as a fusion candidate during one of the intermittent periods in which Tammany had fallen into disfavor. In making appointments, his first priority, it seemed, was to find people who were upright in their public posture and whose names bore not even a suggestion of taint. If a man was disdained by the Tammany crowd, that accrued to his favor. Whitman, who had all the qualities Low was looking for, was appointed assistant corporation counsel, the number two man in the city's legal office. He served creditably and was rewarded for his effort. Tammany reclaimed its position of power in the 1903 elections, but Low saw to it that Whitman was taken care of. On his last official day in office, he named Whitman to a position on the magistrate's court. For the next three years, Whitman served as judge in the Jefferson Market Court, the Victorian Gothic landmark at Sixth Avenue and Tenth Street in Greenwich Village, where women defendants, mostly streetwalkers, were sent for the speedy, if not entirely equitable, dispensation of justice. Whitman soon discovered that a carefully honed strain of corruption ran through his court.

By the nature of their offense, most of the women brought before him were arrested at night, when court was no longer in session. They would be held in jail until the next morning when their cases would be heard. At that time, the arresting officer would offer insufficient evidence, Whitman would be forced to dismiss the case, and the defendant would be returned to the streets. The punishment for the presumed offense had already been meted out—the accused had to spend a night in the slammer. To avoid being sent to jail, many of those arrested would pay five dollars to a bail bond broker who would guarantee their appearance. The five dollars was split three ways: the bail bondsman kept two, the arresting officer got one, and the precinct captain received the remaining two, which often was shared with a Tammany operative.

It did not take Whitman long to discern a pattern, and he believed he had a solution. He collected the details on four hundred cases in which he suspected a payoff had been made and delivered the evidence to the state legislature in Albany. With an eye to the future, he also stopped by to visit with Governor Charles Evans Hughes, who later would be named to the U.S. Supreme Court. Both the lawmakers and the governor were impressed. Not only had Whitman fully documented his case, he also brought with him a plan to resolve the problem. His solution, which eventually was passed by the legislature and signed by the governor, was the creation of a night court which allowed defendants to have their cases decided immediately, making it unnecessary to post bail. Night court became an integral and permanent part of the criminal justice system.

Named a magistrate in 1907, Whitman became something of a judicial activist. It had come to his attention that the saloons in his neighborhood, which happened to be in the heart of the Tenderloin, were in the habit of remaining open long past the prescribed closing hour of one A.M. It was a circumstance that Whitman learned of at first hand. A man with an unrepentant thirst for a late-night nip or two, he sometimes went from bar to bar well past the witching hour, ordered himself a drink, and then called the local precinct to have the saloon keeper arrested. His one-man sorties soon earned him the sobriquet of "the raiding judge."

Whitman's moralistic zeal did not escape the notice of Governor Hughes, himself known to be something of a purist, and when an opening arose on the Court of General Sessions Hughes offered Whitman the opportunity to fill it on an interim basis. Whitman eagerly accepted, but the interim for which he served turned out to be very brief. Four months later, in November 1907, he lost his bid for reelection. His defeat was little more than a speed bump on his climb to the top. In 1909, running on a fusion, anti-Tammany ticket, Whitman was elected district attorney by a wide margin. That was the same year that Gaynor was elected mayor as Tammany's compromise candidate, and the two men, who ostensibly had the same goal, also had some interesting differences.

While both were committed to "cleaning up the city," they did not necessarily agree on what it was that needed to be cleaned up. Gaynor thought it was official graft—both political and in the police department—that was the corrupting influence. "The law does not commit the supreme folly of making [the police] the custodians of the private morals of the community," he had famously said. Establishments that did not present themselves to open view, whether brothels or not, should be left undisturbed.

Whitman's moralistic tendencies moved in an altogether different direction. His contempt for ladies of the night was harsh enough to raise questions about his own attitudes regarding the moral texture of life in the city. While the new district attorney proclaimed his distaste for gambling houses, police corruption, and the bribing of civil officials, it was the practice of prostitution that most seemed to inflame his sense of purity and virtue. As quoted by Jonathan Root, in his book *One Night in July*, Whitman stated his position on the subject unambiguously:

"Women of the streets are the most dangerous factor in the spread of crime," he said in an exercise in hyperbole. "[A streetwalker] seldom reforms, for she is criminal in all her instincts. She is the greatest of unfortunates, but she is also the recipient of much misplaced sympathy. It will be impossible to drive all of them from the streets, but their operations can be confined to a restricted area. The grafting of the police in this regard will be stopped."

But not strictly by chance had prostitution survived through the ages as the world's oldest profession. It was after all an intimate business that was conducted by only two people at a time in circumstances as clandestine as could be arranged. Gambling, by contrast, depended upon large numbers of players plying their trade in spacious rooms that were open to the public and as visible as possible, even to the unpracticed eye. It was the gambling industry that fed the System and kept it running; that was where the action was, and if Whitman was not quite aware of its reach and its drive, Swope was more than ready to bring it to his attention; Rosenthal's affidavit would do the job.

Swope, of course, knew every bend in that road with the canniness that is the special province of the insider. He was acquainted with all its intricacies and he understood how it ran and who ran it and, being a man of large ambition, he was quick to sense the same appetite in others. It was the one trait that he and Whitman shared. Whitman was not so alert to the possibilities that common ground offered, but Swope had an unerring instinct for the soft side of every proposition. He understood that political ambition was a hunger that had no limits, and he knew how to feed it.

The lead headline in Monday morning's edition of the *World,* on July 15, noted that both Whitman and Waldo were returning early from their summer respites to pursue the allegations made by Rosenthal in his affidavit. Deputy Commissioner Dougherty also was recalled to duty. The drop-head noted that Waldo resented the statement that New York has been wide open and that he wanted his administration cleared of stain. He said he would demand a thorough inquiry. The Commissioner was understandably irate on being called home from Toronto. He was to be one of the featured speakers at a police chief's convention. The subject of the conference was, "How to Wipe Out Police Graft." It was Whitman, however, who would lead the investigation.

The text of the article read:

"District Attorney Whitman is cutting short his stay here in Newport so as to be ready to take up to-morrow morning the investigation into the Police Department brought about by the publication in the *World* of the charges of Herman Rosenthal.

"'Rosenthal has told a story full of accusations and possibly full of truth, but as yet he has done nothing more than tell the story—he has not in any way substantiated it,' Mr. Whitman said to-night.

"'I have seen and am seeing to it that he is given the fullest chance to make good his charges, not because I am eager to see any scandal uncovered in the Police Department, but because his accusations are so serious as to call forth the utmost efforts of my office to determine their weight.'"

Whitman returned to the city and met with Rosenthal that night in the Criminal Courts building. By all accounts, the D.A. welcomed Rosenthal's testimony, which reprised much of what he had said in his affidavit. In only his third year as district attorney, Whitman was about to break open one of the biggest scandals in the city's history. He assured his informer that he would convene a grand jury to hear the charges. Rosenthal had finally found himself an advocate. His name was in the headlines of every newspaper in town. Now, he felt as big as the System itself, for he had his finger on the power switch, and he could flick it whenever he chose. Like him or not, every gambler in the city would be obliged to pay homage. Beansie had become the district attorney's main man. They agreed to meet again on Tuesday morning at eight. Never more pleased with himself, Rosenthal stepped out into late-night streets and headed uptown to the Metropole.

5

Lying lifeless on the pavement, Beansie Rosenthal attracted more attention than he ever had while living. Now past two A.M. on Tuesday, July 16, a crowd of some size had gathered around his fallen body. At first, they were mostly denizens of the night—streetwalkers and their johns, gamblers, assorted drifters—who happened to be nearby. But their number soon was swollen by customers from hotels and clubs that operated well into the night and by random insomniacs, perhaps kept awake by the heat, who had heard the shots and ventured out into the streets. By some estimates, several thousand people had converged on the scene. As the crowd grew, so did the contingent of police who were trying to keep order and sort out the details of the shooting. Days later, there would be reason to take account of who in particular might have been there, but at the time, events seemed to be sweeping by too quickly.

One of those at the scene was William J. File, an off-duty police detective and a Metropole regular. Billy File, as he was known, was a one-time sparring partner of James J. Corbett's who looked every bit the part. When File heard the shots, he drew his gun and headed for the entrance. He saw the gray Packard sedan turn south on Sixth Avenue, but the streets were too crowded to risk firing his revolver. Instead, he ran to a taxi stand at the Cadillac Hotel, near the corner of Forty-third Street and Broadway. There, he met with two other officers, and the three of them piled into a cab and sent the driver in the direction of the fleeing touring car. But when they turned into Sixth Avenue, the Packard was no longer in sight. The police queried passersby who directed them east and finally north on Madison Avenue, but when they got as far as Central Park with still no sign of the Packard, they turned around and went back to the Metropole. At just about that time, a police patrol wagon arrived and carted Rosenthal's body to the Forty-seventh Street station house.

The police pursuit of the getaway car impressed no one, least of all District Attorney Whitman. In a statement the following day, he would characterize the car chase as "little more than a pretense of pursing the killers." Even more disturbing was the matter of the hit car's license plate number. The police had brought back several versions of the number, but none was quite exact. The correct number—the critical bit of evidence that would lead to the arrest of the killers—was jotted down by a passerby who, after offering it to the police, was first ignored and then abused

Charles Gallagher, an out-of-work café singer, was on his way to the Metropole to speak with Jim Considine, the club's manager, about a possible booking when he heard the shots and saw the Packard speeding down Forty-third Street. He made a note of the number: New York 41313. He offered it to police at the scene but was pushed aside. "We already have the number," he was told. But Gallagher had overheard the numbers that were given to the police. "All those numbers are wrong," he said and repeated the correct plate number. As a reward for his offer of help, Gallagher was taken forcibly to the station house, booked as a material witness, and thrown into a jail cell for safekeeping.

While police set to work tracking the car, the Forty-seventh Street station house had become the nerve center of operations. The building that housed it was a hard-edged structure that looked much the way a police station might be expected to look. There was a forbidding sense about it, both inside and out. Its sturdy brick façade served as a shell for a structure that was rotting at its core. Paint that had been laid on too many years ago was peeling from the walls. The wooden floorboards groaned beneath one's step. The desks, stained from spilled coffee and scarred by cigarette burns, testified to long nights of bookings and interrogations, and the unseen minutiae of police work that proceeds round the clock every day of the week. Decades later, it would be difficult for the untrained eye to differentiate between a police station and a nursery, as form ceased to reflect function. But in 1912, on the west side of Forty-seventh Street, there was no mistaking the building that housed the Sixteenth Precinct. Now, even as the clock inched toward dawn, the feeling of unease that was so much a part of the structure was heightened by the relentless heat that radiated from the brick walls and became trapped inside. The open windows offered no relief. And this was as cool as it would get. In just a few hours, the sun would be up.

The word of the shooting spread quickly. Rosenthal's body had barely cooled when the ring of telephones began rousing from sleep newsmen who would soon be racing to the scene; gamblers who would make it their business to stay away; and high-ranking police officers and city officials, many of whose lives would now never be the same. Police Commissioner Waldo got the word in his suite at the Ritz-Carlton but did not think his presence was needed. Whitman also was reluctant to interrupt his night's sleep. Swope called the D.A. at his apartment on Madison Square and urged him to get to the station house, but Whitman thought morning would be soon enough. Swope knew it would not; he could hear destiny calling. He took a taxi to Whitman's home and personally escorted him to the station. It was just past three A.M. when they arrived.

Becker's informant was a young police reporter for the *New York Sun* by the name of Fred Hawley. Becker had spent the evening at Madison Square Garden watching Buck Crouse beat Joe Worthing in the main event. With him were Deacon Terry, a police reporter who covered the Criminal Courts Building for Hearst's morning paper, the *New York Journal,* and Jacob Reich, alias Jack Sullivan, a newspaper distributor who was known among the Broadway crowd as King of the Newsboys. After the fights, the three men, riding in a car Becker had borrowed for the occasion, went for drinks at the St. George Hotel on East Twenty-eighth Street. At some time past midnight, they let Terry off at Thirty-third Street and Sixth Avenue, where he took the Hudson tubes to his home in Jersey City. Becker dropped Reich at Forty-fourth and Broadway and then drove to his own home on the northern end of Manhattan. He had barely settled into sleep when Hawley phoned him.

Hawley was to Becker what Swope was to Whitman, but in any such pairing Whitman had the edge; Swope was by far more seasoned and more adept at turning events to his favor. In the final summing, however, Becker might have proved to be his own best counsel. Wiser in the ways of the street than either Waldo or Whitman, he understood immediately that he was confronted with a Hobson's choice. Unlike the police commissioner or the district attorney, he had no official call to rush to the scene. The murder of Rosenthal had followed by a matter of hours the dead man's accusation that Becker was the king of corruption in the police department. It was not much of a stretch to think that he would be considered a suspect. The consequences of his decision about whether to go to the station house therefore could well be profound. If he went, it might appear that he was trying to deflect suspicion by helping to initiate a search for the killers. If he did not show up, it might look as though he was unconcerned, perhaps even gratified, by the silencing of his accuser. He decided he would be best served by going to the station house. At the very least, that would place him on the inside; he would be in a better position to know what the official thinking was and where he stood.

He met Hawley at the Metropole, now dark and abandoned, and together they walked to Forty-seventh Street. It was not yet four o'clock, but newsboys were already hawking "extras," early editions of the morning papers. The headline in the *World,* in three decks, read: GAMBLER ROSENTHAL SLAIN / BY THREE MEN IN FRONT / OF METROPOLE AT 2 A.M. The five-line drop-head beneath it carried more detail: Man Who Made Charges Against Police Lieutenant Becker Was in Conference in Hotel with Several Men—Assassins Drive Up in a Touring Car and Begin Shooting as Soon as Their Victim Appears on Street—Four Policemen Hear the Shots and Run to Scene—Two Commandeer a Taxicab and Chase the Murderers Whose Car Speeds Up Fifth Avenue and Disappears in Central Park. Just below was the same head shot of Rosenthal that was used in Sunday's paper, topped by the cutline, "GAMBLER MURDERED IN POLICE FEUD." Not all of the details were entirely accurate, but the paper was on the streets just about two hours after the killing. There remained some confusion about how many men had been involved in the shooting and how many were in the escape car, but the investigation was clearly being put on the fast track.

Whitman understood that this was a case that could not be entrusted to the police, since the police were to be the chief object of the inquiry. The D.A.'s office would have to conduct the investigation itself. So it should not have been a total surprise that when Becker arrived at the station he found Whitman sitting behind the desk that belonged to Precinct Captain Day. It did not take Becker long to realize that his presence was neither needed nor welcome. He stepped back into the street where he was immediately surrounded by a throng of newspapermen. It was an opportunity not to be lost. Intuiting that he might be considered a primary suspect, Becker made a preemptive statement to the press:

"Coming as this does at this psychological moment, it is most unfortunate. It ought to be needless for me to say—and I think I ought not to be asked to say—what you newspapermen know to be the fact that I know absolutely nothing about the crime—who perpetrated it, what the motive was, or what was to be gained by it. I want to say now that I have said this much—and perhaps I am violating a rule of the department by so saying—that it was to my best and only advantage that Rosenthal should have been permitted to live for many years. I bear this man no malice. He set himself up as my enemy. I have explained every move I made with this man to the satisfaction of my superiors."

He went on to refute, glancingly, some of the charges Rosenthal made in his affidavit, including their meeting at the Elks' Club and the $1,500 he had loaned Rosenthal for his mortgage. Though obviously self-serving, his statement was not altogether lacking in substance. With Rosenthal alive, Becker would have been able to confront his charges directly and perhaps impugn his credibility. He had in fact already begun gathering evidence for a libel suit against Rosenthal and the *World*. Toward that end, he had retained an attorney by the name of John Hart, who previously had worked for the district attorney's office. Now, with Rosenthal dead, the statements he had made about Becker assumed a life of their own. When the case came to trial, Becker would be deprived of the opportunity to confront and question his chief accuser. Of course, those who would make the case against Becker were not without arguments in their own behalf. Rosenthal's murder, it could be said, sent a message to others that lining up with the district attorney could be dangerous to one's health. If there was no one to corroborate Rosenthal's allegations, Becker could well find himself in the clear.

With Whitman orchestrating the investigation, events began moving quickly. Deputy Commissioner Dougherty had traced the license plate of the gray touring car, and within two hours of the murder, it was in the possession of the police. Before long, so were the owner and the driver. The car was registered to Louis Libby, who ran the Boulevard Taxi Service at Second Avenue and Tenth Street. It was one of the autos Libby offered for hire and by far the most popular. Its original owner was John L. Sullivan, the first heavyweight champion of the world, and there was no shortage of customers who took delight in touring the city's streets in the same stylish elegance as the great John L.

Libby was snatched from sleep in the early hours of morning at his apartment on Stuyvesant Street, a few blocks north of Greenwich Village. A slightly built man and of timid disposition, Libby was not ready to play fast-and-loose with New York's Finest in the midst of a murder investigation, especially when he was nowhere near the car at the time of the shooting. Yes, he owned the car, but it was driven that night by his partner, William Shapiro. Shapiro had taken the car out at about ten the previous night and returned it shortly after two the next morning. One more thing: Shapiro told him that the car had been used in a shooting. Shapiro was picked up at around daybreak as a material witness and later charged with homicide. Libby's candor did him little good. He too was charged with homicide, and both men were sent to the Tombs.

The tug-of-war between the police department and the district attorney's office had just begun, but it was gathering momentum swiftly. Dougherty had refused to allow Whitman to question Libby and Shapiro. Until the case was fed into the judicial machinery, he contended, it was the police who had jurisdiction. For his part, Whitman believed that turning the case over to the police was akin to having a suspect interrogate himself. He believed the police bore responsibility for Rosenthal's murder, and on that very afternoon, still July 16, he put his views on the record in a hastily called press conference. After apologizing to Charles Gallagher for the way he was treated, Whitman submitted his indictment of the police department:

"I accuse the police department of New York, through certain members of it, with having murdered Herman Rosenthal.

"Either directly or indirectly it was because of them that he was slain in cold blood with never a chance for his life. And the time and place selected were such as to inspire terror in the hearts of those the System had most to fear. It was intended to be a lesson to anyone who might have thought of exposing the alliance between the police and crime.

"Just as he was about to give important additional evidence and to give the names of eight or ten men who could and would support his charges; just as the situation shapes up most dangerously for the police involved, he is killed and with him dies his evidence.

"But the case against Lieutenant Becker will be pushed through with all possible vigor, even though it is apparent that no conviction can result."

The conviction Whitman was referring to of course was for Becker's role in the police graft system. At this point he was not yet officially a suspect in the murder case, but that would not be long in coming. The net was being cast widely now, and a growing number of names was being added to the list of those who were either directly implicated or believed to be harboring valuable information. Bridgey Webber and Harry Vallon had been seen in or around the Metropole at the time of the killing. Other names were thrown into the mix—Bald Jack Rose, whose monitoring of the Hesper Club made him a natural enemy of Rosenthal's; Big Jack Zelig, who frequently rented the same car that was used in the shooting; and Sam Paul, head of the eponymous Sam Paul Association, a social club spin-off of Tammany Hall whose members were connected to the gambling industry in one way or another. Zelig had been arrested a few weeks earlier on a gun charge, but he was said to be seen talking to Rose on the night of the murder. Paul was a man of some influence in the gaming world and no friend of Rosenthal's. On Sunday, July 14, the day Rosenthal's affidavit appeared in the *World,* the Sam Paul Association held an outing at Northport, Long Island, and Rosenthal was the subject of much discussion. Word surfaced that during a poker game aboard a ship called the *Sea Gate,* a prediction was made that if "Herman did not keep his mouth shut, someone would get him and get him for keeps."

Among those taking part in the outing was Bridgey Webber, a long-time rival of Rosenthal's and the man who fingered him at the Metropole minutes before the shots were fired. Webber, named Louis at birth, had acquired his nickname following an abbreviated marriage to a 200-pound prostitute named Bridget. He was the first East Side gambling impresario to open a casino in the Tenderloin. Bridgey had made his earlier jump to the East Side from Chinatown, where he was reputed to have supplemented his gambling income in the opium trade. When Rosenthal followed him to the West Side and opened a place not far from his, Bridgey did not welcome the competition. His resentment of Rosenthal (it might as easily have been called hatred) was intense, and he made no attempt to hide it.

Webber was an obvious choice to be among the first brought in by the police for questioning. His prominence in the Tenderloin was well documented, and he was readily accessible. On the night of the murder, he was taken directly to the commissioner's office for questioning. He gave this account of his activities on the night of July 15:

"I went to the Garden and saw the fights, returning to my clubhouse about 11:45 P.M. I remained there until about 12:50 A.M., then walked to Broadway and to the Metropole . . . I saw Rosenthal sitting with Boob Walker, Hicky, Butch and Moe Brown . . . I returned to the club and sat in front of the door until about 2:30, when I heard Herman was shot. I don't know who told me . . . I didn't see Rose on July 15 and he was not at my clubhouse between 11 and 11:45 that night. I don't know anything about the murder."

After making his statement, Webber was taken to police headquarters where he was booked on what the *New York Times* called the enigmatic "suspicious person" charge. Webber was now the third person in police custody. It was not yet twenty-four hours since the crime had been committed, so it appeared that the authorities were moving with dispatch. But while the list of possible suspects kept getting longer, the focus had gotten no sharper. The gun that fired the fatal shots could not be placed in the hand of any of those being held. So far, Libby and Shapiro were the only ones who could be tied directly to the events, and the investigation would have to begin with them. They certainly knew who had leased the car, and if Shapiro did not know the names of his passengers, the man who rented the car would be the next best source. The picture brightened late Tuesday morning when Aaron J. Levy, a Tammany attorney, walked, unannounced, into police headquarters. He said he was representing Libby and Shapiro.

Levy, who was on his way to becoming a power in the New York State legislature, indicated early that he knew how the pieces fit. He announced that his clients were prepared to make a full statement, but it would have to be directly to the district attorney. Doubtless briefed by Tammany, Levy was aware of the hazards involved in dealing with the police. He also insisted that his clients be transferred to cells in the Criminal Courts Building where Whitman had his office. It would be more convenient for Whitman and probably safer for his clients. Whitman was more than eager. Libby and Shapiro were shepherded into his office, and Levy read the district attorney a prepared statement. After a bit of revision, Whitman had the statement retyped and invited a bevy of waiting reporters in to hear it directly. Levy read them the revised statement. In substance, it said:

Libby turned over the car to Shapiro at about ten o'clock on the night of Monday, July 15, at the Café Boulevard, on Second Avenue and Twenty-first Street. A few minutes later, a call came in to the café to have the car sent to Tom Sharkey's saloon on Fourteenth Street and Third Avenue. Shapiro drove to Sharkey's where three men got in the car and told the driver to go to Bridgey Webber's poolroom at Forty-second and Sixth. There, all the passengers exited the car and Shapiro was told to wait.

Half an hour later, seven men came down the stairs, and six of them got into the car. The other remained on the sidewalk and said to those inside the car, "Now make good." Shapiro was then told to drive to the Metropole and pull up opposite the entrance. Two men got out of the car, told Shapiro to wait, and entered the hotel. Two others left the car and stood on the sidewalk, blocking Shapiro's view of the entrance.

A few minutes later, Shapiro said, he heard loud voices and several shots were fired. Two of the men jumped back into the car and ordered Shapiro to "get out of here." When Shapiro hesitated, one of the men in the back seat leaned over and struck him on the side of the head with a pistol, shouting, "Go on, you bastard. The cops are all fixed. It's a clean getaway."

Shapiro drove to Sixth Avenue, then headed east and turned north on Madison Avenue. He was driving as fast as he could, thirty-five miles an hour, hoping he would be stopped by a policeman for speeding. Somewhere in the Eighties, he was ordered to stop. All the men got out of the car and told him to "beat it." He was never paid for his services.

The statement itself shed no new light on the killing, as Shapiro insisted he did not know the identity of any of the passengers; he had never seen any of them before. But another piece of information was yet to come. A reporter asked if Shapiro knew who had rented the car; Levy responded, "Yes, he does. The car was hired by Bald Jack Rose."

Now, the investigation was about to pick up speed.

Herman "Beansie" Rosenthal was laid to rest on Thursday, July 18. The service was held at his home-cum-gambling club at 104 West Forty-fifth Street. The city was still sizzling. At ten o'clock in the morning the temperature was already in the eighties. Still, the street fronting the brownstone was crammed with the curious. Not every day did a neighbor's death capture front-page headlines in every paper in town. Beansie's murder was big-time stuff; there were certain to be some familiar faces attending the service. As it turned out, there were not very many. Though a number of the city's gambling fraternity helped Rosenthal's widow meet the funeral expenses, they did not deem their presence to be necessary. Having no volunteers, members of the undertaker's staff acted as pallbearers.

The undertaker had done a commendable job restoring what was left of Rosenthal's face, but his widow, Lillian, was not impressed. Sobbing hysterically, the second Mrs. Rosenthal leaned her massive frame over the coffin and shouted, "That's not Herman! There's been a mistake. Isn't it a mistake? Tell me it's a mistake. Tell me it isn't my Herman." But it was her Herman, clearly recognizable and laid out decorously in evening dress.

The brief service was conducted by Rabbi Samuel Greenfield from the Washington Heights (Reformed) Congregation. According to the account by Jonathan Root, the rabbi made an oblique reference to the circumstances that brought Rosenthal down. "It is not given to us," he said, "to round out the term of our creation, and Herman Rosenthal was cut down at a time when he was most needed." He then compared Rosenthal's travails to those of King David who "also had no place to hide his weary head from the darts of his enemies." The body was finally carried away in a hearse drawn by two chestnut horses.

To no one's surprise, Bald Jack Rose, the dead man's bête noir, did not attend the funeral. To everyone's surprise, Rose had taken the occasion to turn himself in at police headquarters, jarring the nerves of every member of the gambling fraternity. He had acted on the advice of his Tammany-connected attorney, James Mark Sullivan, but it was a maneuver that was not out of character. Rose had a reputation as the shrewdest of poker players, and now it was as if he had chosen to risk something in order to get an idea of what cards the opposition was holding. Splendidly turned out in a medley of gray suit, shirt and tie, wearing a panama hat, and carrying a walking stick, he strolled casually into headquarters and asked to see Commissioner Waldo. Remarkably, though the police had been looking for him and his photo had been featured in every paper in town, he attracted no attention. Told that Waldo was not in, Rose left as nonchalantly as he had entered, only to return about an hour later. This time, he walked directly to Waldo's office and found Deputy Dougherty filling in for the commissioner.

Rose admitted having leased the car on the night of July 15, but he insisted that he was nowhere near it at the time of the murder. Early in the evening, he said, he had gone to the Lafayette Turkish Baths on the Lower East Side, a regular haunt of the uptown gambling crowd. There he met Harry Vallon and Sam Schepps, a gambler and reputed opium dealer who was known as Rose's flunky. The three of them, together with Charles Plitt, walked up to Twenty-third Street to the home of Dora Gilbert, Rosenthal's first wife. Rose's mission was to gather evidence attesting to flaws in Rosenthal's credibility that could be used against him in any future legal proceeding. Rose explained that he, as well as Becker, had been named in Rosenthal's sweeping indictment. He emphasized, however, that he had gone to see Gilbert on his own, not at Becker's urging.

Having obtained what he wanted, Rose said, he called for a car and had Shapiro drive him to his brother-in-law's house on West 143rd Street and then to Bridgey Webber's gambling room. After playing a few hands of poker, he dropped in to Jack's Restaurant at Forty-third and Sixth where he had a drink or two. It was there, he said, that he heard about the shooting. "I wasn't very surprised," he said, "for it was in the air that Rosenthal was running a big risk acting the way he did." Rose acknowledged that there had been bad blood between him and Rosenthal, but he maintained he knew nothing of any plans to silence the talkative Beansie. Dougherty was not overly impressed. He charged Rose with complicity to murder and sent him to the Tombs, where he joined Libby and Shapiro.

The Tombs was beginning to fill with suspects, but none of them could be tied directly to the crime. The police said they had a good idea who the killers were. They had pieced together information gleaned from the suspects they had questioned and descriptions and nicknames provided by Shapiro. They believed the four shooters were hired assassins, probably some of Big Jack Zelig's men. Word was making the rounds in the Criminal Courts Building that Zelig had been seen in serious discussion with Rose at Third Avenue and Twelfth Street on the night of the murder. Rose, the story went, was trying to get Zelig to do something for him in return for a significant reward that had nothing to do with money. Zelig would be freed of a charge of illegal possession of a handgun that was still pending in the courts.

The law Zelig was charged with violating had been passed just a year earlier and was part of the legacy of Big Tim Sullivan who had ushered it through the state legislature. The statute made carrying a concealed weapon a felony punishable by seven years in prison. Its purpose was to give the police additional leverage in rounding up and holding suspected criminals. If there was insufficient evidence to charge a suspect with robbery, assault with a deadly weapon, or even homicide, the gun possession charge would do just fine. Furthermore, it served as a bargaining tool during interrogation. Looking at a seven-year sentence, many a suspect was inclined to be unusually cooperative if the charge was made to disappear. The law became known as the Sullivan Law and still stands as Section 1897 of the New York State Penal Code.

In the days following its passage, no one was more adept at using it than Lieutenant Becker. His strong-arm squads kept a supply of revolvers at the ready and thought nothing of planting them on a suspect who wanted things his own way. Zelig, for one, insisted that the illegal firearm he was convicted of possessing had been planted in his pocket by police. From that time on, he sewed up the pockets of his jackets to prevent a recurrence. The question nonetheless remained: if Rose had promised Zelig he could have the conviction expunged, how did he propose to get it done? It would have required the cooperation of either the police, the district attorney's office, or the courts. The police would have been anyone's first choice.

Thus far, there was no testimony that tied Becker to Rosenthal's murder. But the suspicion was on everyone's mind. Dougherty referred to him as "a figure" in the case, and while Waldo told the press there was no evidence to justify suspending him, he obviously believed that some action had to be taken to reflect his possible implication. The commissioner summoned Becker to his office and relieved him of his duties as head of the strong-arm squad. He assigned him to do clerical work at police headquarters and named Lieutenant Daniel Costigan to take over the squad that had defined Becker's career.

After scrupulously following his attorney's advice to remain silent on the case, Becker now felt compelled to make a statement. Rumors had been circulating that he had more financial assets than a police officer was likely to acquire, that he owned much valuable real estate and was a big-time player on Wall Street. He responded in an interview with reporters:

"I have been working hard as a policeman for nineteen years and my wife has been working for seventeen years as a school teacher. For three years of her service in the schools she has been a night-school teacher. Last February I learned that there was some property for sale in the Olinville section of the Bronx and that the man who owned it was willing to sell it cheap. The price of the property was $6,000 and that of the two adjoining lots, which I also acquired, $1,500, making the total cost $7,500. I told Commissioner Waldo what I wished to do, for I realized that as the head of the strong-arm squad I might be criticized for acquiring property, and I wanted everything about the purchase of the property to be open and above board. To purchase the property, I borrowed $3,000 from my brother, who is a broker with offices at 80 Wall Street, and the rest of the money I had myself. We are building a modest home on the property, and there is also a garage, but there is nothing extravagant about it."

Guilty or not, Becker had become the pivot of the investigation into Rosenthal's murder. The number of suspects kept growing, their ranks swollen by material witnesses, and the actual killers—four of them—were still on the loose, whereabouts unknown. Still, Becker, not yet officially a suspect, had been the focus of attention from the very beginning, and so he remained. For the case was freighted with political baggage, and nothing could snarl an inquiry so completely and irrevocably as the struggle that ensues when men of station and ambition believe their future is the stake in the outcome.

Here, Whitman and Waldo were engaged in something of a turf war as they seemed to pursue their investigations from opposite poles and perhaps with different objectives. As district attorney, Whitman could look to a bright future if he could prove that the police were behind Rosenthal's murder and finally take credit for cleaning up a force that was corrupt to its core. Waldo, for his part, could hardly welcome a scandal of such dimension festering on his watch. What, one might ask, had the police chief been doing these past three years while his men were taking graft and planning murders?

The in-fighting had begun almost immediately. Just one day after the shooting, Waldo, on the defensive, wrote a curt, accusative letter to Whitman, and the district attorney replied in kind the following day. Mayor Gaynor, caught in the crossfire, leaned toward Waldo whom he had appointed. He sent the commissioner a sympathetic letter in which he made reference to the "corrupt scamps who are trying to defame you ...," an obvious reference to Whitman.

The warring factions were drawn somewhat closer by the intervention of a third party. William Jay Schieffelin, a civic-minded industrialist and chairman of the well-heeled Citizens Union, offered to finance an independent investigation into corruption in the New York City Police Department. Schieffelin, a great grandson of John Jay, the first chief justice of the United States, was not concerned about funding; the Citizens Union was backed by the banking magnate J. P. Morgan. The first infusion of money was used to hire the noted private detective William J. Burns, head of the Burns Detective Agency, to spearhead the investigation. The next installment leased Whitman a suite at the Waldorf Hotel, then at Fifth Avenue and Thirty-fourth Street, which would serve as headquarters for the investigation. With Whitman clearly in charge and Swope at his side offering "all the help in the 'World,'" Waldo was ready to concede the battle if not the war. He dispatched Deputy Commissioner Dougherty and Chief Inspector Hughes to Whitman's office.

"Commissioner Waldo has instructed me to work under the direction of the district attorney," Dougherty told Whitman. He then asked the D.A., "Do you want me to arrest Lieutenant Becker?" "Not yet," Whitman said. Then, tellingly, Dougherty noted, "All right. I see we agree as to who is back of this killing."

Whitman took command eagerly, with as broad a range of public support as an elected official could hope for. The press too was an ally. His campaign against corruption had the support of every newspaper in town, and Whitman obligingly provided them with details of the investigation and perhaps even morsels that might have been snatched from the secret hearings being conducted by the grand jury. His office was open to the press, and he welcomed visits from the cadre of reporters who were assigned to the case. Swope, of course, was the lead voice in the chorus and, quid pro quo, he often seemed to have the most precious nuggets of information just a tad sooner than his competitors. Given his unofficial mandate, Whitman was under even greater pressure to begin getting results.

Of the three men already in custody, reason dictated that Shapiro, who had driven what was now commonly being referred to as the hit car, would be the most likely source of new information. He was the only one who knew for certain who was in the car and at what time. Furthermore, since he was not directly involved in planning the hit, he was in a good position to bargain with the authorities for his freedom. Whitman decided to strike first, where the odds were most in his favor. He offered Shapiro immunity from prosecution on the conditions that he was not found to be one of the killers and that he would divulge all that he knew. Levy, Shapiro's attorney, was quick to accept the offer.

Shapiro's account of the night of July 15 was much the same as the one Levy had given a few days earlier, but a stay in the Tombs appeared to have freshened his recollection and he now was able to add names to some of the descriptions. The three men he had picked up at Sharkey's were Harry Vallon, Jack Rose, and Sam Schepps. He drove them to Bridgey Webber's place, then up into Harlem where a man known as Dago Frank joined them, and back to Webber's. There, Rose, Vallon, and Schepps left the car, and a few other men got in. Shapiro said he didn't know them, but he heard three of them referred to as Lefty, Whitey, and Gyp. All three men, as well as Dago Frank, were known to the police as gunmen for hire. What they did not know was where they could be found and, more important, who had hired them.

The police appeared to have adopted a strategy that, though cumbersome, would eventually lead them where they needed to go. They were picking up anyone who might have had a connection, no matter how tenuous, to the local gambling establishment, stashing them in the Tombs, then shaking and squeezing to see how much information could be obtained. Their latest catch was Bridgey Webber. Webber had been held as a material witness before being set free on one-hundred-dollars bail. But on Monday, July 22, he was placed at the scene by a local barber named John Reisler. Known in the neighborhood as John the Barber, Reisler was a part-time fight promoter whose shop, at Broadway and Forty-fourth Street, was just a few blocks from the Metropole. As chance had it, he had been at the Metropole on the night of July 15, and as he left, he heard gunshots and saw Webber move quickly past him from the direction of the hotel. Webber was brought back in, booked as being "implicated in the murder of Herman Rosenthal," and given a cell in the Tombs. Arrested and booked on the same charge was Sam Paul, at whose Sunday maritime outing police suspected the murder plans had been hatched. Also brought in was Jacob Reich, aka, Jack Sullivan, the newsboy manager, who was held as a material witness.

Reich was viewed as a critical piece to the puzzle. He was the link that could connect Rose to Becker on the night of the shooting, for he was the only man who had ridden that night with both of them. Reich told the police he had gone to Sam Paul's room that evening to return $150 he had borrowed from Paul. Not finding Paul there, he left word that he would meet him later that night at Webber's place. He and Rose drove across town to Madison Square Garden for the fights. He ran into Becker outside the Garden, and after the fights they drove to Park Row to pick up the first editions of the morning papers. The lieutenant was anxious to know what the newspapers would be saying about him in connection with the charges Rosenthal had made. At about one-thirty, Becker dropped Reich outside Webber's place at Forty-second and Sixth, which police had begun referring to as "the rendezvous corner."

As Paul had already left, Reich stopped in at a soda fountain in the Cohan Theatre Building in Times Square. It was there that he heard the shots and joined the crowd at the murder scene. He told the police, "I shoved my stick-pin in my undershirt, for I knew what sort of a crowd would be around, and then I worked my way through and saw it was Herman Rosenthal. I leaned over and shook him and whispered, 'Who done it?' But Herman was dead."

After giving his testimony, Reich was released on one hundred dollars' bail. The five men being held on the homicide charge—Libby, Shapiro, Webber, Paul, and Rose—were less fortunate. They were arraigned before Coroner Israel M. Feinberg, who was sitting as magistrate, and sent back to the Tombs. Shapiro, by all accounts more victim than perpetrator, was badly shaken when he was remanded. He had broken down at the arraignment, perhaps moved by the presence of his mother, who attended the hearing. The other four seemed not much troubled by the turn of events; Webber and Paul, in particular, had shown little interest in the proceedings and appeared almost cheerful when ordered back to prison, as if they were returning to their frat house with good times on the way. Indeed, it would not be long before another member of the fraternity would be added to their number.

At just before midnight on Monday, July 22, a taxicab pulled up in front of police headquarters on Centre Street and out stepped a short, dapper man who walked in and casually identified himself as Harry Vallon, nee Harry Vallinsky. Vallon, Webber's gofer and partner in a few East Side stuss houses, had been named as one of the riders in the gray hit car on the night of the murder, and the police had been searching for him as another suspect and possible source of information. The information Vallon offered was of little help. He admitted having ridden in the hit car and seeing Rose, Webber, and Paul on the night of the shooting but said he had left them at around midnight and gone to the Lafayette Turkish Baths. He said he knew Sam Schepps but had no idea where he was and denied knowing any of the four suspected hitmen. He told the police he had heard they were looking for him, and having nothing to hide, he decided to give himself up. As his reward for good citizenship, Vallon was charged with "acting in concert with others in the murder of Herman Rosenthal." He was given a cell in the Tombs where he was quick to renew acquaintances with Rose, Webber, and Paul.

Whitman was pushing his investigation hard but so far without tangible results. While he relished his role in spearheading the inquiry, he was less inclined to be on his own if things did not go well. He told the press that he had made it clear to Dougherty that "the police work in the Rosenthal case must be done by the police." He believed his best hope was to find among the suspects one who had direct knowledge of the crime and was ready to give it up if the charges against him were dropped. He was convinced that the murder had been the result of a conspiracy and that it had been plotted by the police rather than any of the gamblers. In the meantime, the hunt was on for Schepps and the four gunmen. Word had it that Schepps had left the country. Gyp the Blood apparently had been spotted in Fitchburg, Massachusetts. Local police there notified New York police that a man known as Harry Horowitz (Gyp's real name) had been seen there the previous Thursday, two days after the killing. He was in the company of a man named William Friedman, who was killed when the pair tried to board a moving freight train. Another one of the hit-men was said to be in Vancouver, British Columbia, in Canada. The other two were rumored to be in the Chicago area, and William J. Burns himself was said to be on his way there.

While the police were seeking the gunmen, the grand jury was hearing evidence in the case initiated by Rosenthal in his affidavit—that a partnership existed between gamblers and police, and that Lieutenant Becker was the man who ran the show. Reasonably enough, the grand jury thought it would be a good idea to hear from Becker and directed Whitman to invite him to appear voluntarily and without the protective shield of immunity. John Hart, Becker's attorney, noted that he had not received a request for his client to appear and he would not make a decision until he had.

Whitman recognized an opportunity when he saw one. "It would be a sad situation, wouldn't it," he said, "if any policeman in uniform should refuse to answer questions on the ground that they might incriminate him?" He pointed out that a witness who waived immunity and then was asked a question he did not wish to answer would risk being held in contempt of court if he did not respond. No one, certainly not Whitman, expected Becker to put himself in that position. His star was fading quickly enough. Two days after being placed on desk duty in the squad office, he was transferred to the Bathgate Avenue Station in the Tremont section of the Bronx, the Sixty-third Precinct. The East Bronx was the boondocks in 1912, and if being shunted to desk duty in Midtown Manhattan was comparable to a starting ballplayer's being benched, a move to the Bronx was the equal of being shipped from the majors to a farm team. From so remote a post would Becker follow the grand jury hearings into the charges of graft-taking. But he was no doubt aware that that was the least of his troubles. He would keep a close eye on the investigation into Rosenthal's murder. Thus far, no charges had been leveled against him, no accusations had been made; none of those arrested and interrogated, no one in the police department or the district attorney's office, and none of the gamblers still at large had suggested that he was in any way implicated. But everyone on the street was waiting. As they had known a week ago that Rosenthal was marked for death, they knew now that eventually someone would point the finger at Becker and that he would have no better chance of finding his way clear.

It was Tuesday, July 23, one week since Herman Rosenthal was gunned
down, and the police and district attorney had made reasonable headway
in their investigation: They had possession of the car that carried the killers
to and from the murder scene, and they had in custody the owner of the car
(Libby), its driver (Shapiro), and the man who leased it that night (Rose). They
were also holding two men who had been nearby at the time of the shooting and who might have set up the hit by fingering Rosenthal (Webber and
Vallon). A sixth man (Paul), suspected of providing the venue where the murder was planned, also was in custody. The investigators had succeeded in learn-
ing the identities of the four gunmen: In addition to Gyp the Blood and Dago
Frank Cirofici, they were Whitey Lewis (Jacob Seidenschner) and Lefty
Louie (Louis Rosenberg). There were clues to the four men's whereabouts,
but the hard fact was that no one directly involved in the shooting had yet
been captured. More critically, the police did not have a direct line to the man
or men responsible for setting up the hit and paying the killers. The grand jury
was hearing testimony on the charge that Becker was guilty of taking graft
and being a partner in a gambling casino, but as of July 23, police officials said
that "absolutely no evidence had been produced showing that Becker had any
guilty knowledge of the plot that ended in the murder of Rosenthal, and that
until some such evidence is produced he will not be interfered with."

Another "missing person" in the investigation was Big Jack Zelig. In any crime that has conspiracy at its center, the truth is always fathomed on the streets and in the pool halls long before it is perceived by the authorities and works its ways to the courts. Of course, no solid proof is required in such informal tribunals; there, on the inside, justice is calculated in more muted tones. And in the Tenderloin that hot July, everyone in the know was snickering and wondering why Zelig was not high on the police's list of suspects. It was common knowledge that Zelig was Becker's number one agent of persuasion when collections became difficult and that the four gunmen the police were searching for worked for Zelig. So where was Big Jack?

The second week of the investigation did not begin auspiciously. John J. Reisler, the barber who had placed Bridgey Webber at the murder scene, recanted his testimony when he appeared at a hearing before Coroner Feinberg. On Wednesday, July 24, Reisler was served with a subpoena, and he was escorted to the district attorney's office. Questioned by Whitman, with First Assistant District Attorney Frank Moss present, Reisler repeated his earlier statement that he had seen Webber running from the direction of the Metropole shortly after the murder. He indicated, however, that he did not relish the opportunity to tell his story in public. It would, he said, be "all his life was worth" to take the stand and testify against Webber. He did not know it at the time, but that was exactly where he was headed.

Whitman and Dougherty led him down the stairs, through the justice's chamber, and they emerged, to Reisler's surprise, in the coroner's courtroom. The courtroom was filled with spectators whom Reisler recognized, and he knew why they were there and that their presence did not bode well for his future. When he took the stand, he saw some shake their heads, at very least in disapproval, perhaps in warning. Others whispered to one another behind cupped hands. Reisler, a short, stout man with a ruddy complexion, began to sweat, and the color seemed to drain from his face. He admitted having seen Webber in front of the Hotel Cadillac shortly after the murder, but then he became evasive.

"Was Webber running when you saw him?" Whitman asked.

Reisler hesitated until Coroner Feinberg prodded him to answer the question. Finally, he said, "I don't know."

"Didn't you tell me ten minutes ago that he was running?" Whitman asked.

Again the witness hesitated, then asked that the question be repeated. When it was read back to him, Reisler responded, "I don't remember what I told you. I was excited."

"Well," Whitman said, a touch of irony in his voice, "are you sure this was Webber that you saw?"

Reisler thought he might have been handed a way out. "I think it was," he said. "Maybe it was somebody else."

Here, Whitman decided to go straight for the nerve. His voice growing more accusative, he asked, "Didn't you tell me, in the hearing of Mr. Moss, that you were afraid to testify because you thought they would kill you if you did?"

"No," Reisler protested, "I didn't tell you any such stuff."

"Didn't you say that you knew what kind of a bunch you were up against?"

"No, I didn't tell you anything of the kind." Reisler's voice was unconvincing, his tone that of a schoolboy denying what everyone knew to be true.

At that point, Whitman called Moss to the stand. The assistant D.A. testified that Reisler had, in fact, said he saw Webber running from the scene and that he did say that he feared for his life, that no one could testify against Webber and live.

With Reisler back on the stand, Whitman maneuvered him into a corner from which there was no easy escape. "Now," he asked, "will you swear that you did not say that you would be killed if you should testify in this case?"

"Yes," Reisler said, "I'll swear it."

"Do you know what perjury means?" Whitman asked.

"Yes," Reisler replied, "I guess it means a long term in jail."

When his testimony was concluded, Reisler headed for the door, but Whitman called him back, and Dougherty arrested him for perjury by order of the district attorney. Looking at a "long term in jail," Reisler retained an attorney, Frederick Goldsmith, and before the day was over, Goldsmith assured Whitman that, given the opportunity, his client would swear under oath the following day that he had seen Webber running from the scene if the perjury charge was dropped. Reisler's fears, he said, were more for his wife and six children than for himself.

Whitman eagerly accepted the offer. Webber was of critical importance to his case. While it seemed clear to those who were investigating that Webber was at least peripherally involved in setting up Rosenthal's murder, no one suspected that he had inspired or arranged it. The man in everyone's sights was Becker, but both Whitman and Waldo had made it clear that no action would be taken against him until there was enough hard evidence to make the charge stick. The gathering of such evidence is what made Webber so valuable to the prosecution. He—and in all likelihood Rose and Vallon as well—might be in a position to make the case against Becker if they had enough to gain in the process. If Webber was indeed spotted running from the scene, a resourceful district attorney could make a reasonable case for his involvement in the shooting. For the D.A., such a possibility was a bargaining chip of incalculable value. Webber, whose record and reputation would do him no good in court, might well be inclined to tell the state what it wanted to hear in exchange for immunity from prosecution. With progress in the case somewhat stalled, Whitman sensed it was time to make his position as clear as possible.

"I don't want the small fry in this murder," he told the press. "I want the big fish. I'd give anybody immunity if he will lead me to the real culprit. That goes for Rose, or Webber, or anybody who can help me show how far they were aided by influences and activities outside their own circles—by the police, for example."

Whitman's statement was, in its way, an invitation and an offer to the six men who had spent the past week languishing in prison. The Tombs itself should have been invitation enough. It was a fortress-like structure that seemed to have been designed to encourage its residents to cooperate with the police, the district attorney, or anyone else who might grant them release. The original Tombs, so named because it was modeled in the style of an Egyptian tomb, was built in 1838 at Centre Street. It was replaced in 1902 by a prison that was no less forbidding. The new Tombs was a massive stone structure with 591 steel cells that measured about seven feet long and not quite four feet wide. They were all without windows; the only light a prisoner saw came through the bars of his cell from windows on the opposite side of the corridor. Sanitary facilities consisted of tin pails, and the only ventilation came by way of small chutes resembling chimney flues that ran to the roof. The drainage was poor; cells on the lower level were often ankle-deep in water. The main building (there were two annexes) was connected to the

Criminal Courts Building by a second-story enclosed corridor called, despairingly, the Bridge of Sighs.

Such were the quarters in which the state accommodated the six men being held in connection with Rosenthal's murder. However, the authorities recognized a significant distinction between the three regarded as suspects and those who were seen chiefly as witnesses. Libby, Shapiro, and Paul could provide useful information, but no one believed they were implicated in the conspiracy. Rose, Webber, and Vallon, on the other hand, had been directly linked to the killing. Rose and Vallon were identified by Shapiro as having ridden in the hit car on the night of the murder. John the Barber and another witness—Louis Krause, the Brooklyn waiter who happened to be passing by at the time—had named Webber as the man they saw fleeing from the scene. During his testimony, Krause also spotted Jacob Reich, erstwhile King of the Newsboys, then free on bail and watching the proceedings as a spectator. But he did not remain a spectator for very long. Krause identified him as having also been present, and he was summarily seized by Dougherty, taken back into custody, and returned to the Tombs where he renewed acquaintances with Libby, Shapiro, and Paul.

The three suspects—Rose, Webber, and Vallon—were clustered together in a separate section of the prison where they were visited regularly by members of the D.A.'s office who prodded them for information. The trio was well aware of the prospects that confronted them. Few are better acquainted with the workings of the criminal justice system than those who earn their living outside the law. As accessories to first-degree murder, they were subject to the same penalty as those who did the shooting, and in 1912 that meant a seat in Sing Sing's electric chair. The death penalty was much in vogue in those years. In New York City, nine men had been sentenced to death in just one week in July.

But the three suspects recognized that, though bleak, their future was not necessarily hopeless. The prosecution, they knew, was hunting for larger game, and they did not underestimate their value to the district attorney's office. What they had to say could make or break his case. Their stories therefore had to be sound, convincing, and above all, exactly the same. Given their proximity in the Tombs, they had ample time and opportunity to agree on the precise content of their testimony. Their description of the events that led to Rosenthal's murder would be unwavering and rock solid, and it would be delivered with one voice.

On Thursday, July 25, the state's investigation received an unexpected boost when an anonymous caller tipped Dougherty that Dago Frank could be found in a Harlem rooming house at 523 West 134th Street. Dougherty and three well-armed detectives rushed to the apartment and found him lying in bed in a drug-induced stupor. A warm opium pipe was on the floor beside him. So were two suitcases that apparently were to accompany him to parts unknown. Dago Frank was not alone when the police arrived. With him was a woman by the name of either Rose Harris or Regina Gordon, depending on who was asking and when, and a man name Abie Lewis, commonly known as Fat Abie. Both accompanied Dago Frank to police headquarters where they were held as material witnesses. The three were questioned at length, but the opium had left them dazed and largely incoherent, and the police said they learned little that they did not previously know. They already knew enough.

Frank Cirofici, twenty-eight years old, lived at 360 East 184th Street in the Bronx. He was a steamfitter by trade, but the bulk of his income was earned in other pursuits. A small, deceptively quiet man, he was a hired gun who often was seen providing protection for Kid Benson, a big-time Harlem gambler. He was a close associate of Gyp the Blood, and both were members of Big Jack Zelig's armed cadre. In 1905, he was arrested for burglary and served an indefinite sentence at the penitentiary in Elmira. He was sufficiently well known to be picture #B9,027 in the Rogue's Gallery.

The arrest of Dago Frank broke new ground in the investigation, as he was the first of the murder party to be apprehended. His associates also took it seriously. Just a few days later, two men walked into a saloon adjoining the rooming house where Dago Frank had been arrested and pumped eight bullets into the bartender whose name was either George Hendricks or George Fredericks, but whose name was of little consequence to the gunmen. What mattered was that it was his hoarse voice on the other end of the phone when Dougherty received the tip that led to Dago Frank's arrest.

There was other good news for the state that Thursday afternoon. While Dago Frank was being interrogated, the grand jury was hearing testimony from two witnesses that punctured the alibis of Vallon and Webber. Christopher

"Boob" Walker and John J. Hickey, who were with Rosenthal briefly on the night of the murder, said they saw both men in the Metropole shortly before the shooting. Walker told the grand jury that it was Vallon who had summoned Rosenthal into the vestibule of the hotel. Webber had been seen exchanging greetings with Beansie before he went outside. The testimony of the two witnesses was critical, since both Vallon and Webber had denied being at the Metropole that night. Whitman, elated, announced that their alibis were no longer credible.

Putting together bits and pieces of information provided by various witnesses, the D.A. was beginning to fashion a coherent scenario of what had occurred that night. It now appeared that the hit car had brought three men to the Metropole—probably Rose, Webber, and Vallon, whose role it was to make certain Rosenthal was present, lure him outside, and finger him for the gunmen. After the shooting, the car carried four away—Gyp the Blood, Lefty Louie, Whitey Lewis, and Dago Frank. Where Sam Schepps fit in was not exactly clear. Some believed that five men were taken from the scene; one, possibly Schepps, riding on the outside running board. In any event, the squeeze on Rose, Webber, and Vallon would now grow tighter, and the investigation would sharpen its focus on Becker.

The July grand jury had been extended through August so it could continue hearing the Rosenthal case. Speculation was that Becker would be the first witness to be heard the following week, on July 29. The question to be answered was under what conditions would he testify. Becker told Commissioner Waldo that his attorney had advised him not to appear unless he was subpoenaed. Waldo warned him that unless he appeared voluntarily he would be suspended from the force. The difference was more than cosmetic. A witness who appeared voluntarily could be held in contempt of court if he failed to answer a question; a subpoenaed witness could not. Whitman told the press that under no circumstances would Becker be allowed to testify without a statement that he did so freely and had waived all immunity. At a press conference later that day, Dougherty was asked directly, "Are you going to arrest Becker?" He responded just as directly, "No, I don't expect to."

In fact, Waldo had written to Mayor Gaynor that very day, asking whether Becker should be suspended and put on trial. In a lengthy, detailed response that included a frontal attack on "corrupt newspapers" and an oblique criticism of the district attorney for pressing the case against Becker, the mayor emphatically told the commissioner that no legal action must be taken against Becker in the Rosenthal case until there was sufficient evidence to support the charge. The letter was written on Friday, July 26. Waldo, as it turned out, would not have long to wait.

On Monday night, within the span of two hours, Lieutenant Charles Becker would be indicted on a charge of first-degree murder, arrested, arraigned, and sent to the Tombs. He was placed in Cell 112, on the prison's lowest level. He would never walk free again.

It was just about a week since he had been placed on desk duty at the Bathgate Avenue Station in the Bronx, and Lieutenant Becker was still trying to adapt. He was working the night shift on July 29, tidying up, cleaning a typewriter in the reception area, when two detectives from the D.A.'s office walked in. They knew Becker and greeted him in a friendly manner. "How are you, Lieutenant?" one of them asked. "Welcome to the Bronx," Becker said. It was past eight o'clock, and Becker knew it was not a social call. One of the detectives stepped inside the rail, leaned over toward him and asked politely if he would come with them. Becker was given permission to change into civilian clothes. In all likelihood, he knew where he was headed and did not wish to be arraigned in his police uniform. He stepped into a back room and emerged minutes later, neatly dressed in a tan suit and carrying a Panama hat. The two detectives led him to the Tremont Avenue station of the Third Avenue elevated subway line. Only then did they tell him he was under arrest.

By the time they arrived at the Criminal Courts Building, a fierce storm had hit the city, breaking the heat wave that had gripped it through almost all of July. Rain was falling heavily, splashing hard against the windows. Rolls of thunder echoed through the empty corridors, and lightning lit the grand jury room in eerie flashes, illuminating the faces of the sixteen jurors who had been hastily assembled. The extraordinary night session broke new ground.

It was the first time in the history of the county that such a session had been held, and never before had the members of a grand jury been summoned with as much urgency. No sooner had the detectives been dispatched to arrest Becker than General Sessions Judge J. P. Mulqueen ordered his special aide, John Klinge to begin phoning each of the twenty-three jurors. He was instructed to send taxis for those who did not live within easy distance of the Criminal Courts Building. Klinge managed to round up sixteen members, sufficient for a quorum. They began hearing routine testimony from other witnesses several hours before Becker arrived, ushered into the building through a side door. He tried to affect a casual demeanor, swinging his hat in his hand, smiling at reporters, but he nonetheless appeared to be edgy and tense. The muscles in his face twitched nervously. Still, as he stepped forward to face the judge, he grasped the rail firmly and stood up straight, stoic and defiant. His attorney, John Hart, was at his side.

The voice of the court clerk seemed to come from far off: "Charles Becker, you are charged with murder in the first degree. Do you demand a hearing?" Hart told the court that, having no previous knowledge of a pending indictment, he had not conferred with his client and asked for more time before entering a plea. The judge gave him a week to prepare for a further hearing and suggested that until that time a formal plea of not guilty be entered. Hart complied. "I plead not guilty for the defendant," he said. Becker was placed in the custody of Joseph Flaherty, a former policeman who had once served under him, and led across the Bridge of Sighs to his cell in the Tombs.

It was chiefly the testimony of Bald Jack Rose that put Becker away. Webber and Vallon, to no one's surprise, corroborated what Rose said, but it was Bald Jack who spelled it out, detail for detail. The district attorney wasted no time informing the press of what Rose had to say, although it did not come all at once. It was doled out in bits and pieces, on a daily basis, until the full transcript of his testimony was finally released on August 15.

Most of what Rose told the grand jury was already known, or suspected, by the police. But his testimony served as confirmation and provided a tight narrative of events that until then had been randomly chronicled. He began at the very start, with his meeting Becker for the first time in August 1911. At the time, Rose was part-owner of a gambling casino on the East Side that had been raided by Becker's strong-arm squad. Rose paid two hundred dollars to have the case thrown out of court, and that was the beginning of a lucrative partnership. Becker told Rose that he was planning a series of raids on stuss houses all over the Tenderloin, and after each raid, the owner of the house would be offered the chance to pay three hundred dollars a month for protection. He offered Rose a commission of 25 percent to act as collector. Rose accepted, and Bridgey Webber assisted him in making the collections.

Things went smoothly, Rose said, until Becker met Rosenthal. They soon became fast friends. Rosenthal's intimate acquaintance with the map of the gambling world enabled Becker to fill out his list of establishments to be targeted for raids. In return for Rosenthal's aid, Becker helped him open his Hesper Club on Forty-fifth Street, giving him $1,500 in exchange for a chattel mortgage on his furniture. The two men maintained their friendship until Becker told Rosenthal he had been ordered to raid his club. As the club was located on the ground floor of his home, Rosenthal objected to the raid taking place at all, but he became enraged when a policeman was stationed on the premises. It was then, Rose said, that Beansie first threatened to go public regarding Becker's "System." Becker shrugged it off at first, but as Rosenthal became more persistent and his threats more urgent, Becker began to sense that his entire operation was in jeopardy. He told Rose that he wanted Rosenthal killed.

As early as May, Rose said, Becker told him, "I want Rosenthal murdered, shot, his throat cut, any way that will take him off the earth." He told him to get Big Jack Zelig's gunmen on the case. He also brought Webber and Vallon into the loop. Rosenthal had already "lived too long," he said, and promised protection to anyone who got the job done. He also vowed dire consequences for those called upon to perform who did not follow through. "If you don't kill this man," he told Rose, Webber, and Vallon, "I'll put guns in your pockets and send you up for seven years for carrying a concealed weapon." The same went for Zelig's gunmen, he made clear. Zelig had already been arrested on a gun-possession charge, and he suspected that Rose had played a part in planting the weapon on him. Zelig was not a man whose ill-will promised long life, and Rose, eager to display his good intentions, had posted bail and secured his release. However, Zelig, with a felony charge and the prospect of a seven-year prison sentence looming, told Rose that he did not wish to get involved in a murder conspiracy at that time, and Rose gave him money to get out of town until business with Rosenthal was settled.

With Zelig out of the picture, arrangements to deal with the gunmen would be left to Rose, Webber, and Vallon, and that was a proposition that left Rose feeling on edge. He was hoping that Becker would let the matter drop, but he didn't; in fact, he was becoming impatient. "Why isn't he croaked yet?" he kept asking Rose. "You're all a bunch of damn cowards."

As Becker pushed harder, Rose, Webber, and Vallon were becoming desperate. A few days before the actual killing, they failed in an impromptu effort to get the job done. Rose's testimony was somewhat sketchy in describing the abortive murder attempt. He said that he and Vallon were having dinner in a Third Avenue restaurant when Webber came in and said there were three men (presumably three of the four gunmen) waiting for them at the Lafayette Baths, and Rosenthal was seen dining at the Garden restaurant at Seventh Avenue and Fiftieth Street. After a brief discussion at the bathhouse, the three gunmen headed uptown toward the Garden. But when they got there, Gyp the Blood spotted a man they took to be a Burns detective and the plan was scrapped.

When Becker was told what had happened, he became enraged. Rosenthal seemed to be attracting the interest of the district attorney, and Becker felt the danger was growing. "Tell those fellows to drop everything else," he told Rose. "There is nothing to worry about and nothing to fear. I will take care of anybody and everybody who has a hand in this thing. . . . All that's necessary is to walk right up to where he is and blaze away at him and leave the rest to me. Nothing will happen to anybody who does it. . . . Walk up and shoot him before a policeman if you want to. There ain't nothing to fear . . ."

Rose said that he and Webber, feeling the pressure, met with Becker to plan the murder. It was Webber who was supposed to put the plan into effect, and when he expressed his uncertainty to Rose, Becker took charge. "Rose says that you won't do this for him," Becker said to Webber. "You've got the money and I've got the power. I want you to give the order." And, according to Rose, Vallon, and Webber himself, he did.

The gunmen were hired and assembled in Webber's place on Forty-second and Sixth. They were all seated at a table, having something to eat. Then, Rose stated, "Webber went out and when he returned he said, 'Rosenthal is at the

Metropole.' Everybody got up from the table and started for the door. I remained behind and insisted that Schepps stay with me, which he did. After a while Schepps, too, went out. I waited around, when soon someone came in with the report that Rosenthal had been murdered."

Rose said he then went to Times Square and called Becker from a public telephone. Becker said he already had gotten the news from a newspaperman. Again he assured Rose that there was no reason to worry and said he was coming right down to Webber's place. Meeting Rose there, Becker told him that earlier in the evening he had driven slowly by the Metropole, with the intention of shooting Rosenthal through the window if he was there. When Rose asked Becker if he had seen Rosenthal's body, he replied that he had seen it at the Forty-seventh Street Station, and according to Rose, he added: "It was a pleasing sight to me to see that squealing Jew lying there, and if it had not been for the presence of Whitman I would have cut out his tongue and hung it on the Times Building as a warning to future squealers." Rose then went to Fiftieth Street and Eighth Avenue, where he met Webber and received one thousand dollars to be distributed among the killers.

There was room for much conjecture about why Rose had given himself up and then decided to tell all to the grand jury. As is often the case, the simplest and most direct explanation is probably closest to the truth. Rose knew that the net had been cast for Becker and that if he went down Rose would likely go with him. Yet worse, Becker might try to slip between the cracks by contending that it was Rose, whose relations with Rosenthal had been contentious right from the start, who had planned and orchestrated the murder. He, after all, as well as Becker, had been named by Rosenthal in his confession to Whitman. Perhaps most important was the convenience of proximity—their cells bunched together—that afforded Rose, Webber, and Vallon the opportunity to create an ideal scenario. It must have occurred to each of them that there was at least a possibility that at some point any of the three might seize the opportunity to turn state's evidence in exchange for a plea bargain. If the stories they told in any way conflicted, the credibility of all of them would be called to question. How much sturdier would their case be if they agreed to tell the same story and feed Becker—the D.A.'s chief quarry—to the hounds?

They understood of course that the testimony they offered was not without risk. Given the range of detail contained in their confession, the Tombs might not be the most hospitable place for them to lay their heads that night. All three pleaded with the D.A. for alternative lodgings. Whitman, acknowledging the justice of their fears, allowed them to spend the night in his office, guarded by three detectives. Becker received no such consideration. When he arrived at the Tombs, there was an empty cell waiting for him. Earlier that day, Sam Paul, at whose outing some believed Rosenthal's murder had been planned, was released. He had been held for a week, but at a hearing that afternoon, Whitman said there was not enough evidence to continue holding him, and there seemed to be no prospect of getting anything more convincing to justify further confinement. As for Becker, by contrast, Whitman was more than satisfied. He said he considered the information conveyed by Rose and corroborated by Webber and Vallon to form a perfect chain of evidence identifying Becker as the instigator and secret director of Rosenthal's murder.

The day after Becker's arrest, the city was awash in newsprint covered with the likeness—in photos and sketches—of the indicted police officer and tens of thousands of words devoted to the first New York City policeman ever to be charged with first-degree murder. It was the featured headline in all of the city's daily papers. Not unexpectedly, *Pulitzer's World*, with Swope's hand on the wheel, led the pack. The story occupied all of page one, followed by page after page of sidebar material complete with timelines, background articles, and sketches of other suspects in the case, broken only by an advertisement for Palma de Cuba cigars which were being offered at the price of four for twenty-five cents. Hearst's *American* was doing its best to keep pace, and even the staid and sober *Times* and the almost equally staid and sober *Tribune* were playing it prominently and in great detail.

It was not as if the story was being used to fill column space during a sluggish summer with little of consequence to report. The Becker case was pushing aside events of major dimension. By the summer of 1912, Germany had become a growing menace, and it seemed likely that a global conflict was on the way. Communism, the "specter" that was "haunting Europe," was fast approaching in the form of a revolution that, five years later would shake the world. Eight years before the Nineteenth Amendment gave women the right to vote, suffragettes were staging regular demonstrations throughout the country, but chiefly in New York. Athletes across the United States were competing for the right to represent their country at the summer Olympic Games, to be held in Stockholm in August. Locally, the New York Giants, defending National League champions, were in a heated pennant race with the Pirates and the Cubs. They would win that race but lose the World Series to the Boston Red Sox on a seventh-game, ninth-inning error.

The biggest story to be elbowed off the front page was one of the most interesting, and possibly the most significant, presidential elections in the country's history. It was a four-way race featuring a sitting president, an ex-president, a soon-to-be president, and an outsider who would run better than his party ever had before. President William Howard Taft, whose conservative policies had split the Republican Party, found himself confronting ex-president Teddy Roosevelt, who overrode his 1904 declaration that "under no circumstances" would he seek a third term. In the end, Roosevelt succumbed to the urging of the progressive wing of the party and ran as the candidate of what became known as the Bull Moose Party. The split among Republicans opened the gates for the Democrats, and the scholarly president of Princeton University, Woodrow Wilson, won the closely contested election. Eugene V. Debs, the Socialist candidate, drew nearly one million votes, running on a platform that, twenty years later, would be embraced by another President Roosevelt as the New Deal.

One might have thought that with Teddy Roosevelt, a native son and former New York City police chief, running a renegade campaign against an incumbent president, he would have had first claim on the headlines. But it was the Becker-Rosenthal affair, as it was sometimes called, that had the glitter. Police and political corruption always had a purchase on the public imagination, and here it was embellished by a gangland assassination that took place on the most brightly lit street in the city. The ingredients were all there, and the newspaper moguls knew what sold papers.

The early part of the twentieth century was the hey-day of newspaper reporting. Radio was still relatively new, and the news of the day was invariably imparted via ink and newsprint. Most papers put out several editions a day, often as many as five, and newsboys hawked special editions, or "extras," on the streets when big news broke. The cry of "Extra, extra, read all about it" became part of the folklore of the time. A "beat," or a "scoop," was every publisher's quest for the Holy Grail. Subsequent editions carried what were called "second-day leads," updating the story, with sidebar articles exploring other angles.

So powerful were the publishers of the day that a crusading paper could, on occasion, turn the country in a new direction. Not much more than a decade earlier, Hearst's *Journal* and Pulitzer's *World* had helped push the United States into the Spanish-American War with inflammatory editorials and news reports that often split the difference between fact and fiction. A major story, particularly a local story, which could be covered on the spot, was oil for the machine. The Becker-Rosenthal case could have served as a textbook sample of how competing newspapers scratched and scraped to make a story their own.

There at the start, Swope had delivered the Becker-Rosenthal saga to the *World*. Not only did he assiduously follow the events and report them, he was, some maintained, the story's producer and director. It was even suggested that he himself had written the three major documents in the case—Rose's initial affidavit, his expanded statement, and his confession before the grand jury. Pulitzer, of course, knew hard coin when he saw it. When the full transcript of Rose's grand jury testimony was released, the *World* carried the entire thirty-eight-page document verbatim, beginning with boxcar-size headlines on the front page. The *Times,* for its part, noted that not much new had been revealed and ran its story with a one-column headline on page two.

But no matter how quickly the papers got their extra editions out on the street, it was usually old news to those who traveled on the inside track. The story of Becker's arrest was flashed across the network of police stations so swiftly that it was known to virtually every member of the force by the time Becker arrived at the Criminal Courts Building for arraignment. It made the rounds of the gambling casinos almost as quickly. Some operators decided to close their rooms until matters were settled. Becker's indictment cast a shadow across the entire police/gambling/political complex known as the System. If Rose, Webber, and Vallon could send Becker to the Tombs based on their testimony, what influence might Becker be able to exert? And If he decided to talk, no one would be safe—no cop, no gambler, no hired thug, no city official who might have been in the know. And what greater inducement could Becker have to turn state's evidence? Charged with first-degree murder, he was facing the death penalty.

Whitman wasted no time in defining the alternatives. He announced that Becker's only chance of saving himself from the electric chair was to tell all he knew about the System. Rose had already told the D.A. that Becker knew it all: who the higher-ups were in the police department; who divided and distributed the payments; and which city officials helped forge the alliance between the men who dealt in vice and graft and those who were paid by the city to eliminate them. It was made clear that his confession would have to be not only complete but one that would hold up in court and facilitate Whitman's campaign to purge the police department of even the slightest taint of corruption. The possibility of Becker turning informant chilled the blood of everyone involved in the System, but there were many who insisted that the lieutenant would withstand the pressure and keep his silence. Those who knew him best said, with a degree of prescience, that he would contest the charges to the end and, if necessary, go to the chair protesting his innocence.

Rose, in the meantime, was compiling a list of those he knew who had paid for protection and the amount each was assessed. He was preparing to show how hundreds of thousands of dollars was funneled through the System's machinery into the pockets of those who were paid to provide protection for illegal activities. He estimated that the annual handle was about $2.4 million, which was divided into four parts for distribution.

One part, he said, went to an Inspector of Police, who was higher than a district inspector and whose power exceeded anyone's in the department except for the commissioner. Every man he paid was a member of the force who worked under him. A second share of approximately $600,000, Becker told Rose, went to an inspector who commanded one of the most important districts in the city. In addition to policemen, some politicians profited from that distribution. Another payment was said to have been given to a man who was not on the force, but who was a confidante to a high police official believed to represent an influential state senator (probably Big Tim Sullivan). Becker distributed the fourth share himself, Rose said, with most of it going to the bagmen who collected the payoffs each month. Rose agreed to provide a full and detailed accounting—the names of those from whom he collected, the size of their monthly assessments, and the dates when the collections were made.

Both Webber and Vallon corroborated every aspect of Rose's story. Webber noted, however, that he was never a collector. He was among those who paid for protection, but he had no quarrel with how the System worked and had little patience for those who would upset its operation. Webber agreed to make out a list of his own payments and tell all he knew about the payoffs made by other gamblers. Vallon, of course, told the same story, though he admitted acting as a collector for a police officer other than Becker.

Becker, who had been scheduled to go before the grand jury before he was arrested, now had no such plans. Having been charged, he could not be summoned to testify without violating his Fifth Amendment right against self-incrimination. He could volunteer to share what he knew with the grand jury, but that would come in the form of a confession and only after cutting a deal with the district attorney. A spokesman for the D.A.'s office thought that would accrue to his advantage.

"Becker," he said, "has just one chance, and that is to tell the truth, and enough of it to make possible the destruction of the connection between certain members of the force and the criminal world. Mr. Whitman has the goods on Becker, and he knows it, and if Becker wants to get something less than the electric chair he will have to come across, so to speak, with the information that Mr. Whitman believes he can deliver. The conditions of the Police Department were never worse than now, and what the district attorney most desires is to get the men who are behind the 'System.' Becker can give the information that will make that possible, and therein lies his sole chance of mercy."

James M. Sullivan, Rose's attorney, expressed confidence that Whitman would be able to extract a full confession from Becker in short order. "The Tombs," he said, "is well named. . . . The place is a hole of depression. It got Rose, it will get Becker too. Forty-eight hours in the Tombs is usually enough." He understood, however, the danger involved in Becker's telling what he knew and the magnitude of his testimony. If Becker talks, he said, it will be "in spite of strong urging and whatever influence can be brought to bear on the lieutenant to keep his mouth shut and thereby save others." A full confession, he added, "will make the entire police structure of the city collapse like a house of cards. There is more than one man in the Police Department today who is wearing his honors with extreme uneasiness."

The most immediate effect of Becker's presence in the Tombs was to afflict Rose, Webber, and Vallon with a case of the jitters. Having spent the first night after Becker's arrest in Whitman's office, they pleaded with the D.A. to be sent to another jail, insisting that being in the same facility with Becker put them in grave physical danger. Whitman needed little encouragement to protect the safety of his three key witnesses. They were transferred to the West Side Prison on Fifty-fourth Street where the quality of their lives improved immensely. By all accounts, they were treated regally, fed with food from nearby restaurants, and visited regularly by friends, relatives, their lawyers, and the D.A. himself.

To hear Sullivan tell it, another important witness would soon be in tow. He said that Sam Schepps, who was now being described as the "murder paymaster," was in touch with his friends in the city and would turn himself in within the next few days and testify in exchange for immunity. Sullivan said further that Schepps was in the hit car along with the four gunmen, although he did not take part in the shooting. " . . . it is most unlikely that he will be indicted," Sullivan said. "There is no desire, so far as I know, to prosecute him if he comes forward willingly."

Schepps did not turn himself in willingly. Neither the police nor the district attorney had any idea where he was. Whitman said he would not be surprised if the killers were still in New York and had never been outside the city limits. But not long after he had gone public with that bit of conjecture, word came from Syracuse that police there had arrested a man they thought was Gyp the Blood. He had been identified as a gambler from New York, and a blackjack and a bottle labeled "poison" were found in his hotel room when he was taken into custody. For a brief time, Whitman thought he had caught a break. But he soon learned that the man's name was Harry Lewis, not Horowitz, and he bore no resemblance to the suspect. Gyp the Blood, along with Schepps, Whitey Lewis, and Lefty Louie, were still on the loose.

The four men being hunted were all directly implicated in Rosenthal's murder. Three of them had fired the fatal shots. The fourth, Sam Schepps, was believed to have distributed the cash among the shooters and possibly had ridden with them in the hit car. But a fifth fugitive was perhaps even more essential to the state's case. Big Jack Zelig was officially not a suspect; no one had connected him to the conspiracy. In fact, Rose testified that he had solicited his help but that Zelig, with a gun possession charge pending, wanted no part of it. When Zelig turned him down, Becker pressed Rose to go directly to Bridgey Webber who had a working relationship with Zelig's boys. The chain of command went from Becker to Rose to Webber to the four gunmen. Schepps was peripherally involved. Zelig, by all indications, was in the clear, but he had first-hand knowledge of the plan to assassinate Rosenthal, and that made him a potentially devastating witness.

The heart of the evidence against Becker was being offered by Rose with the concurrence of Webber and Vallon. But the testimony of accomplices, particularly in a capital case, was always suspect, for it was understood that their cooperation would be rewarded by the state. It was for that reason that New York State law required corroboration from someone who had no stake in the outcome. Zelig, then, was the prosecution's perfect witness. He knew of the plan to murder Rosenthal but was free of any involvement. The D.A.

believed that Zelig's testimony could clinch the case against Becker, and Whitman's mood brightened when he was told by Zelig's attorney that it would be provided. Charles G. F. Wahle, a former city magistrate who was representing Zelig, informed the D.A. that he would produce his client whenever he was wanted and that he would assist the prosecution in any way possible. There was just one catch; Zelig was free on ten thousand dollars' bail, and no one knew where to find him.

In the meantime, Sam Schepps was becoming invested with almost as much importance as Zelig. His part in the affair had never been clearly defined. Some said he had ridden in the gray touring car, others said not. His chief role was believed to have been as paymaster, but as circumstances developed, Schepps increasingly took on the cast of a shadowy presence. Rose had begun telling anyone who would listen that although Schepps was often around while the crime was being planned, he was kept outside the loop; he knew nothing of the murder until after the shots were fired. With ample time to refresh his recollection, Rose also recalled that it was not Schepps who had distributed the money, but one of the gunmen, probably Lefty Louie. Webber and Vallon also discovered that prison life was tonic for their memories; Rose had it exactly right. Schepps would, therefore, make a remarkable witness for the state: Like Zelig, he knew Becker had arranged for the murder but he himself was uninvolved. He too could provide the third-party corroboration needed to convict Becker.

While the police and the D.A.'s office tracked down clues and sifted random reports that might lead to Zelig and Schepps, one of the missing gunmen fell into their net. No sooner had July turned to August than three detectives under the command of Inspector Hughes reported that they had captured Whitey Lewis as he was about to board a train in Fleischmanns, New York, a Catskill Mountain resort. Fleischmanns was at the far end of a chain of resort areas—the heart of which was Monticello—that provided respite and entertainment for inner-city residents looking to escape the throbbing heat of summer. It also was known as a place where a fellow on the lam might find shelter.

Conjecture had it that Vallon had provided the tip that led police to scour the area in Sullivan County, about one hundred miles northwest of the city. Lewis, twenty-seven years old, short, and slight of build, had an alias for all occasions and a rap sheet that dated back to his teens. His most recent arrest, in 1907, resulted in a conviction for grand larceny and a four-year term, first at Sing Sing, then at Dannemora. The record also showed that he had served briefly in the United States Army and was imprisoned and dishonorably discharged for stabbing another soldier. Lewis was unarmed when he was picked up, but a trunk that belonged to him contained two revolvers. One of the guns was of the same caliber that had been used in the Rosenthal shooting and, according to ballistic experts, it had been fired within the past two weeks. Lewis denied having any knowledge of the crime he was accused of and said he had no idea where Lefty Louie or Gyp the Blood might be.

Police were fairly certain that the remaining two hit-men would be found not too far from Lewis's hiding place. They drew a cordon around the entire Catskill area and more than a dozen detectives began an intensive search. Just a few days later it appeared that their dragnet was about to snare the two missing men and possibly Schepps as well. From Tannersville, New York, came a report that a detective had spotted Lefty Louie in that mountain hamlet, and an arrest seemed imminent. But Hughes, who was in charge of the mountain search, ordered his men to hold off, hoping that Louie would lead them to the other fugitives. He said he had reason to believe that they were all in that area, and he assigned three detectives to shadow Louie and not let him out of their sight. A small cadre of detectives was dispatched to the area to join in the hunt, and their ranks were soon swollen by members of the local constabulary. Virtually every deputy sheriff, every village policeman, and every town constable put themselves at the disposal of the New York police, combing the mountain sections of Sullivan, Ulster, and Greene Counties.

Reports of sightings came from everywhere. Two members of a boys camping party in Kingston, New York, were certain they had spotted Gyp the Blood. In Camden, New Jersey, three policemen arrested a man they thought was Lefty Louie; it wasn't. Police in Auburn, New York, had taken into custody a man who "looked like one of the missing gunmen"; he was soon released. The suspect being tailed by detectives in Tannersville also proved to be no more than a Lefty Louie look-alike. Still, the manhunt continued to center on the Catskills. Police were posted at the intersections of every key roadway. Grocery stores in the area were canvassed to see if the fugitives had been in to buy provisions. Dozens of men answering the descriptions of the suspects were followed, some by police, others by adventurous citizens playing detective. The summer resort haven had been turned upside down by the police dragnet. The belief that two dangerous killers were in the neighborhood (the name Gyp the Blood itself served to instill fear in the hearts of most vacationers) put a chill on nighttime entertainment. The owner of the only movie house in Tannersville said that business was down nearly fifty percent since police invaded the area.

The summer boarders in the Catskills were not the only ones with a case of the jitters. Rose, Webber, and Vallon, apparently safely ensconced in the West Side Prison, were fully aware that the city crawled with people who would prefer to see them dead, and they understood that some of them might be in a position to do them harm. Fearing the possibility that their food might be poisoned, they declined to eat anything that was not prepared for them by their wives. Beyond that small inconvenience, their lives were as agreeable as life behind bars could be. If the police could not be trusted to protect them, they certainly had the heart of the district attorney, who bent every effort to ensure the comfort of his key witnesses. They were afforded every privilege available to prison inmates, including unrestricted visits by family and friends.

Becker, by contrast, remained isolated in his cell at the Tombs. Of the nine men being held in the case, only Becker was under indictment on a charge of first-degree murder. His only visitor was his wife, Helen. She came every day, traveling by subway from their home at Olinville Avenue in the Williamsbridge section of the Bronx. They had barely taken residence there when Becker was arrested. Helen, earnest, endearing, and loyal, was a favorite of everyone involved in the case. Her unflagging dedication to her husband served to enhance his public persona. How could a man so callous and brutal earn the devotion of a woman whose every attitude seemed imbued with the spirit of a saint?

As events unwound, the support she offered was more than moral. She was instrumental in obtaining for Becker's defense the preeminent criminal attorney in New York. The question of who would represent the defendant at trial had become a matter of contention. The politicians who were close to the scene favored a local congressman, Martin W. Littleton, who had successfully defended Police Inspector Max Schmittberger when he was up on charges of taking graft six years earlier. Becker's brother had taken it upon himself to solicit the services of Robert H. Eider, an ex-assistant district attorney for Kings County. Becker appeared to be satisfied with John D. Hart, who had been representing him zealously since Rosenthal made his accusations. But Helen Becker felt that her husband needed a high-octane advocate who was more accustomed to the pressure that filled a courtroom when the defendant's life was at risk, and no one in New York had handled more murder cases than John F. McIntyre. Mrs. Becker called on McIntyre at his office in the Broad Exchange Building and asked him to visit her husband in the Tombs. Ever conscious of legal protocol, McIntyre agreed to visit Becker but only at Hart's invitation. The two attorneys went to the Tombs together. When they emerged, Hart was still the attorney of record, but the inference was clear that McIntyre would soon be joining the defense team.

It was becoming increasingly apparent that Becker was going to need all the legal help he could get. A rumor had begun to circulate that Hart had visited Rose while he was still in hiding. Hart refused to address the charge, claiming attorney-client privilege. In an extraordinary maneuver that was, if not unprecedented, certainly unorthodox, Whitman subpoenaed Hart to appear before the grand jury. When he balked, the district attorney hailed him before Judge Mulqueen for a disposition. "It is most unusual," Hart said, "to ask an attorney to testify against his own client." But that is how Judge Mulqueen ruled. Hart testified and answered the questions put to him. Two days later, perhaps as a gesture of defiance, he was back before Mulqueen with Becker at his side, placing before the court two motions he was certain to lose. He began by withdrawing the plea of "not guilty," which allowed the motions to be put before the court.

The first asked that the indictment be dismissed as illegal because the grand jury was not properly convened and "seven members of the jury were not even summoned." The second was a request to inspect the grand jury minutes to search for infractions that might invalidate the indictment. The judge did nothing to hide his irritation. "The grand jury meets when and where it pleases," he said. "It met at my orders, and as long as there were sixteen present and twelve voted for the indictment, the indictment is legal. I dismiss the motion on those grounds."

Hart persisted: "I move that the clerk of the court be instructed to produce the tally sheets showing the attendance of the grand jurymen for the month of July, during the time these proceedings against Charles Becker were pending."

Snapping off his words, each pronounced distinctly as if it could stand on its own, Mulqueen responded: "There is nothing before this court."

"Then I understand my motion is denied?" Hart said.

"You understand nothing." Mulqueen was close to shouting now. "There is nothing before this court," he repeated.

Though he could not have expected any other outcome, Hart clearly resented the peremptory treatment he received from the court and the bond he might have sensed between the district attorney and the judge. On the way out, he told the reporters who had covered the hearing that his client was being framed. Rose, Webber, and Vallon, he said, "have been told again and again that if they will swear that Becker conspired with them they will be granted immunity. They showed yellow and they threw Becker to the wolves. They have nothing on him and they made the story up. We won't have any trouble proving it."

There was little doubt that the three men would be granted immunity, but their cooperation had its price. Rose, convinced that an attempt would be made on his life to prevent him from testifying, had worked himself into what his brother Morris described as "a state of nervous collapse." He had been scheduled to be arraigned for examination immediately after Becker's appearance before Judge Mulqueen, but James M. Sullivan, his attorney, obtained a postponement on the grounds that Rose was emotionally incapable of leaving his cell.

"He can't eat, he can't sleep, and all he can think about is the murder," Morris said. "I tried to cheer him up today by talking about his family to him, but he sat there in his cell with his head in his hands, brooding over the crime and the part he was terrorized into taking in it. His condition is pitiful, and he firmly believes that his enemies will get to him if he is taken out of the prison."

Webber and Vallon were faring only slightly better. They said they expected to be killed if they were taken to court through the streets. Each day's mail brought death threats, they said, and Webber provided an example:

"Mr. Webber: In case you have an interest to live a few years more it would be advisable for you to keep your mouth shut. Don't do like Rose, as he is on our death list, with Assistant District Attorney Moss. Whether he leaves prison or not he dies before the month is over. You understand he involves high officials, and they will not stand for exposure. The less you say the more you live." It was signed, "THE CROWD."

There was of course no question but that the trio would testify. They had a better chance of escaping the wrath of the streets than the state's taste for retribution. Besides, others would have to testify if the state was to make its case and that would diffuse, to a degree, the impact of any one man's testimony. The case against Becker was gathering momentum. Other witnesses, whatever their reasons, were beginning to come forward.

Not long after being transferred to the West Side Prison—where he joined Rose, Webber, and Vallon—Jacob Reich, the Newsboy King, declared that he was ready to tell all he knew about the plot to kill Rosenthal. Reich, who also used the name Jack Sullivan, had been expected to testify on behalf of Becker, his long-time friend and patron. He had consistently maintained that neither he nor Becker had any "guilty knowledge" of the slaying, but on August 10 he notified Assistant District Attorney James E. Smith that he was prepared to reverse field and tell all. The principal piece of testimony he had to offer was confirmation of Rose's claim that the two of them, together with Becker and Webber, had met in front of the Murray Hill Baths on the night of the murder. Events that had placed Reich and Becker with known suspects on the night of the crime, formerly described by Reich as coincidences, would now apparently be depicted as part of the plan to eliminate Rosenthal. Needless to say, Reich would be accorded a degree of immunity, though how much was not certain. Rose, as key prosecution witness, had been granted total immunity, on the condition that his testimony resulted in an indictment and it was found that he himself had not fired any of the shots that struck Rosenthal. Since the indictment had already been returned and it was clear that Rose was not one of the shooters, he was theoretically a free man. He was simply being held by the state for safekeeping until after the trial. It was uncertain whether Reich would be given a similar deal, for he was expected to add nothing new. Of greater significance than what he had to say was the fact that the defense had lost one of its chief witnesses. But Reich's turnabout was not the worst news Becker received that day. Far more critical was an entirely unrelated occurrence. Sam Schepps, the fugitive paymaster-turned corroborative witness, had been arrested in Hot Springs, Arkansas.

Schepps was arrested late in the afternoon on Saturday, August 11, at the Hot Springs post office as he was about to mail a letter to Jack Rose. He had been under constant surveillance by private detectives for more than a week. The arrest was made by Postmaster Fred Johnson, who held a commission as a Deputy United State Marshal. Johnson immediately turned the prisoner over to local Police Captain George Howell. Schepps was searched and then escorted, under heavy guard, to the Marquette Hotel where he would be watched closely until detectives from the D.A.'s office arrived to take him back to New York. A personal guard at the hotel was considered more secure than holding him in a jail cell, as prisoners were known to escape from the county jail fairly often and with relative ease. In the meantime, Schepps was treated like precious cargo. Escape was not the principal concern of those charged with watching him. The prisoner was a quarry for any number of hunters, and no one knew it better than Schepps. He also knew which hunters posed the greatest threat.

"There are more than ten thousand police officers in New York City, and nine thousand of them would not hesitate to put me out of the way if they had a chance," he told Howell. "I do not want to go back with those Burns detectives or with Whitman's representatives. I will give you five hundred dollars, Captain Howell, if you will take me back right away and not say anything to them as to when you will arrive there with me."

Howell turned down the offer and assured Schepps that he would have to return to New York in the custody of New York officers. The following conversation was reported in the *New York Times*:

"Looks like I had just about as well take a chance out of this window for a run," Schepps said to Howell.

"Well, it wouldn't be much chance," Howell said.

"Would you shoot?" Schepps asked.

"Yes," Howell said, "and I can hit a rabbit running."

"Well, then," Schepps mused, "I will think it over. With the electric chair on one side, the gang and the police on the other, and a bullet that would go straight and end it all here, it is hard to tell which is best. I might run and settle it here. I don't know what to do. It looks like either the Dutch route or squeal. I am not a squealer. I don't know why they did all this. Sometimes I don't give a damn and am glad it is this far over. I might as well be dead as driven from New York and exiled in some other part of the world as a squealer. If I told, I couldn't live in New York; they would not let me. And if I don't tell, God only knows what will become of me. I never sanctioned the killing of Rosenthal, and I only wanted to serve all my friends; they are all my friends."

Schepps paused briefly and then addressed his chief concern:

"Dougherty won't get me, will he? There is nothing he can do to me but kill me, and I guess they won't stand for that."

Schepps's fears were not the product of paranoia. They were shared by everyone involved in the case, most notably the district attorney's office. On the night of the arrest, Whitman sent a telegram to Tom Pettit, acting mayor of Hot Springs and proprietor of the Marquette Hotel, where Schepps was being held, requesting that under no circumstances should the prisoner be turned over to any New York officer unless he shows credentials from the district attorney's office. He said that a D.A.-appointed officer was on his way to Little Rock, the state capital, to see the governor on Monday morning and obtain extradition papers. He would then head straight to Hot Springs where he would pick up Schepps and return him to New York. Pettit took Whitman at his word. When Assistant D.A. Robert G. Rubin and Robert Stewart, a process server in Whitman's office, arrived the following day, Pettit asked for their credentials. They didn't have any.

Rubin explained, "We just had two minutes to catch our train after Mr. Whitman ordered us to come down here, and we could not wait to have credentials prepared."

"In that case," Pettit said, "the city cannot turn Schepps over to you, for we do not know you, and we are not going to take any chances. Schepps will be turned over to Mr. Whitman's men, but they must be identified properly."

It was a temporary setback for both men. Pettit could not be more eager to get the prisoner out of his jurisdiction safely and forever. Earlier that day, Schepps had indicated his willingness to head back to New York where, he said, he would "look the district attorney in the eye and tell him all of it." Rubin, for his part, would have been just as pleased to get the job done with as little trouble as possible. Rubin resolved the issue by suggesting that Pettit wire Whitman asking for complete descriptions of the two men from his office. Whitman complied, and Schepps was on his way back to New York.

The question now was what was he going to say when he got there. He was obviously conflicted on whether to remain silent or tell the D.A. what he wanted to hear, but he had at least a layman's understanding of his options. "It's up to me to make the best bargain I can," he said. "I have something to sell, and District Attorney Whitman wants to buy. I will tell all to him in a room where there are none but we two. He alone can make the deal. Two men already have confessed, the one corroborating the other, but they need a third confession, and mine is that one."

He had already received some guidance in the matter. The letter he was about to mail when he was arrested was a response to one he had gotten from Rose. In it, Rose said:

"I don't know what you have heard or read, but it has got down to a stage where the electric chair stares us in the face. The first man to try to get from under was Becker. There was [sic] many people who saw everything that night, and the next day the District Attorney knew what part everybody played in the thing, and nobody could have got away.

"I was deserted like a dog by Becker. When I saw what the situation was I opened up negotiations with the District Attorney, who offered me a sort of cover that I could not go into details by writing. I insisted that the same protection given me be extended to Harry, 'Bridgey' and you, to which he finally agreed. We are all pleased with the arrangement, and our worry has been to get you to come in to get the same benefits we got before it is too late.

"My advice is to let me send a representative of the District Attorney to bring you back here. That would prevent the police getting you, and putting you through a third degree."

While Schepps was being transported back to the city, the case against Becker was playing out on another front. Periodic reports were emanating from the district attorney's office regarding Becker's finances. One report said he had three bank accounts in as many banks in New Jersey. Another said he had more than $65,000 squirreled away in various New York banks. Savings that large for a man earning $2,150 a year would have been difficult to explain, even with his wife's school-teacher salary added to it. But no documentation was ever produced, and McIntyre, who was now officially acting as Becker's chief counsel, described those reports as nothing but lies.

"There is not a single word of truth in that story.... There isn't a lie that has been told against Becker—and there have been scores of them—that I will not be able to expose." He then went a step further and proclaimed his client's innocence of all the charges being leveled against him, including first-degree murder. "I am well versed in the criminal law," he said, "and I know something about criminal procedure, and I stake my reputation on the statement that I will prove that Becker is an innocent and persecuted man. I was asked the other day if the public excitement now was as great as it was during the days of the Lexow investigation. I replied that there was just as much excitement now. And what became of that investigation? Thirty-one policemen were indicted at that time, but only six were tried. Only one of the indicted men served a term in prison, and that term was for the period of one month."

What McIntyre failed to mention was that the officers indicted in the Lexow investigation were charged only with taking graft. His current client was struggling to stay afloat in much deeper waters. Enlarged bank accounts were the least of his problems; there was a corpse to be dealt with this time around, and anyone at all involved was running for cover. Schepps was quick to take the immunity deal the D.A. offered him, and he now marched in lock step with Rose, Webber, and Vallon, except for one detail; all agreed that he was the only one of the four who had no prior knowledge of the plan to kill Rosenthal. His identity had been indelibly established—he was the third-party corroborator.

The prosecution fully understood that it would require more than a little finesse to sell to the jury the notion that Schepps was around while the others planned the crime but managed to remain oblivious to it. A second outside corroborator would help their case immensely. Big Jack Zelig, who fit that role perfectly, was still at large; but not for long.

On Thursday, August 15, a man who identified himself as James Golden was arrested on a streetcar in Providence, Rhode Island, for picking the pocket of another passenger. The victim, Thomas Griffiths, told police that he was just leaving the car when he felt a tug at his pocket, reached down, and saw that his wallet was missing. He suspected a man standing next to him who immediately boarded another car. Griffiths followed him aboard and accused him of stealing the wallet, which contained sixty-five dollars. The man denied it, and when an argument broke out, a traffic cop who was posted at the corner interceded. The wallet was found on the same seat occupied by

Golden, who was taken into custody and committed to the county jail in default of two thousand dollars' bail. From the outset, Providence police suspected that their prisoner might be something more than a common pickpocket; he bore an unmistakable resemblance to the much sought-after Jack Zelig. A few days later, their suspicions were confirmed, and on August 20 Big Jack was in the Criminal Court Building in New York, voluntarily testifying before the grand jury.

Accompanied by his attorney, Charles G. F. Wahle, Zelig strolled breezily into the hearing room wearing a big smile and appearing as cheerful as a man would be if he knew for certain that the performance he was about to give would play to rave reviews. Zelig testified that Becker not only plotted the murder of Rosenthal but insisted on its being carried out. He said that Rose approached him at Becker's urging and asked him to provide the killers. When he refused, he understood that Becker kept the pressure on Rose and Webber to put together a hit team composed of some of Zelig's men. He was not informed of how successful their attempts were, and he was out of town when the murder took place.

Though Zelig's appearance was widely heralded, the starring role that day was played by Sam Schepps. As Becker claimed to know nothing of the plan beyond its earliest stages, Schepps insisted that he was in the dark until after the fact. He testified that he acted as messenger between Becker and Rose for two days following the murder and before Rose turned himself in at police headquarters. He related to the grand jury the substance of numerous conversations that took place between Becker and himself and between Becker and Rose. Based upon those conversations, he was able to state categorically that Becker was fully involved in planning and carrying out the assassination.

Jointly, Schepps and Zelig had begun to seal the prosecution's case. As given, their testimony was presumed to be untainted by any charge of complicity in the crime, thus fulfilling the legal requirement of third-party corroboration. The district attorney's office appeared to have all the pieces in place now except for the two fugitive gunmen—Gyp the Blood and Lefty Louie.

The ease with which Gyp and Lefty were able to elude the police had begun to wear on the district attorney. In a move clearly derisive of Commissioner Waldo and the police department, he offered a reward of $5,000 for the "apprehension of Louis Rosenberg, alias "Lefty Louie," and Harry

Horowitz, alias Gyp the Blood, or $2,500 for the apprehension of either one," to anyone other than a member or an employee of the police department. Though he said his offer indicated no "feeling of unkindness" toward the department, he went on to say it was his "belief that if proper police work had been done, these men would now be in custody." Then, in a caustic indictment, he added, " . . . I cannot escape the conclusion that some members of the police department have known, if they do not know now, the whereabouts of these murderers."

Whitman's hostility toward the police, never a secret, had been fueled by a recent report that, weeks before his arrest, Schepps had been cornered in the Catskills and allowed to escape. As the story had it, five men from the department's Central Office had found Schepps asleep in a barn near Fallsburg, New York. When they awakened him and asked if he was Schepps, the man reportedly grunted, "My name is Schmidt. Go away and don't bother me." And they did.

Two days after Whitman issued his statement, the police reported that they believed Gyp was hiding in a girl's apartment near 116th Street and Lenox Avenue in Harlem, that he had never left the city, and that Lefty Louie was not with him. The truth of that view seemed to be subverted a day later when police in Greeley, Pennsylvania, a small town about one hundred miles from Scranton, announced that they had caught Gyp the Blood. The officer who made the arrest, Constable G. R. Rosencranz, said he was "perfectly certain" that he had caught the right man. The suspect had been staying at a local hotel, the officer said, he was a stranger in that part of the country, and was a regular reader of New York papers. Already counting the reward money, Rosencranz sauntered into the hotel, put his hand on the man's shoulder and said, "You are Harry Horowitz, my friend. You are Gyp the Blood, and you're coming with me." The man went along, but he turned out to be someone other than Harry Horowitz. In Rosencranz's defense, the man, who was not otherwise identified, bore a striking resemblance to Gyp except for a difference in height and the color of his hair.

The false identification was one of many. On August 15, dispatches had been printed in newspapers stating that Gyp and Lefty were believed to be aboard a ship on its way to Duluth, Minnesota. Two days later came reports that they had arrived in Duluth and disappeared. On August 19, a report from

Rochester, New York, said the two men had passed through the city and were headed west. Other "sightings" had placed them in Massachusetts and as far away as Colorado. The fugitives appeared to be leading the police on a merry chase.

Then, on Saturday night, September 14, a contingent of officers led by Deputy Commissioner Dougherty got their men. They were not in Harlem or the Catskills or anywhere in the Midwest, and they were very much together. They were arrested that evening in an apartment in the Glendale section of Queens, just over the Brooklyn line at Ridgewood. They had been there for about a month, having fled the Catskills when they learned that police were searching the area. Their apartment was in the rear of the second floor of a three-story house on the north side of the Ridgewood elevated train tracks. Certain that they had the right men this time, Dougherty and his cadre were taking no chances. They didn't ring the bell and announce their presence. They kicked in the door and found exactly what they hoped to find; Gyp and Lefty were sitting at a table in the dining area with their wives. The captives offered no resistance. When they were searched they were found to have twenty-eight dollars between them. Both were wearing khakis, and they asked for permission to change into more formal attire. For the occasion, they dressed nattily in suits and shirts and ties. Gyp was upset that he could not find his hat, and Dougherty loaned him his own automobile hat. Neither was a man of imposing stature. Gyp was about five-foot-three, Lefty some three inches taller. Gyp gave his age as twenty-four; Lefty said he was twenty-two. They would not get to be very much older.

The arrests helped to vindicate Commissioner Waldo and his force, as they were the result of intensive and prolonged investigation. Dozens of detectives under Dougherty's command had been keeping tight surveillance on every member of the fugitives' families for many weeks, hoping they would eventually be led to their hiding place. They trailed the men's wives all over the metropolitan area but never got close. It was, however, bits and pieces of conversation dropped by the two women that allowed the detectives to narrow their focus. Dougherty would not reveal how these tidbits were picked up, but he explained in some detail what they were.

The first clue was a remark that the tedium of the men's seclusion was eased because they were able to watch open-air movies from the rear window of the hideout. With that bit of information, police began searching the neighborhood around every open-air theater in Greater New York. The next clue narrowed the area considerably. A detective heard it mentioned that the men also had the convenience of a laundry in the building in which they were housed. The final tip was that the name of the laundry was something like Brighten or Bright or Bridgetown. An industrious detective by the name of Frank Cassassa found a Brighton Hand Laundry located in the basement of 756 Woodward Avenue in the Glendale section of Queens, and after canvassing the neighborhood discovered the Woodbine Open Air Moving Picture Show just behind the house. As he began making subtle inquiries in the area, he noticed a woman he was sure was Mrs. Rosenberg, Lefty Louie's wife, leave the building and return some time later carrying a bag of groceries. He then placed a phone call to Dougherty.

Dougherty notified the D.A.'s office and was told to send the prisoners to the Tombs. There was no need to indict them, since they had been named, in absentia, in a blanket indictment that also included Whitey Lewis, Dago Frank, Becker, Reich, and Shapiro, the driver of the getaway car. Libby, the owner of the car, had been turned loose after satisfying the district attorney that he was not involved in the crime and had nothing of consequence to offer the prosecution. Rose, Webber, Vallon, and Schepps were still in custody but only as material witnesses. There were no longer any suspects at large. All of the state's witnesses were present and accounted for. The case was now completely in the hands of the district attorney's office and the courts. There was still a long road to travel.

THE TRIAL:

CONVICTION

AND SENTENCING

10

Trial by jury is a blood sport. Though there may be no better system for teasing justice from the tug between guilt and innocence, a jury trial has little to do with the quest for truth or the passion for justice. It is, in every nuance, a competition between prosecution and defense for the hearts and minds of twelve jurors. Each side is committed to a particular result and is pledged to pursue those facts that will support its case and present only those witnesses whose testimony will further its ends. The jury is the finder of fact, determining which version of the truth is more credible. The judge interprets the law and instructs the jury on how to apply it. But, as is the case with other competitions, the outcome is often determined, or at least influenced, by what has occurred before the contest begins: the strategies that are to be employed, which witnesses will be called and in what sequence, exhibits that might be placed into evidence or withheld. Perhaps nothing is more critical than the makeup of the jury, except possibly the identity and disposition of the judge. For while the jury is the final cause in determining the fate of the defendant, the judge may have more to do with shaping the mood of the jury than either of the advocates, as he is perceived by the jurors as being neutral and fair. It is an attorney's nightmare therefore to learn that the judge who will hear his case has a long history of appearing to favor the opposing side. So Becker and

McIntyre doubtless felt their throats constrict a bit when they learned that the judge they would be dealing with was John W. Goff.

Goff was known as a prosecutor's judge. His reputation as a relentless foe of police corruption dated back to 1894 when he served as counsel to the Lexow Committee, and the intervening years, including the last six as a justice on the state supreme court, had done nothing to soften it. Goff was named to preside over an Extraordinary Session of the Criminal Branch of the State Supreme Court of New York County which had been called at Whitman's request. Even before the last two gunmen were in tow, Whitman had begun to sense that he had come upon his defining moment. The biggest scandal in the city's history was being peeled open, layer by layer, and only he could be trusted to clean it all up and set things right. The next election for governor was three years down the road. He was already being spoken of in Republican circles as a possible candidate, and if he could bring justice to bear on the Becker case and cleanse the city of police corruption, the timing could not be better. It was clearly in the state's interest to move quickly.

In mid-August, Whitman sent a messenger to Albany with a formal application, requesting the Extraordinary Session, which would begin on September 3, about a month before the supreme court was scheduled to begin hearing cases. Governor John Alden Dix readily granted the request, and for an added fillip named Goff to preside over all cases arising from the Rosenthal murder. That Goff would be more than willing to interrupt his summer vacation to take on a high-profile case probably came as no surprise to Whitman. Given the early session and with Goff presiding, the trial seemed to be setting up in favor of the state. There was little the defense could do to counter such events, but it might have hoped that the choice of John F. McIntyre as Becker's lead counsel might offset a measure of the prosecution's advantage.

Now in his mid-fifties, McIntyre had tried more homicide cases than any lawyer in history. Most of them had taken place in the 1880s and 1890s when he was in the district attorney's office. He had prosecuted 614 cases of murder or manslaughter and obtained 580 convictions. As a defense attorney, he had made his reputation in 1896 when he went to London and won an acquittal for Edward Ivory, an Irish revolutionary who was accused of plotting to blow up the Houses of Parliament and kill Queen Victoria. McIntyre had come by his commitment to Irish independence naturally enough. His grandfather had been exiled to the United States in 1878 for taking part in the Irish Rebellion. Such a background suggested the possibility that McIntyre might yet find common ground with the judge. Goff, about ten years McIntyre's senior, was an Irish Nationalist of long standing. Both were said to be members of a secret society that believed freedom from England could be achieved only by violent action. But any notion that Goff and McIntyre might bond over such shared sympathies was dispelled from the outset.

The two men clashed at their first meeting in court, on Tuesday, September 3, when McIntyre and Whitman appeared before the court to make various motions. One of Whitman's first motions was that Becker be tried separately from the other six men who were covered in the blanket indictment and that Becker be tried first. Trying Becker first would circumvent the prospect of the other defendants' testimony—presumably proclaiming their innocence and denying a conspiracy with Becker at its head—being used by the defense. Goff granted the motion over McIntyre's objection. It set a pattern that would be followed throughout the hearing. Whitman's motions were uniformly granted; McIntyre's denied. With Becker's case now separated from the other six, the judge ordered that he be brought before him to plead to the indictment. Again the defense objected. McIntyre asked for a week's adjournment.

"There are certain motions to be made," he said. "We desire to have these motions heard before the pleading in this case is heard. Does Your Honor deny the application?"

"I have already done so," Goff ruled.

McIntyre asked again; Goff denied again. "Then the defendant refuses to plead," McIntyre said.

Goff summoned the court clerk and whispered something to him. The clerk then announced to the court: "In the charge of murder against Charles Becker, the court directs a plea of not guilty be entered."

Whitman promptly requested that the trial be scheduled to start on September 10, one week away. McIntyre sprang to his feet: "The defendant will not be ready for trial," he said. "The defendant needs ample time. This case is important to him. His life is in danger. Your Honor has ordered him to plead before the case was ready. There are men in the Tombs charged with murder in the first degree who have not been put on trial. Why should this case, important as it is, be rushed to trial so? . . . I submit now that to force us to go to trial on next Tuesday will work hardship and injustice to Lieutenant Becker. I ask that the same rights be given to him as to any other defendant arraigned here."

Goff's response was brief: "Trial of the defendant is set for Tuesday next, September 10." Moments later, Becker got two extra days when it was pointed out that the law required that a defendant must have two days' notice for pleading prior to the opening of the trial term of any court. The trial date was then set for Thursday, September 12.

Undeterred, McIntyre appealed to another supreme court justice, George Bischoff, asking that a stay be granted until October 7. He also applied for a commission to be sent to Arkansas to take depositions from three men regarding statements made to them by Sam Schepps. While luxuriating in Hot Springs, Schepps reportedly had told a number of people—among them Mayor Pettit and the editor of a local paper, Douglas Hotchkiss—that Becker had no knowledge of the plan to kill Rosenthal.

"These three men stand high in the community," McIntyre told Justice Bischoff, "and Schepps solemnly declared to them, according to our information, that Becker had nothing to do with the death of Rosenthal. A human life is dangling in the balance, depending on the testimony of three informers and this man Schepps, and if Schepps made statements tending to exculpate Becker, it is necessary to have this evidence."

Assistant D.A. Moss was quick to protest. "If this motion is to be heard, in my opinion, it should be heard by Justice Goff," he told Bischoff. "This motion can be addressed to the justice holding the Extraordinary Term when it meets tomorrow. That would be orderly practice."

Justice Bischoff did not take kindly to Moss's observation. "It is not the convenience of another judge," he said. "It is a matter of justice to the accused man. Is the accused man to be deprived of testimony on a mere technicality? I think not. It becomes my duty to decide this case, and I shall do so as speedily as possible."

On the day before the trial was scheduled to start, Bischoff granted the stay and the commission to Hot Springs. "I am satisfied," he said, "that the testimony sought to be secured by the moving party is material and that he should be given the opportunity to obtain it."

Bischoff's decision was a direct response to McIntyre's spelling out the importance of Schepps to the prosecution's case. He noted that Rose, Webber, and Vallon had all confessed to their roles as assassins in the slaying of Rosenthal. Later, he pointed out, Schepps was implicated as the paymaster, and he fled to Arkansas. While there, he told several people that Becker was not involved in the crime. But, McIntyre emphasized, the district attorney was aware that Becker could not be convicted on the testimony of accomplices alone. Outside corroboration was needed, and the D.A.'s response was to create a shield of "constructive innocence" around Schepps, allowing him to slip free along with the other three accomplices in return for their testimony against Becker.

Now, even if Schepps played his part well, there would be reason for a juror to doubt the truth of his testimony. The defense would be certain to make much of the benefits that accrued to the witness when he was converted from suspect to corroborator of fact. With a shadow cast across Schepps's credibility, the significance of Big Jack Zelig grew increasingly critical. He had never been a suspect, never altered his story, and had nothing to gain if he pointed the finger at Becker. As the trial date approached, the prosecution was counting heavily on what Zelig had to offer.

As it turned out, the state would have to do without it. On Saturday evening, October 5, two days before the trial was to start, Big Jack was shot dead on a Second Avenue streetcar. The assassin, apprehended as he fled, was a nickel-and-dime hood known as "Red Phil" Davidson, thirty years old, who gave his occupation as fruit peddler. Actually, he was a no-account hanger-on who had tried to work his way into Zelig's gang but was never taken seriously. Those on the inside described him as a petty crook and a stool pigeon who made his way stealing from pushcart vendors, snatching the purses of old ladies, and even taking money from children.

The motive for the killing was immediately subject to speculation. Davidson told the police that he had shot Zelig in retaliation for Zelig's roughing him up and taking four hundred dollars from him earlier in the day. But some saw it differently. The news spread through the underworld that Zelig had been "put away" to keep him from testifying for the state. Some might have seen it as the fulfillment of a prophecy. Earlier that day, no more than three or four hours before the shooting, Bald Jack Rose told the district attorney, who was discussing the upcoming trial with his prime witness in the West Side Prison: "Zelig will never live to see the trial start. Watch! He'll be the next one they get."

Whitman therefore was twice stunned when he got the news at about ten o'clock that night upon returning home from dinner at the Waldorf. "My God, what next?" he said. "What next? I don't know what to do."

The incident had occurred little more than an hour earlier. Zelig apparently had been called out to his death in the same fashion that Rosenthal had. He was in a café on Second Avenue, between Fourth and Fifth Streets, when he responded to a phone call from someone who asked to meet him at Fourteenth Street. He boarded a trolley at Fifth Street and headed north. Davidson apparently had been watching for him. After seeing Zelig take a seat, he hopped on to the running board and as the car approached Fourteenth Street he moved up behind him, placed a .38-caliber revolver behind his left ear, and fired a single shot. Zelig slumped forward in his seat. Davidson jumped off the car and began running east on Fourteenth Street. Patrolman Paul Schmidt, of the Twenty-second Street Station, heard the shot, saw Davidson in flight, and took off in pursuit. About halfway down the block, Davidson suddenly stopped, swung around to face the policeman, and shouted, "Stop where you are or I'll shoot." Schmidt didn't stop. He kept moving forward, and drawing his own revolver, pointed it directly at Davidson's face and said, "Drop that gun. Drop it or I'll blow your head off." Davidson's nerve failed him. He tossed his gun aside, raised his hands, and said, "I give up. I give up. Don't shoot."

Back at the scene, Patrolman Robert Locke, of the East Fifth Street Station, found Zelig slumped in a heap in one of the trolley's long cross seats, his head bloody and pressed forward on his chest. Locke called for an ambulance from Bellevue Hospital, but it was already too late. Zelig was pronounced dead on arrival.

Among the items found in his possession were letters from each of the four gunmen, expressing their devotion to Big Jack and their trust that he would do the right thing when he testified. Lefty Louie's sentiments were representative of the others. "Zel," he wrote, "you tell me [referring to a letter he had received from Zelig] you are going to stick to me and the boys to the end. I know that, Zel, as I know what you are made of, having full confidence in you, old boy ..."

Clearly, they expected Zelig to testify that Rose had come to him at the behest of Becker who was planning to have Rosenthal killed, that Becker wanted Zelig to provide him with the killers, but that he, Zelig, would have no part of it. Thus he had no idea who the shooters were, just that it was Becker who was making the arrangements.

Exactly what Zelig might have said on the stand was left to conjecture, and the district attorney's office and the police department were as far apart on the issue as the prosecution and the defense. It served Whitman's ends to depict Zelig as a key witness whose mouth had been shut as part of a grand design. For if it was true that Davidson was a hired gunman, there was a real possibility that he was acting as an agent of the police department. The department would have been the first casualty of Zelig's testimony if he told all he knew about the operation of the System as well as the murder plan. Dougherty, speaking for the police, contended that there was no frame-up. "No," he said, "Davidson did the thing alone, and I believe he thought it out all alone. When Zelig punched him it was probably the last straw in a load of such assaults and keyed Davidson to the murder pitch." The defense, of course, sided with the police version of the shooting. McIntyre, noting that Zelig had not been subpoenaed by the D.A., went so far as to say that he would have called Zelig as a witness for the defense. Zelig would have refuted, not corroborated, Rose's story, McIntyre insisted. The only man who knew the truth about Zelig's murder, Red Phil Davidson, clung to the story that he acted alone. Whatever his motive, he eventually pleaded guilty to second-degree murder and served twelve years of a twenty-year sentence at Sing Sing.

The jousting between the two sides was over now. One thing the prosecution and defense agreed on was that there would be no delay in the start of the trial. It was Monday, October 7, and Police Lieutenant Charles Becker was about to go on trial for his life.

11

The Criminal Courts building in which Becker would be tried had the look of a middle-aged dowager drifting toward a premature death. It was only twenty-seven years old, but there were those who said it should have been condemned on the day it opened. Andy Logan, in her book *Against the Evidence: The Becker-Rosenthal Affair,* quotes the lawyer/novelist Arthur Train's description: "It is one of the gloomiest structures in the world. . . . Tier on tier it rises above a huge central rotunda, rimmed by dim mezzanines and corridors upon which the courtrooms open, and crowned by a . . . glass roof encrusted with soot, through which filters a soiled and viscous light. The air is rancid with garlic, stale cigar smoke, sweat, and the odors of prisoners' lunch." The walls, according to Logan, had begun to buckle soon after the structure was completed, and city officials responded as city officials often do in such circumstances—they declared the building unfit for occupancy and a threat to human life—and promptly turned their attention elsewhere.

Yet the cheerless setting seemed appropriate to the occasion. There were no heroes on the premises, no good guys. Guilty or innocent of Rosenthal's murder, Becker was clearly a dirty cop who ran a graft-taking enterprise that sullied the department, turned sections of New York into pockets of illegal gambling casinos and dens of prostitution, and helped buy and sell city officials as if they were merchandise in a wholesale market. The men who would bear witness against him were in no way his betters. They were, by and large, two-bit gamblers and thugs who were every bit as corrupt as he was. Even the judge and the district attorney were men whose actions were questionable and whose motives were suspect.

The first critical decision made by the prosecution was a bold one, which was challenged by the defense and subjected to much speculation by reporters and other courthouse connoisseurs. Whitman requested that Becker's case be separated from the trial of the four accused gunmen and, to the consternation of many, that he be tried first. McIntyre of course objected to the ruling, and normal courtroom procedure seemed to favor his cause. Trying Becker before the gunmen introduced a legal paradox that could not easily be resolved. Since Becker was accused of hiring the four men to kill Rosenthal, reason suggested that the gunmen should be tried first. For imagine the consequence of Becker's being convicted, while his four presumed hirelings were later acquitted. Becker would have been found guilty of an act that legally never took place; to wit, hiring the four men to commit murder. But the prosecution apparently found the maneuver to be worth the risk. Trying Becker first offered some obvious benefits to the state. Having already pled guilty in an earlier trial, the four men would certainly deny having been hired by Becker; they might even contend that they had never met him, as there was no evidence of any direct interaction between them. In effect, their testimony would serve the interests of the defense. Then, too, there was the catastrophic possibility that the quartet would be found not guilty, in which case Becker would in fact be on trial for engaging in an act that a jury had already found never occurred.

The advantages that accrued to the state did not escape the notice of McIntyre, nor did the logic determining the order of prosecution. He had already objected to separating the two cases, only to be overruled by Goff. Now, he raised an objection to the sequence of the two trials. "I submit," he said, "that the defendant Charles Becker cannot in justice be tried for arranging the murder of Herman Rosenthal unless the persons who, it is alleged, acted at his direction are themselves found guilty of having so acted." His argument fell dead on the judge's ears. Goff lost no time in denying the motion. It was just the beginning of a war of words and a test of wills between the judge and the defense attorney that the attorney was destined to lose.

Indeed, McIntyre had a subtle stratagem of his own that he was ready to spring on the court. He was planning to ask that much of the testimony of the state's four witnesses—Rose, Vallon, Webber, and Schepps—be excluded on the ground that if a conspiracy to kill Rosenthal existed, by its nature it ended with Rosenthal's death. Therefore, all evidence regarding the events that followed the murder was immaterial and irrelevant. It was an interesting bit of legalistic manipulation, but it had no chance of getting by the judge; it didn't.

The trial began on schedule, on Monday, October 7, but only over the strenuous objection of the defense. McIntyre began the day by asking for a week's adjournment because co-counsel Hart had suddenly fallen ill and was unable to appear. It was Hart, McIntyre noted, who had done the preliminary investigation of jurors, and his absence placed the defense at a distinct disadvantage. Goff would have none of it. He let it be known that expedition was a priority in his courtroom, and his subsequent actions left no doubt that he meant it. He urged both attorneys on as voire dire—the examination of prospective jurors—proceeded. But at the end of the day thirteen talesmen had been examined, and only one had been chosen. McIntyre had used four of his thirty peremptory challenges, and Whitman had used three. At the rate they were proceeding, it would take twelve days to fill the panel. That was unacceptable to Goff, and he took no pains to hide his displeasure. In a stern lecture to the court, he said that the delay in picking juries was becoming a public scandal, and he warned that if a jury was not in place by five o'clock the next day he would hold night sessions until all twelve members were chosen. Goff suspected, perhaps not without reason, that McIntyre was prolonging his interrogations to gain time until Hart was well enough to return to court.

Despite the air of open hostility that flowed between the bench and the defense table, there was from time to time a touch of humor that leavened the atmosphere in the courtroom. Prospective juror Robert McEwen provided such a moment when he told the court it would be difficult for him to serve because it was his busy season and he could not spare the time. Asked his occupation, he said he was secretary of the Woodlawn Cemetery Company. McEwen seemed a reasonable prospect in all other respects, but Becker insisted that McIntyre dismiss him. Becker played an active role throughout the selection procedure. As the *Times* reported it, "He studied each talesman closely, and time and again consulted with Mr. McIntyre, or with Lloyd Stryker, or George W. Whiteside, Mr. McIntyre's associates. And frequently it was upon the recommendation of Becker that Mr. McIntyre employed one of his precious peremptory challenges."

Becker had entered the courtroom looking stoic and exuding confidence. Still, three months in the Tombs had exacted its price. It was a slimmed-down version of the muscular lieutenant who now sat beside his attorneys at the defense table. His suit was at least one size too large for his frame, and his face was speckled with grooves that reflected the loss of weight. But the swagger was still there. He felt that the state's case was weak, resting almost entirely on the testimony of witnesses who would be brought to the courthouse directly from their prison cells, witnesses who already had confessed their part in the conspiracy with which the defendant was charged. On his way out of the courtroom, Becker asked a newspaper reporter, "Well, how do you chaps think it's going?"

The reporter said that most of them thought the jury was likely to be divided and unable to reach a verdict.

"What?" Becker responded. "Do you mean to tell me that I shan't be acquitted? Why, this is worse than Russia if they convict me on such testimony."

Had there been any doubt that Judge Goff meant it when he threatened to keep the court in session well into the night, it was removed on the second day of jury selection. The proceedings moved slowly through the morning and early afternoon, principally because Becker continued to be fastidious in his judgment of candidates. McIntyre later explained that his client sometimes overrode his own judgment, insisting that a juror that McIntyre found acceptable be dismissed for reasons that only Becker knew. He operated chiefly on instinct, on one occasion asking McIntyre to use a peremptory challenge on a candidate whom he saw smile in the direction of the district attorney. But McIntyre was well aware of the priorities. It was Becker's life that was at risk, and he had the right to decide in whose hands he would place it.

By six o'clock, eight places had been filled in the jury box; there were four to go. Good to his word, Goff ordered a nighttime session beginning at eight, after a two-hour recess. Three additional jurors were selected by nine-thirty, leaving the panel just one short. McIntyre asked the court for an adjournment, saying that he had been working eighteen hours a day and was physically exhausted.

"There are eleven jurors in the box," Goff said. "Go on with the examinations."

An hour later, McIntyre renewed his request. "Your Honor," he said, "the defense is entitled to my very best efforts, and I do not feel that I can do justice to my client unless the case is adjourned soon. I am very tired and under the strain of this night session I do not feel that I shall be keen and on edge tomorrow morning." This time the judge relented. He adjourned court until eleven the following morning.

With only one more juror to be picked, and day-long and evening sessions once again scheduled, it appeared certain that the panel would be complete on the third day. But it wasn't. From eleven in the morning, candidate after candidate was rejected, either for cause or peremptorily, and by six o'clock the blue-ribbon list of 250 prospective jurors was exhausted. Goff had no alternative but to adjourn until Thursday when an additional one hundred prospects would be on hand. McIntyre had four peremptory challenges left and Whitman had just one, so it was certain that the twelfth man would be selected, but not until every peremptory challenge had been used by the defense, for McIntyre deemed it essential that none be left.

"As an actual fact," he told the press, "I've got to exhaust all my peremptory challenges, even if it should be necessary to challenge talesmen for the twelfth seat in the jury box a dozen times, and even if by so doing I were to lose a juror whom I might prefer above all others. The reason is a technical one and is based on various decisions of the higher courts."

He quoted a ruling by the Court of Appeals which said that "no injury could be done to a convicted man by reason of mistakes of the court provided all of the peremptory challenges of the defense had not been employed. Were any of these not used, the court held, a remedy ready at hand had been neglected by the defense, and consequently the claim of injury by court ruling could not hold."

McIntyre also noted that Becker had been responsible for a number of challenges. "In one or two instances," he said, "I passed over men whom personally I should have liked, but they were not acceptable to Lt. Becker, and he is entitled to have his opinion in this regard respected. On the other hand,

I accepted at least one man on his suggestion whom I should have challenged. In this respect also, however, Lt. Becker is entitled to his opinion and choice, for in the selection of a jury it is simply a matter of the study of human nature, and he may be a keener student of this than I."

McIntyre's first priority, and the most difficult to achieve, he said, was to choose men of exceptional intellect and discernment, for they would be called upon to distinguish among the crimes of murder, extortion, and graft. "Without a jury that can keep the murder charge—the charge upon which we are being tried—distinct from the allegations of extortion and bribery, which are sure to be introduced by the prosecution, we should stand a mighty slim chance," he said.

An accountant by the name of Samuel H. Haas filled all of McIntyre's requirements. He was the twelfth man, seated as the noon hour approached. The full panel, to no one's surprise, was of a piece: They were all men (women were not yet permitted to vote in 1912, let alone sit on juries); all white (a black panelist sitting in judgment of a white defendant in a capital case would have been unthinkable); and they were all married, substantial citizens as the world might judge them (Becker had insisted that all jurors be married, in the belief that married men take their responsibilities more seriously). In addition to the accountant, the jury included: a branch manager for the New York Edison Company, a chemist, a retired rice merchant, an auditor for a collar company, two real estate brokers, a wholesale lumber merchant, a commissary agent, a baker, a mechanical engineer, and the manager of the Bonwit Teller department store.

With the jury box filled before noon, Goff called for opening statements. In his brief remarks to the jury, the district attorney demonstrated that McIntyre's concern about mingling the murder charge with accusations of extortion and graft was not misplaced.

"We are going to claim," Whitman said, "that in spite of the fact that Becker did not use the fatal weapons, notwithstanding the fact that he may not have been present at the scene of the crime, conceding, of course, that others are guilty of the awful crime of feloniously taking human life, that the real murderer, the most desperate criminal of them all, was the cool, calculating, scheming, grafting police officer who used the very office with which the people had entrusted him, the very power which was his for the enforcement of law and order, to tempt and force others into the commission of crime, to extort, graft and blackmail from lawbreakers, and finally, for the protection of his infamous traffic in the purchase and sale of law enforcement, wantonly to sacrifice human life for the protection of which the very office which he held was created."

Addressing the critical issue of motive, Whitman noted, "So far as we can learn, none of those four [gun]men knew Herman Rosenthal at all. There was no cause for them to fear him living. There was no normal reason for them to desire his death."

Through it all, Becker appeared impassive. He leaned back in his chair, his right arm cast leisurely over its back, his head tilted slightly to the right, listening carefully but with a restless detachment. He affected the posture of a student impatient for the instructor to conclude and eager for the bell to sound, ending the class

Opening statements rarely have a serious affect on the outcome of a trial. They are designed to allow each side to state its case and outline what it proposes to prove through the testimony of witnesses. Days or weeks later, only the most attentive juror is likely to remember what was said prior to the avalanche of testimony that followed. The avalanche of testimony linking Lieutenant Charles Becker to the murder of Herman "Beansie" Rosenthal would begin in the afternoon session, immediately after a lunch break.

POLICE LIEUTENANT CHARLES BECKER,
tried and convicted twice for the murder of
Beansie Rosenthal, is the only New York
police officer ever executed for murder.

HELEN BECKER remained steadfastly loyal to her husband and continued to insist on his innocence throughout his three-year struggle with the law.

HERMAN "BEANSIE" ROSENTHAL, a Times Square gambler, was shot down and killed after he went public with a tale of police graft and corruption. *Courtesy of David Pietrusza*

ROSENTHAL'S FUNERAL attracted a large group of onlookers as his body was carted away from in front of his home and gambling parlor at 104 W. 45th St.

DISTRICT ATTORNEY CHARLES WHITMAN (seated) prosecuted Becker zealously and was twice elected governor of New York State.

**POLICE COMMISSIONER
RHINELANDER WALDO**
tried to clean up the West
Side gambling industry
but made the mistake of
appointing Becker to
head the effort.

BIG TIM SULLIVAN, a New York State
senator and U.S. congressman, was
the kingpin of virtually all organized
graft and bribery operations in Manhattan.

BALD JACK ROSE, Becker's bagman and accomplice in Rosenthal's murder, turned state's evidence and was the prosecution's chief witness against Becker.

BRIDGEY WEBBER (front left), also an accomplice, was assigned by Becker to round up the gunmen. It was Webber who spotted Rosenthal in the Metropole on the night of the murder and notified Rose and the hitmen.

HARRY VALLON, together with Rose and Bridgey Webber, planned the hit on Rosenthal and testified against Becker at both of his trials.

WHT "WHITEY" LEWIS.

THE FOUR GUNMEN who fired the shots that killed Rosenthal were electrocuted in succession: (above) Whitey Lewis being taken into custody by police; (opposite, top) Lefty Louie (seated) and Gyp the Blood; and (opposite, bottom) Dago Frank, shielding his face from the camera.

SAM SCHEPPS, although clearly a party to the murder arrangements, served the state's case by corroborating the testimony of the other accomplices.

BIG JACK ZELIG, leader of the gang that included the four gunmen, was shot and killed while riding on a trolley car two days before Becker's trial was to begin.
Courtesy of David Pietrusza

12

The early testimony in a murder trial is not unlike the warm-up ritual of an orchestra prior to the opening of a concert; the intent is not to make music but to take inventory and make sure all the pieces are in place. Since only sworn testimony is admitted as evidence, the trial generally begins with a series of witnesses who do no more than create a foundation that allows the trial to proceed. Until the first witness takes the stand, nothing is assumed, nothing taken as fact; no crime has been committed until someone puts it on the record; there has been no shooting unless someone heard the shots or found the bullet holes. Herman Rosenthal is not presumed dead until an authority on the subject says he is.

So the first witnesses were called solely to establish the most basic facts. Officer John J. Brady was on his beat when he heard the shots, rushed to the scene, and saw Rosenthal sprawled on the sidewalk. Another policeman, William J. File, was in the Metropole at the time, rushed outside, and saw the getaway car speeding away. Dr. Dennis Taylor, of Flower Hospital, testified that he saw a man lying dead in the street in front of the hotel, covered with a white tablecloth. Dr. Otto H. Schultze, a coroner's physician, performed the autopsy and found that Rosenthal died of two bullet wounds to the head, both of which penetrated the brain. Jacob Hecht, a waiter at the Metropole, said he heard the shots and saw Rosenthal fall to the ground. He saw the men who shot him but did not get a look at their faces and would be unable to identify any of them. After each of these witnesses testified for the prosecution, McIntyre said simply, "No questions." There was nothing yet to contend, and McIntyre, as it developed, did well to husband his energy.

The first witness of consequence was Louis Krause, the Hungarian waiter who had happened by the scene on the night of the killing and was told by police to move on. No mystery attended the testimony Krause would deliver. A witness at the coroner's hearing, he had identified Bridgey Webber and Jacob Reich as being at the scene. Now, under direct examination by Assistant D.A. Moss, he affirmed that he had indeed seen Reich lean over the body, then stand erect with a smile on his face. He also identified three of the gunmen Justice Goff had ordered brought into the courtroom. Instructed by Goff, Krause left the witness stand and approached the shooting suspects. He touched Whitey Lewis on the shoulder and said, "I saw him there." He did the same with Lefty Louie and then with Gyp the Blood. For some reason, he failed to identify Dago Frank. Moss put Krause through his paces pointedly and with little hesitation. All he wanted was a positive identification of the suspects at the scene, and Krause was quick to oblige. He said he was opposite the hotel when he saw two men emerge. The second man lifted his finger to his head and then four others came out from behind a large touring car and started shooting. All four men had revolvers, he said, and he saw at least three of them fire. They then ran back into the car and Krause saw it start toward Sixth Avenue. He also explained that he had seen Webber with a group of men near the Metropole just before the shooting and again stated that he saw Reich lean over the body. After Krause completed his person-to-person identification, the prosecution was finished with him. He stepped back to the witness stand and prepared for what would be an unexpectedly lengthy cross-examination.

It was clear from the start that McIntyre had determined that it was important to discredit the first eyewitness to the murder. He seemed also to be a bit overconfident. Krause, after all, was an itinerant waiter who had changed jobs often, who was living apart from his wife and son, and who, not yet a citizen of the United States, spoke with the accents of Eastern Europe still on his tongue. But McIntyre had miscalculated badly. Krause proved to be cool, totally at his ease, and unflappable during a heated, two-hour frontal assault by the defense attorney. Even his fairly recent acquaintance with the English language seemed more an asset than a liability. Like many another early twentieth-century immigrant, he learned to speak English precisely, directly, and with a syntax that was unadorned by the argot of the streets and pool halls. And he took special delight in his ability to keep McIntyre slightly off-balance.

He offered reasonable explanations for his changes in jobs, working as a waiter at one restaurant or another since arriving in America in 1907. When McIntyre asked if he had ever worked under "Oscar, the chef at the Waldorf," Krause responded, "He's the manager, not the chef. Yes, I worked for him." But that was a mere parry in a duel that was just beginning to take shape. Looking to cut the legs out from under the witness, McIntyre committed a blunder that every law student is taught to avoid: He asked a question without knowing how the witness would respond. Not having gotten what he wanted with regard to Krause's professional resume, McIntyre turned to his family life in an attempt to depict him as being less than stable. The attorney had learned that Krause had recently moved from his mother-in-law's apartment on East 112th Street to an apartment in Bath Beach.

"Are you living alone there?" McIntyre asked.

"Yes," Krause replied. "I sent my wife and son to her parents, who are now in Westerly, Rhode Island."

"And why did you move to Bath Beach?" McIntyre's tone was accusative, but it would soon grow hostile and defensive because the response he received was anything but what he had hoped for.

"Because," Krause said evenly and without emotion, "I got so many threatening letters that I was afraid to stay here."

"Do you honestly expect to tell these gentlemen that and to have them believe it?" McIntyre asked, motioning in the direction of the jury.

When Krause affirmed, calmly and with assurance, that he did because be was telling the truth, McIntyre tried quickly to recover the lost ground, but he again took the wrong direction. In a tone near the boiling point, he made it clear that he doubted the truth of those threats and let loose a flurry of questions, one following the other so closely that Krause had no chance to reply. Had Krause notified the police of these threats? Had he told the postal authorities? Had he taken any measures to protect himself? The barrage continued until Goff ordered McIntyre to stop. He and the jury then learned that Krause had indeed received such threats, that he had notified the district attorney, and that it had been the district attorney who sent him to Bath Beach, where he had been living in hiding since shortly after the murder. Furthermore, a detective had been assigned to be with him at all times, serving as a body-guard who was sworn to be ready to place himself between Krause and a bullet should that be required. And, when the trial was over, Krause and his family were to be escorted safely to another location.

It was a bad moment for the defense. McIntyre, for his part, must have felt as if he were trapped in a nightmare, and every effort to awaken only drew him in deeper. He might have served his cause better if he had dismissed Krause and saved his fire for later witnesses, but he was determined to at least dent Krause's credibility. He was one of the few prosecution witnesses who had actually been at the scene at the time of the shooting, and it was largely on the strength of his eyewitness account that Webber and Reich had been held by the coroner as accomplices to the murder. So McIntyre pressed on doggedly, but every line of questioning only seemed to reinforce the integrity of the witness. Since Krause had come to the attention of the district attor-ney late in the investigation, his motives for offering his services were sub-ject to speculation. McIntyre chose next to explore those motives. He was preparing the way to question whether Krause actually was at the murder scene and whether he might have been offered something tangible by the D.A.'s office in return for his testimony.

Krause testified that, having witnessed the shooting, he consulted with some of his colleagues at Reisenweber's restaurant in Brighton Beach, where he was working at the time, and with his landlady; on their advice he went to police headquarters and spoke with Inspector Hughes. Hughes, in turn, introduced him to the district attorney. And what, McIntyre wondered, was Krause doing outside the Metropole at that early hour of the morning? The witness explained that he was dissatisfied with the working conditions at Reisenweber's, and he thought he could do better at a restaurant in the city. He had left Brighton Beach at about 12:15 and arrived at Forty-third Street and Broadway at about 1:40. He was on his way to a restaurant called Rec-tor's and the Geneva Club, the headquarters of a waiters' organization, where he hoped to hear of a job opening. As he neared the Metropole, he saw small groups of men milling about. "I thought something was going to happen, and I was curious," he said.

"I suppose you thought there was going to be a shooting," McIntyre said, his voice oozing sarcasm.

"No," Krause said, "if I had I wouldn't have been there."

The response drew laughter from the courtroom. McIntyre shifted ground, hoping to find firmer footing with another line of questioning. He asked Krause if he was acquainted with an officer at Reisenweber's restaurant named Henry Shade. When Krause said he was, McIntyre leaned in toward the witness chair, and in a voice that resonated with accusation, asked, "Didn't you say to Shade, 'I didn't see any one of the murderers that did the shooting?'"

Unshaken, Krause said simply, "I did not."

The attorney persisted: "Didn't Shade say to you, "'Go down to the district attorney and get a piece of the money?'"

Again, the witness denied the charge and went on to say that he did not want any money for testifying.

"I suppose," McIntyre suggested, "you wouldn't take any if the district attorney offered it to you?"

"No, I don't want a cent." Krause said. "I don't expect to be paid. I am doing my duty as a citizen."

Once again, the attorney asked a question to which he did not know the answer. "Are you a citizen?" he asked.

"I shall be soon," Krause said. "I have taken out my first papers."

It was another setback for the defense. It developed that since he had become a state's witness, Krause had been paid a total of seventy-eight dollars, all for legitimate expenses. Stymied again, McIntyre returned to the scene of the crime. It did him no good this time either. Krause testified that there were two small groups in front of the Metropole—Webber in one and Jack Sullivan (aka Jacob Reich) in the other. One of the men warned Krause to get off the street or there would be trouble. "I told him I had as much right as he had and I wouldn't go," Krause said.

"Of course you weren't afraid," McIntyre said in an apparent attempt to needle the witness.

"No," Krause responded, matter-of-factly.

Krause described how the gunmen were in a separate group behind the touring car.

"You mean the men who you thought did the shooting?" McIntyre asked.

Krause did not take the bait. "No," he said, "I mean the men who did the shooting."

McIntyre again questioned whether Krause actually witnessed the incident. "Do you know where Dowling's saloon is," he asked. When Krause said he did, McIntyre again turned accusative: "Weren't you in there the night of the shooting, and didn't you run out when you heard the shots?"

"I wasn't in there," Krause said, "and I never drink."

With cross-examination nearing the two-hour mark, McIntyre had lost every skirmish with the witness. He now seemed desperate to score some points, perhaps for no greater reason than to close on a positive note. Unable to discredit Krause's testimony that he had been at the murder scene, he tried to establish that, even if he was, he was in no position to see the participants well enough to identify them. In rapid succession, he asked how many feet the witness was from the Metropole when he heard the shots, how far from the hotel was the getaway car, how far was he from the gunmen when they did the shooting? Krause explained that he was unable to judge the distances in feet. He said he was about five meters away when he heard the shots. McIntyre, his poise ebbing quickly and his energy exhausted, let loose a barrage of comments, questioning how Krause could identify two months later men he had never seen before and yet was unable to recall simple matters of distance. Krause had the answer: "It's my business to remember faces," he said. "I've been a waiter for fifteen years."

McIntyre continued to try to shake Krause loose from his story, to trap him in inconsistencies, to make it appear that his testimony was fabricated or at least carefully orchestrated by the district attorney. He called attention to a few minor discrepancies between what Krause had told the coroner three months earlier and what he had said on the witness stand, but they were minor points that could be attributed to ordinary forgetfulness. McIntyre's questions had begun to lack substance, and his tone became increasingly caustic until Justice Goff called a stop to the cross-examination. "I can see no necessity for further questioning along that line," he said. "If there is no other question for the witness, I shall dismiss him." And he did.

It was very much like a referee calling an end to a one-sided bout and awarding the victor a technical knockout. The *Times* described Krause's performance this way:

"Throughout the long cross-examination Mr. Moss gave his witness almost no help. Time and again he declined to take advantage of opportunities to object to Mr. McIntyre's questions, and it was clear that he did so in full knowledge of Krause's ability to take care of himself. Lawyers who, hurrying from other courts when their cases were finished, dropped in to hear the Becker trial, declared that Krause made as remarkable a witness as any they had ever seen."

Despite the ease with which Krause frustrated, even embarrassed, the defense attorney, Becker's cause was not seriously damaged during the first day of testimony. His name was never mentioned, and there was no suggestion of a conspiracy. What surprised seasoned observers was the manner in which McIntyre tried to impugn the credibility of the eyewitness. It had been assumed that the shooting itself would be conceded; the defense would not challenge the fact that the four gunmen did the job but would try to demonstrate that Becker had no part in it. Now it appeared that the defense would question whether the four were involved at all. The reasoning seemed clear: If Rosenthal had been slain by professional hit-men, they must have been hired by someone, and who would benefit more from Rosenthal's death than Becker? But if the state's eyewitnesses had not seen four men jump from a car and do the shooting, Rosenthal might well have been killed by one of the many enemies he had made during his gambling career.

The following day, the prosecution opened with two more eyewitnesses. The first did little to help the state's case. He was Thomas Ryan, a young, curly haired taxi driver who had been parked across the street when the shooting occurred. Ryan had seen the action unfold and had said he could identify at least one of the shooters, but on the witness stand he grew less certain. As he had the previous day, Goff had the four accused gunmen paraded into the courtroom. But unlike Krause, who casually walked up and identified three of the men by touching them on the shoulder, Ryan was visibly intimidated. His voice was nearly inaudible. Several times, the judge said he could not hear him and asked if he could speak louder. On one occasion, Goff sent a court attendant to fetch Ryan a glass of water. All four suspects fixed the witness with a steady, menacing gaze, and Ryan appeared to have trouble looking away. He squirmed in the witness chair, his breath came in short takes, and in the final analysis he was unable to identify anyone.

Ryan said that although he had seen four men step up to Rosenthal, he had seen only one of the men fire his revolver.

"Did you notice the man who fired the shot so you could identify him?" Moss asked. "I did not," Ryan said.

It was not the response Moss expected. He had been advised that Ryan would identify one of the men—probably Lefty Louie—as the shooter, but now the witness insisted that "it all happened so quickly that I couldn't remember him."

Aware that the young man was paralyzed with fear, Goff tried to ease him along, displaying a gentle side of his nature that rarely surfaced in his courtroom. But neither the prodding of Goff nor the persistent questioning of Moss could pry loose an identification. Hadn't he told the assistant district attorney that he would be able to identify the shooter? "I only thought I could identify him," he said. Then why was he now unable to name him. Because, he said, he didn't want to pick out the wrong man. It was an explanation that allowed for little in the way of rebuttal, but Moss pressed on.

"Look at them," he said. "Which one did you think was the man?"

"I can't tell you," Ryan said.

"Look at them," Moss insisted, his voice growing louder. "Do you recognize one of them? Remember, you are here in the interests of justice."

Goff asked a question to which he already knew the answer: "Is there any reason why you should be afraid to tell the truth."

"No," Ryan said.

"You swear you cannot identify any of these four men?" Goff asked.

"I cannot," Ryan said.

And that was the end of it. McIntyre had no questions on cross. With a wave of his hand, he dismissed the witness. Ryan had already given him the best he could hope for.

The defense would not do as well with the next witness—an Austrian Count, to hear him tell it—who said he had been standing only a few feet away when the shooting started. The Count's name was Giovanni Stanish, and his English was limited enough to require an interpreter. Stanish testified that he had been standing near the Hotel Cadillac when he saw the hit-car pull up east of the Metropole. Four or five persons got out, he said, and then the shooting began. Goff again sent for the four gunmen, and Stanish, asked for an identification, sidled up to Whitey Lewis, as casually indifferent as Ryan had been terror-stricken, and touched him on the arm. He could not identify any of the others. That was good enough for the prosecution. It was understandable that, given the suddenness of the assault and its brief duration, a witness who had come upon the scene would not get a close look at all four men. It should, perhaps, also have been good enough for the defense. No new harm was done by the identification of a man who already had been pointed out as a gunman, but McIntyre appeared intent upon cracking the credibility of witnesses who identified the killers. It hadn't worked with Krause, and he would fare no better with Stanish.

Cool and detached, a man with no stake in the outcome, Stanish affected the attitude of a nobleman who would abide just so much intrusion from a commoner who asked too many questions. Throughout the cross-examination, he appeared to toy with the attorney, funneling him into lines of questioning that promised much and resulted in nothing. He often refused to answer a question, leading McIntyre to believe that the response, if he could get one, would benefit the defense. But when the judge finally ordered Stanish to answer, the bit of information proved to be of no consequence at all.

At one point, McIntyre tried to pry loose the witness's source of income but was told it was none of his business. Stanish, an electrical engineer, had been in the United States for about six months but had not been employed. McIntyre seemed to suspect that the Count might have been short on funds and had accepted a stipend for his eyewitness testimony. He pursued his hunch as relentlessly as a bloodhound on the trail of its quarry. He implored and threatened, he badgered and cajoled, he framed the question this way and that, but Stanish, appearing somewhat amused, continued to insist that his source of income was no one's business but his own. Eventually, Goff told him he had to respond, and Stanish whispered something to the interpreter, who repeated it to the court: "I brought twenty thousand francs with me when I came to this country."

Stanish set the same kind of trap when asked if he had ever been convicted of a crime in his own country.

"That is my own business," he said.

Again thinking that the witness's refusal to respond implied that he was concealing something significant, McIntyre persisted. "I ask you the same question again," he said.

"I will not answer questions about my personal affairs," Stanish said.

McIntyre would not let go, and each refusal to respond fed his certainty that he was on to something. Stanish continued to lead him on until, with no prodding from the court, he volunteered: "I have never been convicted in my life."

McIntyre kept on squeezing, like a man convinced there was one more dose left in an empty tube. He revisited the crime scene, hoping to find some inconsistencies in the witness's account, but here again Stanish played hard to get.

"Where were you on the morning of July sixteenth at two o'clock?"

"I have told you before."

"Well tell me again."

"I am not a parrot that I should repeat the same things," Stanish said.

Later: "When did the shooting occur?"

"It was the sixteenth of July. I saw the shooting and saw the man who fired the shots. I won't tell it over again."

Finally, McIntyre gave up. Stanish had been on the stand for nearly two hours and had offered nothing that was of any help to the defense. Of course, McIntyre could find solace in the fact that he had offered nothing that would hurt his case either. The same would not be said for the next witness.

Thus far, nearly two days into the trial, Becker had emerged unscathed. All that had been established as certain was that Herman Rosenthal had indeed been shot to death. Evidence had been introduced that at least several of four men had done the shooting. There was no suggestion that they were in any way linked to Becker. His name had not yet been mentioned. Now, all that was about to change.

The first witness to implicate Becker in any way was a man whom the defense had counted on to be one of its own prime witnesses. His name was Morris Luban, and he arrived in court directly from the Essex County Jail in Newark, New Jersey, where he was serving time on a forgery charge. He was a tall, raw-boned man who looked in need of a meal and a shave. A lock of dark hair crossed his forehead and nearly covered his right eye. He spoke in a voice so low that those seated at the defense table complained they could not hear him; what they did hear offered little comfort.

Luban and his brother, Jacob, who also was serving a sentence for forgery, had been subpoenaed by the defense. They were expected to testify that on the evening before the murder, at Sam Paul's place, they heard Webber, Rose, and Vallon discuss plans to kill Rosenthal and then frame Becker for orchestrating the plot. It was a story that would have been devastating to the prosecution's case, for it was consistent with events as they developed and entirely believable. It was, after all, Webber, not Becker, who had solicited the services of the killers. The prosecution was obliged to show that he had acted as Becker's agent. It could also be presumed that Webber, Rose, and Vallon would have been better off with the squealer Rosenthal silenced and the graft-taking Becker no longer on their payroll. True or not, it was a story that, absent compelling evidence of Becker's involvement, would certainly cast reasonable doubt on the state's case, and "beyond reasonable doubt" was the standard of proof needed for a conviction. It was, therefore, a crushing blow to the defense when the Luban brothers flipped and became witnesses for the prosecution.

Under direct questioning, Luban told Moss that he had met Rosenthal inside the hallway of the Metropole shortly before the killing. He was still inside when he heard the shots, and he saw three of the men who did the shooting—Dago Frank, Gyp, and Lefty Louie. Following form, Goff asked that the gunmen be brought in. Also following form, McIntyre objected and was overruled. But this time there was a new turn. Lefty Louie added his own unofficial objection to his attorney's. He spoke courteously, but there was menace in his tone and a snarl on his face.

"We are only too glad to be identified, Your Honor," he said, "and to get this case over with as soon as possible and cleared up. But identify us the way everyone else is identified. Put us in a line with five or six other men. This isn't square."

Gyp added his own voice to the chorus: "Yes, why don't you identify us the way others are identified?"

Surprisingly, Goff offered a token concession. He ordered Jacob Reich and William Shapiro added to the group. But Luban did not hesitate. He identified Dago Frank, Gyp, and Lefty Louie, and each in turn was cited by his legal name—Frank Cirofici, Harry Horowitz, and Louis Rosenberg.

Moss then led Luban into newly chartered territory where Becker became the focus. Luban said he had seen Becker and Rose at the Lafayette Baths two or three weeks before the murder. Asked whom he heard speak, Luban replied, "Becker."

"Give us his exact words," Moss said.

Luban responded: "'If that Jew bastard Rosenthal isn't croaked, I will croak him myself.'" On that note, Moss turned the witness over to McIntyre.

McIntyre was troubled by the turn of events, but in his pocket he had a surprise for the witness that he thought might bring him to his knees. He had four documents—three letters and a post card—addressed to Becker in the Tombs and funneled indirectly to McIntyre, all signed either Jacob or Jake Luban. In a handwriting believed to be Luban's, they said that the brothers could be of significant help to the defense, that they knew of a conspiracy to kill Rosenthal and frame Becker for the murder. But Luban flatly denied having written the letters. McIntyre tried to prove otherwise:

"Isn't it a fact," he asked, "that last week you and your brother sent word to me that if we'd get you out of jail in Newark you'd come here and testify for this defendant, Becker?"

"It is not," Luban said.

"Will you swear that you did not write to Becker that, 'They are trying to frame you up and that reputable persons will bear us out?'"

"I did not write that."

Later: "Did you or your brother cause to be sent indirectly to the counsel for the defendant a letter written to you by Sam Paul?"

"I can't remember. I can't answer for my brother; I did not."

"Did the state's attorney say to you that if you testified in this case you would get immunity in the State of New Jersey?"

"He did not. He said he would help me all he could if I could prove that my case had been a frame-up."

McIntyre had pursued that line of questioning as far as he could without getting the answers he was looking for. The letters had been marked for identification but not entered as evidence. All the same, the jury had heard the defense's contention, and they would have to determine whether they had been written by the Luban brothers and what weight they should be given. (As it developed, shortly after the trial ended, the forgery charges against Morris and Jacob Luban were dismissed "because of assistance accorded to the District Attorney of New York.")

His trumps having been spent, though with little effect, McIntyre now played the only card he had left; he tried to cast doubt on the character and credibility of the witness.

"Would you please tell us," he asked, "exactly what you did between the hours of eight P.M. on July 15, 1912, and two a.m. on July 16, 1912?"

Luban responded that he had taken a young lady named Anna to Hammerstein's Victoria Theater. In response to McIntyre's questions, he explained in great detail that he had paid one dollar for seats that were in the third or fourth row of the balcony, that they had entered by the main entrance and had climbed one flight of stairs. When he had concluded, the attorney leaned over the defense table, shook his finger in the direction of the witness, and fairly roared, "Don't you know that Hammerstein's was closed and that only the roof garden was open?"

Luban was unshaken. "Then it must have been the roof garden," he said.

McIntyre had no place else to go. He had tried every approach, taken every path that beckoned, and they had all led him nowhere. He tried now to backtrack, to revisit places he had already been, hoping that he had missed something, that he might spot an opening that previously was hidden from view. Aware that the attorney had come to the end of the road and that the day was getting late, Justice Goff said that if McIntyre could not open a new line of questioning he would declare the examination ended. McIntyre had no further questions, and Luban left the stand.

It was now six o'clock and both attorneys, McIntyre in particular, were clearly exhausted. But Goff ordered the next witness to be called. It was a dramatic moment, the first time during the trial when no one in the courtroom would so much as clear his throat, for everyone knew that the next scheduled witness was Bald Jack Rose. And, in fact, Rose, looking like he had stepped from the cover of a men's fashion magazine, came forth and strode to the witness stand. His faultless appearance—a freshly pressed blue suit and starched shirt and collar—offered no suggestion that he had come directly from his cell in the West Side Prison.

Looking straight ahead, making no eye contact with Becker, he folded his hands in his lap and waited for the first question. But none was forthcoming. Whitman told Goff that he wanted at least two hours with Rose, and McIntyre said he would need at least three. "If you'll agree to hear the witness through the night, I will continue to sit," Goff told the attorneys. Neither Whitman nor McIntyre had an appetite to continue. Court was adjourned until ten o'clock the following morning, Saturday, October 12, when Rose would again take the stand. Darkness would settle over the city before he would leave it.

All spit-shined and polished, Bald Jack Rose stepped through the court-room with the assurance of a man who knew he was the star of the show and that everything that had come before was just prelude to his appearance. He was dressed and groomed much as he had been the previous day. His bald pate, scrubbed to a high sheen, glistened beneath the ceiling lights, leaving none to wonder why he was often referred to as Billiard Ball Jack. Looking as relaxed as the guest of honor at a banquet, he panned the courtroom, his eyes coming to rest briefly on the jury box and then, for a time, locking hard with Becker's. Becker, for his part, seemed to be holding up well. Though his ruddy complexion had faded to a jailhouse pallor and his muscular frame was now trimmed and somewhat less imposing, he still seemed to emit an air of menace. His gaze, unblinking and unforgiving, fixed on Rose like a promise of doom that needed no further expression.

Rose was unaffected. Not for nothing had he been celebrated as the model of a poker player whose face told no tales. It was a reputation he would bur-nish over the next eleven hours as, throughout a relentless siege of questioning with a break of no more than an hour and a half, he remained unruffled and in full control. In measured tones, speaking his lines precisely and with just enough emotion to make it all believable, he projected to the jury the picture of a reformed apostle of unimpeachable truth while, step by step, he edged Becker toward a fate that had begun to appear inevitable.

Rose recounted his tale from the very beginning, from his first meeting with the defendant. Initially, Assistant District Attorney Moss's questions steered the narrative, but during the course of five hours of direct examination, Rose's testimony began to take the form of a monologue in which he moved the story forward himself with little prodding from the prosecution and only occasional objections from the defense.

Moss began with the ritualistic basics of courtroom procedure, and Rose responded in like manner:

"Do you know Charles Becker, the defendant in this case?"

"I do."

"How long have you known him?"

"Since the fall of 1911."

"Did you have any business relations at any time with Herman Rosenthal?"

"I did. I was in partnership with him at 104 West Forty-fifth Street, a gambling house."

"Did you ever see Rosenthal and Becker together?"

"I did. The first time was at the Lafayette Baths. The second time, as near as I can remember, when they were together on last New Year's Eve at the Elks' Club."

"Did you see Rosenthal and Becker together in conversation at the Elks' Club at the time that you have mentioned?"

Rose said he had but that he could not hear what they were saying. He added, however, that Mrs. Rosenthal was also present and that at one point he heard Becker say to her: "'Now, do not worry, cheer up. Herman and I have a thorough understanding and your troubles are all over. I am his friend and he is my friend, and you have nothing further to worry about, and I will go the route for Herman.'"

Having established the necessary connections, Rose proceeded to carry the story deeper into the relations between the defendant and Rosenthal. He said he met Becker the next day, and Becker told him that Rosenthal had approached him about going partners in the opening of a gambling house on Forty-fifth Street.

"Herman Rosenthal had asked Becker to invest five thousand dollars and told him that with Becker's influence in command of the strong-arm squad and Herman's capabilities in the conducting of such a place, that the possibilities of growing rich fast were very bright. Becker consulted me on the matter and I advised against it. I told Becker that nobody had ever made money with Rosenthal and that for many reasons that I pointed out it was a proposition he had better let alone. I told him that Rosenthal was unreliable in his transactions in the division of the profits of a place, that I knew that, and I told him not to accept the proposition of this investment of five thousand dollars in his place, and Becker said, "'Well, I guess I will turn it down.'"

But Rosenthal kept lowering the price, Rose said, finally telling Becker he could open the club with $1,500. Again, he asked Rose's advice, and again Rose advised against it.

"'It is not a question of the amount, Charley, it is a question of your avoiding tying up in business with him, because it won't take very long before Herman will be telling everybody, "Becker is my partner."'"

Becker said he wanted to avoid that, but that he owed Rosenthal some favors and would like to help him out. He told Rose he would lend Herman $1,500 and "'I will secure myself by getting a dummy to act for me in the matter and get a chattel mortgage on his household things. I will insist on Herman Rosenthal taking you in as a partner in the place, and you are to get twenty-five percent of the profits. Now, do not let Herman know you are representing me in there, and you and I will divide the profits of the place.'"

Rose, continuing to cast himself in the role of mediator and the measured voice of reason, said he told Becker, "'I would rather not represent you or myself or anyone else in any business with Herman Rosenthal.'" But Becker reassured him that whatever Rosenthal had done in the past, he would not tamper with the profits in the new club "'because if he does, he will have me to reckon with.'"

Rose agreed, and the deal was struck, but it was not long before trouble developed. Business at the Hesper Club started slowly but gradually picked up, and after a particularly profitable night, Becker told Rose to get five hundred dollars from Herman as a contribution to the legal defense fund for Charles Plitt, Becker's erstwhile publicity agent. Plitt was facing a charge of murder that grew out of a raid by Becker's strong-arm squad. Rosenthal apparently thought Plitt was none of his concern; he refused to give Rose the five hundred dollars. Becker did not welcome the news. At Moss's prompting to quote Becker's response as accurately as possible, Rose said:

"'Now I will tell you, Jack, this place has given me a lot of worry and trouble. I am being harped on every day at police headquarters about this place. Up to today I have been able to deny its existence, but the time will come very soon when I won't be able to do that. While I was assured I would be dealt with fairly by that fellow, I was willing to go on and do everything I could to protect that place, but this man's treatment of me now when I need money and sent you to get five hundred dollars, and his refusal to do it, relieves me of that worry about that place. The next time my attention is called to that place I am going to raid it.'"

Rose, who apparently had begun acting as a messenger, shuttling back and forth daily between Becker and Rosenthal, now told the court that Herman was openly defiant. He quoted him: "'You tell Becker that he cannot raid this place unless he gets the proper evidence, and he has not a chance to get any evidence against this place, because I know every one of his men and not one of them can get in here.'" Becker responded in kind: "'If I have to raid that place I will raid it; you tell Herman so.'"

The events that followed had about them the inexorable unfolding of Greek drama. Becker could not relent without losing some of his grip on his gambling-collection network. Rosenthal, for his part, seemed to believe that somewhere along the way he had acquired a degree of immunity. Soon, the other shoe dropped. Becker told him, Rose testified, that "'the trouble had started. Commissioner Waldo sent for me and told me he was informed that the place at 104 West Forty-fifth Street was wide open and being conducted as a public gambling house, and told me to investigate it and if he found it was a fact to take the necessary steps to close the place.'"

Rosenthal did not believe it. According to Rose, he said, "'You tell Becker that he cannot bluff me that way. I do not believe his attention to the place has been called by Commissioner Waldo.'"

As Rose told it, Becker was prepared to be patient. "'Well, we'll see,'" he said. But a few days later, he told Rose that Waldo was continuing to hound him. He asked Rose to reason with Herman.

"Becker said: 'I want you to go to Rosenthal and have a talk with him. Tell him that I have helped him, and he must help me out of this predicament I am in now. I want Rosenthal to agree to stand for a raid. By doing that it will help me and it will help him. Immediately the raid is made and I have reported to headquarters that the place my attention is called to has been raided, that ends it. Within a few days he can open up again, and there is a record of the place having been raided.'"

Rose continued, quoting Rosenthal: "'Tell Becker he must think I am crazy to stand for anything like that. Why, here is this place only open a short time, and I am just about building the business up. I have been around telling people that Becker is my friend, and then have him come along and raid me? Why, this is ridiculous. I might as well take and put a torch to the place and burn it up.'"

Rose's coaxing, telling Rosenthal that the raid will help both him and Becker, only caused Herman to dig in harder, the witness said. Again playing the part of Rosenthal, he testified: "'I don't care anything about Becker. It is my place, and I am going to handle it, not give the business away, and Becker is not going to bluff me in standing for any friendly raid.'

"I said to Rosenthal: 'Is that the message you want me to take to Becker?' He said, 'Yes, just that way, and you cannot make it too strong for me.'"

Now it was Becker's turn to up the ante. "'Well,'" he told Rose, "'that place is going to be raided by me and no one else and in the next few days.'"

Rose said he warned Becker that if he delivered that message to Rosenthal it would spell trouble, but Becker assured him, "'Now, don't you worry, there will be no trouble. The only trouble in this case will be for Rosenthal.'" He also told Rose to issue Herman no warning. He said he would compensate Rosenthal for any damage done to the premises by paying out the $1,500 owed on his mortgage, and then "'I am through with him,'" he said.

On the night of the raid, Rose, who had been told it was coming, and Rosenthal, who hadn't, stood across the street together and watched. One might imagine the depths of Rosenthal's mood as he stood by, helpless, while his place was being dismantled at the directions of his partner. He had chosen to go mano-a-mano with Becker, but perhaps now was having second thoughts. The day after the raid, he seemed conciliatory when he met Becker at the Union Square Hotel.

"'That is a tough deal you gave me last night,'" Rosenthal told Becker. "'Well, Herman, it had to be,'" Becker told him.

Rosenthal was particularly offended that his nephew had been arrested along with one of the dealers. Becker, himself adopting a gentler tone, did his best to mollify him, according to Rose. "'Now Herman,' he said, 'if you will do as I tell you to do in this matter, everything will be all right for everyone concerned.'" He told Rosenthal that if he waived examination Becker would see to it that his nephew and the dealer were not indicted and that the policeman stationed at his house would be removed. He also said he told Rosenthal that the only permanent damage that had been done was the smashing of the front door and that would be paid for by returning the satisfaction papers on the $1,500 mortgage.

"Becker told me Rosenthal's reply to that was, 'If you will do that, if you will get that man out of the house within two days, if you will return no indictments against my place and give me the satisfaction papers on that mortgage, why, all well and good. I will waive examination, but remember, if you do not play fair with me and live up to all these agreements that are being made between you and me, you look out for me. I won't stop until I break you.'"

Rosenthal waived examination, but Becker reneged on his part of the deal. The grand jury returned indictments against Rosenthal's nephew and the dealer. The police officer remained stationed at his house, which remained closed. Becker was likely responding to Rosenthal's threat. "What do you think of the nerve of that fellow talking to me that way?" he had asked Rose. Now, it appeared that Becker, presumptive Prussian gladiator, had decided that nothing short of total victory would do. Rosenthal would have to learn that he was just another part of the landscape, that he would play by Becker's rules or not at all. When Becker told Rose that he had backed away from his deal with Rosenthal, "I told Becker, 'I am very sorry to hear that.' He said, 'Why?' I said, 'There will be a lot of trouble.'"

Having learned that Becker had double-crossed him, Rosenthal soon discovered that turning things to his favor would not be easy. He phoned Becker at home and at the station house, but the lieutenant refused to take his calls. He left word that any time Rosenthal called, he was not in. Stymied at every turn, Rosenthal took his case to the streets. He began spreading the word, Rose testified, that he and Becker had been partners in the gambling house and Becker had raided his place on framed-up evidence. The rumors took on added weight when Commissioner Waldo summoned Becker and asked if they were true. Becker denied them, and Waldo believed him. Rosenthal had petitioned the commissioner for an interview but was rebuffed. The facts in the case, Waldo said, speak for themselves: the place had been raided by Lieutenant Becker.

But Rosenthal kept the drumbeat going. "Becker told me that every day he was getting different reports from people to whom Rosenthal had been denouncing him," Rose said, "and I asked Lieutenant Becker if the man had been taken out of the place as yet, and he said, 'No.' I said to him, 'As long as that man stays in that place Rosenthal will keep on talking.' Becker said he did not care much what he said."

Becker was certain that so long as he had Waldo's trust Rosenthal could not touch him. If the commissioner would not give him a hearing, neither would the district attorney or the mayor. At one point, Rose said, he warned Becker that Rosenthal was trying to get his story into the newspapers, but here again, Becker thought his friend Jack Sullivan (aka Jacob Reich) would be able to keep the story out of print. But this time Becker miscalculated. He did not count on the near-reckless ambition of Herbert Bayard Swope nor his power of persuasion. He soon learned that the World had an affidavit signed by Rosenthal in which he told the whole story of police graft in the Tenderloin and how Becker's strong-arm squad ran the operation.

"Well," Becker told Rose, "I guess Rosenthal means to do what he threatened he would—to squeal and break me."

Rose said Becker told him the *World* had offered him a chance to respond to Rosenthal's charges, but that he had turned it down on the advice of his attorney. Furthermore, First Deputy Police Commissioner Douglas J. McKay had advised him that if he could get the affidavit, he could file a legal action for criminal libel. Becker said he intended to follow that advice. Of course, Becker may not have been aware that truth is the absolute defense against libel, and McKay may not have known that most of what Rosenthal attested to was indeed the truth.

In any event, Rose's testimony had gotten Moss to the critical point where a solid motive had been established. Rosenthal's defiance of the Law of the Tenderloin may have provided Becker with reason to raid his casino and to place a police guard inside, but it hardly seemed to justify orchestrating a conspiracy to murder. But Rosenthal's affidavit, sitting in a newspaper office awaiting publication, was more than Becker might wish to deal with. There was little good he could hope for if the affidavit was made public. At best, there would be an investigation that would likely close down his operation; at worst, he could face multiple felony charges.

Becker called and asked Rose to meet him at the Union Square Hotel. Rose recounted the conversation: "'Well, now, this fellow Rosenthal means to do all he said he would do about exposing me, and that I was his partner, and that I am a grafter, and going to show me up and try to break me.' Becker explained that Rosenthal had continued to press Waldo for a meeting, that he had tried to see Chief Magistrate William McAdoo to tell him that the warrants issued against his place were secured on perjured testimony, that he had tried unsuccessfully to meet with Mayor Gaynor, and that now he was trying to get to the district attorney's office. "If he ever gets there, why it means great danger," Becker told Rose. "'Well,' I said to Becker, 'I don't think he can get there. Besides,' I said, 'it is the soreness of a man whose place has been raided.' 'But,' said Becker, 'he means to do me if he can, and I must stop him.' 'Well,' I said, 'it is easy enough to stop him. We will get people to see him and talk with him.' He said, 'Now, Jack, I want to have a frank talk with you and tell you something I want you to do.'"

At this point, an audible silence fell across the courtroom. It had taken on the aura of a theater at the critical moment when the stillness of the audience becomes a part of the play. Everyone knew what would come next, but the reality would not be validated until the words were spoken. Rose proceeded to speak them.

"Becker said to me, 'there is only one thing to do with a fellow like Rosenthal—just stop him so that he will not bother anybody anymore for all time.' I said, 'What do you mean?' He said, 'Well, there is a fellow that ought to be put off the earth.' 'Why,' I says, 'I agree with you. He is no account.' He said, 'Well, no use saying he is no account and all of that, but the idea is now to do something to him.' I says, 'What do you mean?' and he said, 'There is a fellow I would like to have croaked.'"

Rose testified that he balked at the suggestion. "'Why,' I says, 'Charley, there is other ways of handling Rosenthal.'" Rose offered to "send a couple of fellows up there that will give Rosenthal a beating and warn him and tell him the reason of that beating, and if he don't stop there is something worse than a beating in store for him.'" But Rose's solution seemed short of the mark.

"Becker said, 'I don't want him beat up. I could do that myself. . . . No beating up will fix that fellow, a dog in the eyes of myself, you, and everybody else. Nothing for that man but taken off the earth.'" Doing his best impersonation of Becker, Rose's voice became shrill as he portrayed the lieutenant as being more desperate than calculating, his mood stoked to near-hysteria. Rose was nearly shouting as he quoted Becker's injunction: "'Have him murdered, cut his throat, dynamited, or anything.'"

Rose was still looking for an alternative resolution. He said he told Becker, "'This man Rosenthal isn't worth taking any such chances with.'" But Becker assured him that no chances were being taken. "'There is no danger to anybody that has any hand in the murder of Rosenthal,' Becker told him. 'There can't anything happen to anyone, and you know the sentiment over at police headquarters is so strong that the man or men that croak him would have a medal pinned on them.'"

"I said, 'All right, Charley, I will help you. What is it you want?'"

What Becker wanted Rose to do was to visit Big Jack Zelig in the Tombs, where he was being held on ten thousand dollars bail for a Sullivan Law violation, and offer him a quid pro quo. Rose quoted Becker's request: "'Ask him to issue an order from the Tombs to some of his gang to croak Rosenthal tonight, and tomorrow Zelig will be out on the street and relieved of any further worry about the charge against him.'" He handed Rose one hundred dollars to give to Zelig as a token of good faith.

Rose took Harry Vallon with him, and they went to the Tombs to make Zelig an offer they thought he couldn't refuse. But Zelig was not inclined to deal with either Becker or Rose. He was bitter at the way he had been dealt with and not only did he reject Rose's offer, he countered with a threat of his own. As Rose testified, Zelig told him:

"'I don't want that hundred dollars; I want to get out of here. It is you and Becker who got me in this trouble in the first place on that framed-up charge. . . . Now you come and hand me a hundred dollars! I don't want the hundred dollars. I want you to get me out of here. I tell you, Jack, if you are under the impression that if you rush me to trial and give me fourteen years [the sentence Zelig was facing] that that will end it as far as you are concerned you are mistaken. And there will be friends of mine that you will have to reckon with about this thing.'"

When told of Zelig's rejection, Rose said, Becker was unfazed. "'Well, then, let him rot in the Tombs,'" he said.

Rose, however, had some contacts of his own and was ready to share them with Becker. He told the court: "I said to Becker, 'There are some friends of Zelig whom I know, that I have met during the time I was trying to get Zelig out on bail. I will go see them. Perhaps I could get them to act without any order from Zelig.'"

With Becker's encouragement, Rose said he went to a house on Southern Boulevard in the Bronx where he met with Lefty Louie and Whitey Lewis. "I told them I came there to warn them of the danger that they were in," Rose testified, "of the fate similar to what Zelig had met by being arrested on a charge of carrying concealed weapons, and they said 'Well, we don't carry them anymore since this trouble of Zelig's.' 'Well,' I said, 'it don't make any difference. Zelig didn't have one either. Now, if you go downtown at all, you are gone.' They asked me what was the cause of this, and I said, 'Why, Herman Rosenthal.' 'Who is Herman Rosenthal?'" they asked. Rose said he explained the situation, telling them that Rosenthal was trying to see the district attorney and expose the operation of Becker's strong-arm squad. "I said, Becker feels, and has told me so, that all you fellows, whom, on my account he has been taking care of, owe it to him and to yourselves to see that Rosenthal does not appear and make that squeal.' They said, 'You mean by croaking him?' I said, 'Yes.' 'Have you seen Zelig?' they asked me."

Assured that Zelig would have no objection, they agreed to do the job, but as the days passed and nothing happened, Becker grew impatient. Rose said Becker phoned him at home and warned that "' . . . if there is much delay, much further delay by them, there won't be any delay by me.'" Rose again went to see Lefty and Whitey and urged them to hasten the process. He told Becker, "'Those fellows will surely do it. Now they are waiting to get Rosenthal downtown.' 'Well, what is the difference where they do it?' Becker said. 'They need not be particular as to the place or time. Get him anywhere. Break into his house and get him. It is the same thing. I told you there cannot anything happen to anyone.'" When a few more days passed, Becker told Rose

"' . . . either you are stalling me or those fellows don't take any stock in what you told them about anything happening to any one of them.'"

Whichever the case, Becker was not prepared to allow matters to drift any further. He suggested that Bridgey Webber be contacted. Webber seemed the perfect man for the job. He knew everyone involved, his pool hall on Forty-second and Sixth was a nerve center for underworld activity, and most appealing to Becker, he was known to be efficient and reliable. Rose said Becker told him he was going to raid a crap game in Harlem that night and that he should meet him there at about nine o'clock and to bring Webber with him. Rose brought Vallon along as well, and there in a vacant lot in West Harlem, the four men stood together and planned Rosenthal's future.

Rose recounted the conversation. "Becker said to Webber: 'Bridgey, why don't you help Jack in that thing and have that fellow croaked?' And Webber said he didn't want to lay himself liable to these fellows." Becker repeated the pledge he had made to Rose. "'There is no laying liable to anybody or anything. There is nothing to happen to anybody that has any hand in the croaking of Rosenthal,' he said. 'Now you step into this thing, Bridgey, take charge of things and see that this thing is done for me, will you?'" Bridgey agreed. He said "'Leave it to me now. The job will be done and done quick.'"

Now, the wheels were in motion. Bridgey Webber was not a man to pass time idly. Just a few days after the meeting with Becker, he found Rose and Vallon at dinner in Still's restaurant. Rose told the court that Webber called him outside and said, "'There are some fellows around at the Lafayette Baths waiting to see you.'" At the baths, Rose found Lefty Louie, Gyp the Blood, and Dago Frank. They apparently had been well briefed by Webber and were ready to take care of matters immediately. Webber said he would find Rosenthal and get the job done that night. The others went to a chop-suey restaurant, and before long Webber came in and told them that Rosenthal was in the Garden Restaurant, at Forty-fifth and Broadway, with his wife and Jack Sullivan. "We all started to go there—Lefty Louie, Gyp the Blood, Dago Frank, Vallon, and myself." But when they got to the corner, Rose said, he saw a man across the street from the restaurant whom he identified as a Burns detective. He believed the man had been appointed by the D.A. to serve as a body guard for Rosenthal, and he told Louie they would have to call things off. "Wait until you hear from me," he said. The next day, Rose said, when he told Becker what had happened, the lieutenant boiled over. "'A detective?' Becker shouted. 'I told you that there is nothing to fear here. Walk up and shoot him in front of a policeman if you want to; there ain't nothing to fear. But don't let that happen again. When you get him, get through with it and get it over with.'"

On Saturday, July 13, Becker got a copy of the affidavit that had been given to the *World,* and, Rose said, he expressed his displeasure: "'If you had been on this job as you promised it, I would not be facing all this now. While there is still time, why don't you get on the job and do this thing and have it done and over with.'"

Rose said he told Becker that he was going on the Sam Paul outing the next day and would make the final arrangements with Webber and Vallon. He called Becker as soon as the boat docked at East Twenty-third Street, and Becker was insistent. Subpoenas to appear before the grand jury were being issued to anyone named in the affidavit, and Becker wanted the job done before Rosenthal could be summoned or granted an interview with the district attorney. He said to Rose:

"'Well, I told you that this thing would occur if you didn't get rid of that fellow. Now, all this delay and this stalling around—you don't mean to tell me that this could not have been done all this time, croaking Rosenthal. Now, there is still time; tonight is the time, and it will just fit. It will look like the gamblers did it on account of his threatened squeal.'"

Rose testified that when he returned to the city, on Monday, July 15, he rented a car, a red touring car, and went to Tom Sharkey's saloon on Fourteenth Street. When he noticed that a tire had been punctured and gone flat, he sent for another car; the gray murder car was delivered. Now, in response to a series of rapid-fire questions, Rose related, in detail, the events that preceded the murder of Rosenthal:

Rose, Vallon, and Sam Schepps went into the gray touring car, which was driven by William Shapiro. They drove up Seventh Avenue, where they picked up Dago Frank. They then drove down to Webber's place at Forty-second and Sixth. Outside on the sidewalk were Webber, Lefty Louie, Whitey Lewis, and Gyp the Blood. They all went upstairs to Bridgey Webber's poker room where refreshments were ordered. Late that night or early Tuesday morning, Webber left the others and went outside. He returned shortly and said that Rosenthal was around the Metropole. Everyone then rose from the table and started for the door. They all went downstairs except for Rose and Schepps who remained behind. At around two A.M., word came that Rosenthal had been shot near the Metropole. Rose stayed on for about an hour, then went out and phoned Becker and asked if he had heard the news.

"'Yes, and I congratulate you,'" Becker said, adding that a newspaperman had already called to give him the news. Becker said he would come down to meet Rose at Webber's place. Becker didn't arrive until around daybreak, and Rose asked what had kept him.

"'I stopped over at the station house before coming here,'" he said.

"I said, 'Whom did you see over there?' He said, 'District Attorney Whitman is there.' I said, 'Well, that means danger.' 'Oh, no,' he said 'everything will be all right; don't go exciting yourself.' I said, 'Has anything developed new?' 'They have got three or four [license] numbers there, but neither one of them, I understand, is the correct number of the machine.' I said, 'Did you see Rosenthal?' He said, 'Yes, I went to the back room and took a look at him.'" Then, coaxed by Moss to use Becker's exact words, Rose continued:

"Becker said, 'It was a pleasing sight to me to look and see that squealing Jew bastard there, and if it was not for the presence of District Attorney Whitman, I would have reached down and cut his tongue out and hung it up somewheres as a warning to future squealers.'"

A collective gasp could be heard in the courtroom, prompted perhaps by the tone with which Rose spoke the words. A Jew himself, Rose might have been expressing a degree of personal resentment as his eyes narrowed and he hissed the words slowly and evenly through clenched jaws.

After a brief pause, allowing the force of his remark to settle, Rose continued. He said he went to the Lafayette Baths with Vallon and then home to 115th Street to get some sleep. Later that afternoon, he headed down to Fiftieth Street and Eighth Avenue where he met with Sam Schepps. He asked Schepps to go back downtown and get the latest word on the shooting. Finally, he went to stay for a while at the home of a friend named Harry Pollock. Rose was beginning to feel the effects of what had transpired, the growing awareness that he was complicit in an act of murder. He said he was feeling ill. Becker called that afternoon. He said he had just seen Pollock who told him Rose was staying with him. "'He told me you were feeling ill,'" Becker said. "I said, 'Yes, in mind and body.' He said, 'Don't go carrying on and taking things to heart; everything is all right. This will be all over in a day or two.'"

But Rose had reason to worry. He had heard that Shapiro and Libby had been arrested. Becker continued to reassure him. He asked Rose if he could locate the attorney Aaron Levy. Becker wanted him to appear for Shapiro and Libby. "'I think I can,'" Rose said. Again, Becker tried to settle his nerves. "'There is nothing for you to worry about,'" he said. "'I know where you are, and that is a good place for you to rest up. Now, just stay right there.'"

Later that day, Becker called again. This time he was less assuring. When Rose asked what the latest news was, Becker told him: "'News? There is two hundred cops looking for you.' I said, 'Well, I guess I better go downtown or something.' He said, 'No, you stay right where you are until you hear something different from me. Now, I am doing this; don't you go jumping at conclusions as to what you ought to do or ought not to do; you do as I tell you. Now, don't worry and don't get so excited.' 'Well,' I said, 'it is something to worry about, isn't it?' 'Now, don't make it worse than it is,' Becker said. 'It is nothing to worry about. This will all blow over.'"

But Becker, a step or two ahead of Rose, was not waiting for things to blow over. He needed Rose's help with another matter. He wanted Rose to sign an affidavit saying that it was he, not Becker, who advanced Rosenthal the fifteen hundred dollars and took as collateral the mortgage on his household goods. Rose testified: "I said, 'This is rather a poor time for any such things as affidavits, or things like that, Charley, a man murdered—and they are already beginning to talk and pointing at you and pointing at me, and everybody else. What is the use of affidavits now?' 'Now, this is absolutely necessary or I would not ask it.' That was what Becker said."

Becker viewed the affidavit as critical to his case, for it would counter the charge that he and Rosenthal were partners. Rose was still hesitant. "I said, 'Perhaps there will be a question about my having fifteen hundred.'" Becker thought Rose's friend Pollock might be helpful, that he might sign an affidavit attesting that he had loaned Rose the fifteen hundred. Rose finally consented. Becker said he would send his attorney, John Hart, to Pollock's home to obtain the affidavit. He asked Rose if he knew Hart. Rose said he didn't.

"'You don't know how he looks?' 'No.' 'Well, I will arrange with him and he will come there, and whoever answers the door bell, he will say, "Tell Mr. Rose that J. H. is here." Now, you admit him and give him that affidavit.' I said, 'All right, I will.'"

When Hart arrived, accompanied by a notary, Rose said he told him he was not feeling well enough to draw up the document. Hart said he would help him with it. Hart questioned Rose much as an attorney might question a witness, and he formulated Rose's responses in affidavit form. For example: "'Is it not a fact, Mr. Rose, that you did not have this money at this time but that you secured it from your friend, Mr. Pollock, who knew the purpose and the nature of the business that it was to be used for, and at his suggestion and advice you secured yourself with that chattel mortgage?' "'Yes.'" In such a manner did Hart elicit the content of the affidavit, which Rose proceeded to sign.

It was well past one-thirty at this point. Rose had been testifying for about five hours without a break. It appeared that Moss was almost ready to conclude his direct examination, but Justice Goff interrupted and called for a one-hour lunch recess. When Rose returned to the stand, Moss had him identify Shapiro as the driver of the gray touring car. Then he asked him to tell the court how the payoff was made. Rose said he met with Lefty Louie at Fiftieth Street and Eighth Avenue, handed him one thousand dollars and told him: "'You and the rest of the fellows lay low for a few days. Becker said, above all, you must not talk; everything will be all right.'"

Moss turned and walked back to the prosecution table. Rose was now McIntyre's witness.

Rose's testimony left little to the imagination. He had spun his narrative with the self-assurance of a man whose word was beyond question. Guided gingerly by the district attorney and unruffled by the objections of the defense, he had detailed the case against Becker as neatly and as dramatically as if it had been scripted for no end other than to send the defendant to the electric chair. Rose had, after all, dabbled in theater some years earlier, and he had now been cast in the role of his life, a one-man show in which he played all the key parts. His voice grew harsh, and the muscles in his face tightened when he recounted Becker's lines; he sounded earnest when he quoted his own; and at no time did he take on the tone of a man who was desperate to save his own life. Rose was the perfect witness in every respect but one—he had admitted to being an accomplice of the man he was testifying against, and so with every statement he uttered one was obliged to weigh the possibility that truth might not be his first consideration.

Since Rose's story was nearly seamless, McIntyre was left little room to pry loose any admissions that would aid the defense. His best chance was to demonstrate to the jury that Rose was not a man whose word could be trusted; he had lived most of his life outside the law, had taken part in the very murder that was now at issue, and had seized upon the opportunity to spare himself by pinning the deed on an innocent man. McIntyre moved quickly in that direction, but it did not go well. His first question was:

"Did you not counsel, advise, and supervise the murder of Herman Rosenthal?" Whitman's objection was sustained, and McIntyre rephrased the question: "Do you believe you are a murderer?" Rose made the obvious reply: "I do not." McIntyre pressed on, asking Rose whether he had participated in any other murder, citing in particular the slaying of a hood called Kid Twist. Rose responded each time, coolly, that he had not. The defense's opening series of questions seemed pointless unless McIntyre was about to spring on Rose some evidence that he had indeed been involved in other murders. But it was soon apparent that he had no such evidence and that this line of questioning was going nowhere.

McIntyre then changed course. Besides the questionable reputation of its key witness, there was one soft spot in the state's case: It needed the corroboration of a witness who was not involved in the conspiracy. That witness was Sam Schepps, whom the state had struggled mightily to convert from accessory to neutral observer. But the prosecution had made one serious slip during direct examination—Rose had named Schepps as one of the men who rode with him in the gray touring car on the night of the murder. He said Schepps accompanied him uptown to pick up Dago Frank, and they returned together to Bridgey Webber's poker room. The two of them remained there while Webber, Vallon, and the four gunmen went to the Metropole to gun down Rosenthal. They were still there when the news came that Rosenthal had been shot. Later that afternoon, Rose had testified, he met with Schepps at Fiftieth Street and Eighth Avenue and asked him to go downtown and bring back the latest news on the shooting. Rose's re-creation of events appeared to implicate Schepps more directly than the prosecution had counted on. For who would be ready to believe that Schepps had spent the evening in the company of the three admitted conspirators—Rose, Webber, and Vallon—had even ridden in the murder car when it picked up one of the gunmen, then waited with Rose for news of the shooting, and yet was unaware that the murder was being planned and was about to be carried out? It was a lingering irony that all the conspirators but Becker had been on the scene that night, and Becker was the only one on trial for his life.

McIntyre wanted to draw Schepps into the plot as early as possible during his questioning of Rose. He asked if Schepps had been present in Harry Pollock's house when Rose gave Hart his affidavit. Rose conceded he was there, which meant that he had heard Rose relate his story of how the $1,500 chattel mortgage on the furniture in Rosenthal's gambling house was arranged, but it still did not place him inside the conspiracy. McIntyre would bring Schepps back into the picture later during his cross-examination, but now he shifted his focus once again to Rose's past.

He learned that Rose's real name was Jacob Rosensweig, that he was thirty-seven years old, that his attorney of record was James M. Sullivan, and that before moving to New York from Connecticut, he had been active in a variety of endeavors. He had promoted prizefights and spent some time in the hotel business, the printing business, and the theater. He said that he had never been involved in gambling while living in Connecticut. Asked where he was born, he said he had been brought to the United States by his parents when he was two years old. Then, for reasons not easy to fathom, McIntyre tried insistently to determine where Rose had been born. When he said he did not know which his native country was, the following exchange took place:

Q: Were you born in Russian Poland? *A:* I don't know. I think it was.

Q: Don't you know that you were born in Russian Poland? *A:* I don't know.

Q: Don't you know from hearsay and from that which your parents have told you that you were born in Russian Poland? *A:* I assume that was the fact because many of my relatives have spoken of that part of Europe.

Q: Did your father not tell you that you were born in Russian Poland? *A:* He never discussed my birthplace.

Q: Did your mother ever discuss your birthplace? *A:* No.

McIntyre continued to probe Rose's background, toward what end it was unclear. When he asked if, after coming to New York, Rose had lived together with a woman who was not his wife, Justice Goff intervened. He leaned over in the direction of the witness and said, "It is my duty to caution the witness that he may decline to answer the question on the ground that the question may tend to degrade or disgrace him." Rose heeded the judge's advice and declined to answer any questions regarding his earlier years. McIntyre then turned to the present.

"What is your occupation?" he asked. "I am a gambler," came the response.

Rose proceeded to chronicle the history of his gambling operations beginning with his activities on the Lower East Side. In 1911, he said, he was "interested in the Hesper Club," located at the time at 111 Second Avenue, and run under the protection of Big Tim Sullivan. He remained there, he said, until the place was raided. McIntyre then asked a question to which he knew the answer but that elicited a response he did not expect.

"And what business were you in after the Second Avenue club was closed." "I then," said Rose, "became collector for Lieutenant Becker."

Caught off guard, McIntyre let the remark pass without comment. It did not, after all, produce information that was not already known. He continued to press Rose on his gambling career, year for year, month by month, until Goff called a halt. "It is unnecessary to go further on that line," he said. "This witness has acknowledged he was a poker player and gambler, and there is nothing to gain by further inquiry."

As it turned out, McIntyre did have something to gain, though he could not have anticipated it. Rose had testified that between the time the East Side club was closed and he went to work for Becker, he had decided to withdraw from the gambling business.

"When was it," McIntyre asked, "that you concluded to quit the gambling business and become connected with respectable business?" "I made that attempt on several occasions," Rose answered.

"When was that?" "Three years ago, four years ago, six years ago, ten years ago, twenty years ago," and then Rose handed McIntyre his first opportunity to score, "and I hope to do the same again," he said.

"Then you expect to get out of jail?"

The question struck at the most critical weakness in the state's case. The jury was reminded that the witness they had been listening to since early morning, the key witness for the prosecution, was an admitted accomplice to the murder the defendant was charged with, that he had spent the last three months in jail, and that, if tried and convicted, he might never again walk free. But Rose did expect to get out of jail because, the implication was, he had cut a deal with the state, and his freedom depended in large measure on how good a job he did for the prosecution.

Whitman of course was quick to object, and Goff sustained the objection. But the defense made the most of it. McIntyre rephrased the question again and again, and although each attempt was disallowed by the court, it served to remind the jury that they were hearing the testimony of a man whose freedom depended on what he was willing to say. It was the defense's best moment. During the rest of his cross-examination, McIntyre seemed to be probing at random, looking for openings that never developed or closed too soon; there was a dead end at every turn.

He established that Rose's relations with Rosenthal were not cordial after the Hesper Club was raided, but that would hardly surprise a jury. He then turned his attention to the confession Rose had made to the district attorney and to an "alleged confession which appeared in the *New York World*. It is true, is it not, that you were paid two thousand dollars by the *World* for this?" McIntyre asked. "I don't know what confession you mean," Rose said. He insisted that he had never written anything for any newspaper. McIntyre handed him a copy of the paper. The confession covered ten full columns. It was written in the first person, and what was said to be Rose's signature appeared at the end. Rose scanned it for several minutes, then said the statement reflected the information he had given to D.A. Whitman from time to time. He denied having written the document or having been paid anything for it.

McIntyre tried valiantly but vainly to get Rose to admit—if not directly, by implication—that it was he who first suggested that Rosenthal be put out of the way. Noting that Rose was one of those whose names Rosenthal had given to the district attorney, he asked:

Q: You thought then that Herman Rosenthal had squealed on you, didn't you? A: Well, I don't know. I felt whatever interests involved Lieutenant Becker were my interests.

Q: When you found that Herman Rosenthal had told about you and had handed your name to the district attorney for the purpose of having you brought before the grand jury, you became very much incensed at Herman Rosenthal, didn't you? A: I did not.

Q: Did you call him a squealer? A: I may have said he was a squealer.

Q: Did you say to anybody . . . that "the squealer should be put out of the way"? A: I did not.

Q: Did you say anything that bore resemblance to that which I have said? A: Do you mean to Becker?

Q: You said to Becker that because he squealed he ought to be put out of the way? A: I didn't put it in that way.

Q: Did you utter threats of any kind concerning Rosenthal on the Sam Paul excursion? *A:* I did not.

Rose was a well-prepared witness. He parried each thrust by McIntyre as if he had expected it and rehearsed his response. He denied making any remarks that could be construed as a direct threat to Rosenthal or that even suggested a feeling of hostility. Did he tell Becker that Rosenthal was a dangerous man? Did he make such a statement to Mrs. Becker? Did he say that he was afraid of Rosenthal? Did he say that he was afraid that he would be "brought home on a shutter" because of something Rosenthal might have done to him? Did he say that Rosenthal was accusing him of being a stool pigeon? Did he say that Rosenthal had circulated a story that he was responsible for the arrest of Jack Zelig for carrying a concealed weapon? To all of these questions, Rose, with a quiet assurance, simply answered, "I did not."

Only once did Rose lose his composure. McIntyre asked if he had been told that Rosenthal was spreading a false story that Rose's wife was a prostitute and that his children were bastards. Rose grabbed the arms of his chair, leaned forward, and shouted, "No, no, no." But he quickly regained his balance and continued to deflect the questions put to him by McIntyre.

No doubt aware that he had done little to deflate the testimony of the prosecution's key witness, McIntyre worked his way to the night of the murder. He would attempt to tie Rose as closely as possible to the conspiracy, since that would sharpen the perception that he had bartered his testimony for a free ride out of the grasp of the state.

Rose admitted he had known of a "frame-up" to kill Rosenthal.

Q: You knew there was a plan to kill Herman Rosenthal and yet you did not warn him? *A:* No.

Q: Did you warn anybody? *A:* I telephoned Mrs. Rosenthal and told her that her husband was in danger.

Q: Did not your conscience prick you? *A:* I did not consult my conscience.

McIntyre raised the question of why Rose was involved at all. If, as he had testified, Becker told him he would do the job himself if Rose didn't get it done, why didn't Rose just stand by and let the lieutenant do it.

Q: When he told you he would do it, why didn't you withdraw from the conspiracy and let someone else do it? *A:* I was between two fires. On the one side Becker, and on the other side the gang, and I thought I could handle both ends until such time as the matter straightened itself out.

Q: When you were between two fires—Becker on the one side and the gang on the other—did you go to anybody and complain and say that a foul murder was about to be done? A: Not in that part of the world I frequented is there anybody that would have paid any attention to me.

McIntyre pressed Rose to name the gangsters he feared, but Rose would offer no names. He explained that if Becker had carried out his threat to go downtown and arrest every member of the gang who would not cooperate—frame them as he had Zelig, by planting a gun on them and charging them with illegal possession—Rose would be suspected of having helped to set them up; he had already been accused of complicity in Zelig's arrest.

McIntyre proceeded to have Rose reprise the story he had told in the morning—the murder of Herman Rosenthal from conception to execution. Rose repeated it mechanically, with no new shades of nuance and no show of emotion. Having elicited nothing that would favor the cause of his client, McIntyre played what would be his final card. Once again, he tried to draw Schepps back into the conspiracy, to nullify his role as corroborator of the prosecution's case. He had co-counsel Hart read, with all the dramatic effect he could muster, the letter Rose had sent to Schepps when he was hiding in Hot Springs. In it, he urged Schepps to return to New York and avail himself of the offer of clemency that the D.A. was ready to extend to him. The letter having been read, McIntyre asked, "Isn't Schepps what is known as a lobbygow?"

"A what?" Goff asked.

"A lobbygow, Your Honor. This man knows very well what it means over on the East Side." [A lobbygow, in underworld terminology, was an errand boy or messenger, a demeaning term similar today to a gofer.]

Rose shook the question off without answering it directly, and when McIntyre continued to rephrase it, Goff became impatient. "Stop right there, Mr. McIntyre," he said when Whitman objected to any more questions using the term "lobbygow." It was getting late, now past eight-thirty. Aside from the lunch break, Rose had been on the stand for the better part of ten hours. But he appeared to be fresher than McIntyre. The defense attorney had clearly exhausted his resources and expended his ammunition. He resembled a punched-out prizefighter who could no longer lift his arms and needed the respite that the sound of the bell would bring. Hearing no bell, he addressed the judge:

"I must ask Your Honor's indulgence and request that the cross-examination of this witness be postponed until next Monday morning." He was leaning heavily on the counsel table. "I am physically exhausted," he continued. "I cannot ask another question."

Goff was not impressed. "Go on," he said, "you are stronger than you were this morning."

"I have been on my feet for six hours cross-examining," McIntyre said. "I have had to go without my dinner. It is against the interests of justice to force me to go on." McIntyre was looking at the jury as he made his plea, searching their eyes for a sign of sympathy.

Goff was still unmoved. "If you have another question, put it," he said, "otherwise the cross-examination is closed."

"Counsel does not wish it closed," McIntyre insisted. "Counsel states that he is unable to go on. My mind will not work as it should."

Hart now rose to his colleague's defense. "I do not want to hear you," Goff told him. "Sit down. One counsel at a time is enough." Then he turned back to McIntyre: "I should have acceded to your request, Mr. McIntyre, if the nature of the cross-examination for the last three hours had warranted it, but it was not apparent to me that counsel meant to finish."

McIntyre took issue: "I object to the remark of the court implying that I acted in bad faith." Hart took matters a step further. He stepped before the bench and moved for "a mistrial on the grounds that Your Honor's remark is uncalled for and illegal."

"Denied," said Goff. "The cross-examination is closed. Counsel for the prosecution may re-direct after which counsel for the defense may cross-examine."

Moss asked a few perfunctory questions, McIntyre repeated that he was unable to continue, and Rose left the stand, but the fireworks were not yet over. McIntyre drew himself to his feet and said, "I ask that this witness be kept apart from Vallon, Webber, and Schepps. I ask Your Honor to have him placed in the Tombs so that he cannot confer with the other three."

Goff's response was simply to recall Rose and caution him not to discuss his testimony with the other three prisoners.

"What's the use of cautioning a man like that?" McIntyre asked. "I demand, Your Honor, that he be kept apart from them."

Goff explained that he did not have the authority to order Rose transferred to the Tombs. McIntyre, visibly and audibly angry, turned to Whitman and shouted, "You took this man out of the Tombs and put him in the West Side Prison." Just as heatedly, Whitman responded, "I had the power to do so." McIntyre had the last word: "You're not only acting as district attorney but as jail-keeper too."

It was eight minutes short of nine o'clock, nearly eleven hours since Rose had taken the stand, when court was adjourned. The next day, Sunday, would be a day of rest. On Monday morning, October 14, beginning at ten-thirty, Bridgey Webber and Harry Vallon would be called upon by the state to corroborate Rose's story.

15

McIntyre made full use of the day's respite. One might even say it was the best day he had since the trial had begun. He was feeling optimistic because he believed the prosecution's star witness had been unpersuasive and that the state's case could only grow weaker as it proceeded. He told the press that he was thinking seriously about not putting on a case for the defense at all and relying on the softness of the state's case to acquit his client. He was certain that the jury would not believe the testimony of Rose or the other accomplices who would doubtless echo his story. While he admitted that he had not succeeded in breaking him down on any particular point, McIntyre contended that his cross-examination had exposed Rose as a man without scruples who would not hesitate to swear away another man's life.

"I think that under the circumstances I scored pretty heavily on him," he told the press. "He admitted that he was without conscience, never did have one, and hasn't one now. He showed the jury that he felt no repentance, nor remorse, and that he was quite as ready to commit the crime of perjury as he was to commit the crime of murder."

The cross-examination of the other accomplice/witnesses, he said, would demonstrate that they were of much the same character as Rose. McIntyre was certain that their stories had been so thoroughly rehearsed that it was unlikely they could be caught off guard, but it was equally unlikely, he felt, that the jury would be fooled into believing their fabricated testimony. It would become increasingly clear that "all the gamblers and those mixed up with them had a strong reason to wish Rosenthal dead because his squealing would put an end to their living."

McIntyre also said he intended to ask that murder indictments be handed up against Rose, Webber, Vallon, and Schepps based on their own confessions. At the close of the trial, McIntyre said, he would ask Justice Goff to turn the court records over to the grand jury. Told of his opponent's intent, Whitman responded, "Mr. McIntyre is in a position to ask such a thing if he wants to. The matter of granting it, however, rests with the justice. You must remember also that their testimony has already been heard by one grand jury."

Both Whitman and McIntyre revealed that they had received dozens of letters threatening their lives. Only McIntyre, however, had been menaced in person. The incident occurred at the conclusion of Rose's testimony. McIntyre offered this account:

"I had just finished gathering up my papers and was starting to leave the courtroom after adjournment on Saturday night. All the other lawyers had gone, and the police who had been guarding the courtroom had left. When I swung open the gate of the counsels' enclosure, I found myself face to face with a man who had a murderous look in his eyes. He thrust his head forward till his face was within a few inches of mine and said, 'If you drag Mrs. Rose's name into this case, I'll blow the top of your head off.'" When McIntyre threatened to have his assailant arrested, the man repeated his own threat, turned, and walked out of the courtroom. Fearing that he might be waiting for him outside the courtroom, McIntyre was hesitant to leave the building without an escort. Jackson Becker, the defendant's brother, accompanied him back to his office.

McIntyre said that the threats had taken their toll on him, as had the frenetic pace of the trial. While emphasizing that he had the highest regard for Justice Goff, he said that the judge's desire to push the case forward—the long hours of testimony with few breaks—might have disastrous effects for both sides.

"If the danger of proceeding too rapidly is realized," he said, "something may snap. I am on the verge of illness because of the strain, heat, and rush of the last few days. If I should get too sick to proceed, it would result in a mistrial. Becker could not be expected to proceed with the case under such circumstances."

It was clear that McIntyre, in his late fifties, was wearing down, and there was still a long way to go. The prosecution would need another week to conclude its case, and McIntyre's suggestion that he might put on no defense sounded more like bravado than calculation. Bridgey Webber would be the state's heavyweight witness on Monday, and his testimony was deemed critical because he had dealt directly with Becker. He had been brought into the conspiracy when Rose seemed unable to get the gunmen to act, and Webber would not only corroborate the story Rose told, he would add the dimension of someone who had taken orders straight from Becker without an intermediary.

All the same, anyone who had been following the trial closely might have been mystified when he did not find the report of Webber's testimony, or anything else about the trial, on the front pages of the city's newspapers on Tuesday, October 15. For the first time since the trial began, the *New York Times* did not carry the story on page one; it was not on pages two or three either. The front-page headline in the *Times* that morning, across all seven columns and in capital letters, read:

MANIAC IN MILWAUKEE SHOOTS COLONEL ROOSEVELT;
HE IGNORES WOUND, SPEAKS AN HOUR, GOES TO HOSPITAL

Colonel Roosevelt was, of course, Theodore Roosevelt, former President of the United States and one-time police chief of New York City. He was campaigning again for president, on the ticket of the Bull Moose Party, against the Republican incumbent, William Howard Taft; the Democratic nominee and eventual winner, Woodrow Wilson; and the Socialist Party candidate, Eugene V. Debs. He had been shot once with a Colt revolver, the bullet puncturing the flesh just below the right nipple. It was possible that Roosevelt was spared more serious injury by the cold Milwaukee autumn and the length of his prepared speech. The raw weather caused him to wear a heavy army overcoat, and his speech, fifty pages long, was tucked in the right breast pocket of his coat. The bullet had a long way to go before reaching its mark. True to form, Roosevelt insisted on delivering his hour-long speech. He was then taken to the hospital for treatment. The gunman, a man by the name of John Schrank, was arrested on the spot. The three pages of in-depth coverage pushed the story of the trial onto page four, but it was still covered in detail, filling nearly two full pages.

Bridgey Webber was not an imposing presence. Slightly built, short, and nattily dressed in a dark blue suit, high white collar, and black tie, he looked somewhat dainty as took the stand. Before being seated, he bowed ostentatiously to the judge, the jury, and the spectators. His eyes darted from one side of the courtroom to the other, but at no time did they come to rest on the defendant. Throughout nearly five hours of testimony, he was clearly reluctant to meet Becker's gaze.

In response to questioning by Moss, he told the court he "collected from gambling houses for Rose, who was collecting for Lieutenant Becker." Asked if he had ever spoken with Becker about Herman Rosenthal, Webber replied: "Yes, at 124th Street and Seventh Avenue. Harry Vallon and Jack Rose were there. It was in the latter part of June of this year. Sam Schepps met me in front of my place and told me to go up, that Lieutenant Becker wanted to see me. I found Vallon, Rose, and Becker there, and Becker called me to one side. He said, 'Well, that Jew is going all the way. He's tried to see McAdoo, Corrigan, Gaynor, and Waldo, and now he's trying to get to Whitman. He must be croaked before he sees the district attorney. That Jew must be croaked.'

"'It's a pretty hard thing, Charley, to see a man murdered,' I told him. 'Well, if he gets to see Whitman there'll be trouble,' he said. 'He's got to be croaked.' 'There'll be a lot of trouble about that,' said I, but he said that he'd look out for everybody, and there wouldn't be any trouble. He said he would protect everybody and for me to go the limit, so I said, 'All right, Charley,' and then he got in a car and went away."

On the morning of July 10, Webber said, Becker called him and asked that they meet in front of the Union Square Hotel. When they met, Becker asked, "What are you going to do about that Jew bastard Rosenthal? He's making a lot of trouble for me. Why don't you have him croaked?" Webber said he responded, "'Charley, that's all being taken care of. You're liable to read about it any day in the papers.'"

On Monday, July 15, Webber testified, Rose called him about four-thirty in the afternoon and said that subpoenas were out for four men to corroborate Rosenthal's story about Becker. That night, Bridgey met Becker at

Madison Square Garden, and Becker gave him the nod to go ahead with his plans to eliminate Rosenthal. When he returned to his poker room, Gyp the Blood, Lefty Louie, and Whitey Lewis were waiting outside. Soon, Webber said, Rose, Vallon, Schepps, and Dago Frank arrived, and they all went inside for refreshments. Rose asked him if he knew where Rosenthal was.

"I put on my hat and coat and said I thought I could find him. I saw Rosenthal in the Metropole and returned to my place, where I announced, 'Rosenthal is in the Metropole.' Lefty Louie, Gyp the Blood, Dago Frank, and Whitey Lewis went out. Someone else went, too. I stayed behind for about five minutes, and then I went out. I noticed that the gray automobile which William Shapiro had been driving and which brought Rose, Vallon, Schepps, and Dago Frank to my place had gone. I walked to Forty-second Street and Broadway and stayed there about ten minutes, and then I returned to the poker room. I stayed there until 2:10, and then I walked toward the Metropole." When he got there, he said, he saw Rosenthal's body lying on the pavement.

At about daybreak, Webber continued, he met with Becker and Rose at his poker room. Rose was edgy. He noted that Whitman was at the station house. Becker was reassuring: "'There ain't going to be no trouble. I'll take care of everybody. Just tell the boys to keep quiet and everything will be all right. Bridgey, give Jack $1,000.'" That afternoon, Webber said, he and Rose went to Fiftieth Street and Eighth Avenue, where the money was passed to Lefty Louie.

Webber's direct examination lasted less than an hour. McIntyre seemed eager to get at the witness, sensing perhaps that he would be easier prey than Rose had been. He was quick to elicit the admission that in addition to running an illegal gambling room, Bridgey dealt in drugs and operated an opium den on Pell Street. But McIntyre was heading in a more critical direction. With Rose on the stand, he had not succeeded in tying Schepps to the murder plot. He was ready to try again with Webber. After Webber denied that Schepps was present at the meeting with Rose and Becker in front of the Union Square Hotel, McIntyre fired a volley of questions at the witness:

Q: Have you been told to exculpate Schepps as far as you could? *A:* No.

Q: Have you been told that to convict Becker, the testimony of accomplices must be corroborated? *A:* No.

Q: Haven't you discussed the question of corroboration with Rose or Vallon? Do you mean to tell the jury that all cooped up there together you didn't discuss your testimony?

McIntyre did not want a response. He let the implication hang there for the jury to draw its own conclusion and moved right on to Webber's role in the case, beginning with the night of the abortive attempt to murder Rosenthal at the Garden Restaurant. Under direct examination, Webber had testified that he told Rose he would go uptown looking for Rosenthal.

"For what purpose?" McIntyre asked. "For the purpose of having him murdered," Webber responded. He testified further that he was shocked when told of the plan to kill Rosenthal. Then, in rapid-fire cadence:

Q: Did it trouble you? *A:* Yes.

Q: When you say you were shocked, did you tell anyone? *A:* No.

Q: Becker never did you any harm, never raided you? *A:* No.

Q: Did you tell your wife of the plot? *A:* No.

Q: Did you have any trouble with your conscience? *A:* Yes, I did.

Q: Still, you made the arrangements for the murder? *A:* I did.

Now, McIntyre began searching for a motive that would appear to acquit Becker of leading the conspiracy.

Q: Did you want to see Herman Rosenthal killed? *A:* I did not.

Q Have you ever had any trouble with Rosenthal? *A:* No.

Q: Didn't you say that Herman Rosenthal procured the breaking of your jaw? *A:* I did not.

Q: You had your jaw broken? *A:* Yes

Q: Were you friendly with Herman Rosenthal? *A:* Not very.

Q: Why were you unfriendly? *A:* He borrowed money from me and didn't pay it back.

Q: Were you on speaking terms with him? *A:* Yes.

Q: Did you have trouble because he was your rival in the gambling business? *A:* No.

Q: You were willing to see him put out of the way? *A:* Yes.

Q: Were you anxious to have Rosenthal killed? *A:* I was not.

In similar Gatling-gun fashion, McIntyre won the acknowledgment that it was not fear that motivated Webber to have Rosenthal killed. Specifically, he responded that he did not fear Becker or Zelig or Rose or Vallon. "So,"

McIntyre concluded, "it was not fear that caused you to do as you did?" "No," said Webber.

Once again, Schepps became the subject of inquiry. Webber testified that the "Rosenthal squeal" was the main topic of discussion on the Sam Paul excursion.

Q: Did you all discuss the squealing? A: Yes, all except Schepps. He was not interested.

Q: There were some four hundred or five hundred people on the excursion and they all discussed the squealing? A: Yes.

Q: How did you know the squeal did not interest Schepps? A: Because he is a man not interested in gamblers.

It was now two o'clock, and Goff, who seemed immune to the pangs of hunger or any other of nature's demands, was prepared to continue on, but the jury wanted a break, and court was adjourned until 3:15. No one welcomed the pause more than Webber who had begun to show signs of wear as McIntyre's questioning grew more intense. It did not get any easier when he resumed the stand. McIntyre was eager to establish that Webber, as well as the state's other key witnesses, was testifying under a grant of immunity. He got Webber to admit that he had lied when, early in the investigation, he told Deputy Police Commissioner Dougherty that he was not connected to the murder. He later made his confession to the district attorney, and McIntyre wanted to know why. "Didn't you do this in return for promised immunity?" McIntyre asked. Webber denied it, but after insistent prodding said he signed a stipulation.

Q: What was in the stipulation? A: I did not read it.

Q: Is your object in testifying to get immunity? A: It is to receive protection.

Q: Protection from whom? A: The courts.

Q: What was the contents of the stipulation? A: I don't remember it.

Q: Was it read to you? A: It was.

Q: What do you remember of it? A: I would be given immunity if I told the truth and didn't fire a shot.

Q: Do you expect to be tried for murder in this case? A: I don't know.

McIntyre requested that the immunity agreements between the prosecution witnesses and the district attorney be read into the record and introduced as evidence, but Goff ruled that they were not relevant and refused to admit them.

With his examination of Webber near an end, McIntyre was determined to leave the jury with the sense that the witness was a man not to be trusted, that he had in fact played the role of Judas in sending Rosenthal to his death.

Q: Did you speak to [Rosenthal] at all when you went around [to the Metropole on the night of the murder]? A: I did.

Q: What did you say? A: I said, "Hello, Herman."

Q: In a friendly voice? A: Yes.

Q: And at that minute you knew he was going to be murdered? A: I did.

Q: When you got back to your rooms, what did you say first? A: I said, "Rosenthal's in the Metropole."

Q: Did you know they were going to kill Rosenthal? A: Yes.

Q: Did you do anything to restrain them? A: No.

With Webber visibly shaken and his credibility now perhaps at low tide, McIntyre returned to the central issue of Schepps's role in the murder plan. Webber said he was certain that Schepps had stayed across the street and heard nothing of the conversation when Becker met with Rose, Vallon, and Webber at the "Harlem conference" on the night Becker put Webber in charge of carrying out the murder plan.

Q: Are you trying to keep from making Schepps an accomplice? A: No.

Q: Do you know why Schepps didn't attend the conference? A: Yes, he was never let in on any conference. I told him to stay away. We never discussed the Rosenthal case in the presence of Schepps.

McIntyre then let loose a barrage of questions, giving Webber little time to answer one before firing another. "Didn't Schepps tell you that it was he who actually paid the money? Didn't you advance him the money to flee this jurisdiction? Didn't he write to you after he got away? Didn't you know he was gone?" Webber answered "no" to all but the last question. The answers were of little consequence; McIntyre had managed to do to Webber what he could not do to Rose. He had turned him into something of a caricature, a man with no conscience who would lie to advance his own ends, who was capable of greeting an acquaintance in a friendly manner while knowingly sending him to his death.

Harry Vallon was next to take the stand. It was 5:30, and a long night was still ahead. Vallon spent the next three hours and more going over the same ground covered by Rose and Webber. It was tedious, but the prosecution believed it was necessary that each of the accomplices tell the same story by way of corroboration. Vallon obliged on every detail. He added just one piece of new information. It concerned the Harlem conference. "There was," he said, "a little colored boy on the other side of the street, and [Becker] called him over and spoke to him." The remark was made casually, almost as an aside, but it would loom large as the trial proceeded. In the final telling, it would help to convict Becker.

During the first eight days of the trial, Sam Schepps had taken on the aspect of an *eminence grise*. Unseen and unheard, he was the odd piece of the puzzle that the prosecution needed to close out its case; he also represented the defense's best hope for an acquittal. The question turned on whether the jury could be made to believe that Schepps played around the edges of the murder plot but never quite got inside. He was, according to the prosecution's witnesses, often present when Rosenthal's demise was being planned but was never close enough to hear what was being said or interested enough to give it any attention. What manner of man might this unsuspectinig, perhaps somewhat naïve, gentleman be? On Tuesday morning, October 15, the jury and the spectators who packed the courthouse from end to end would make his acquaintance.

Short and stocky, neatly attired and wearing rimless glasses on a black string hung round his neck, Schepps looked like he might have been a bookkeeper or your neighborhood pharmacist. But that was a first impression that did not last long. He entered the courtroom and strode to the witness stand with the brazen swagger of Napoleon back from exile, reclaiming his troops. It was with that same air of confidence that he responded to the questions Moss put to him. From the prosecution's perspective, he might in fact have been too good a witness. So certain was Schepps that he had a full grip on his story, so sure was he of every detail, that Moss at times appeared uneasy, concerned that the testimony, as it unfolded, sounded too glib, as if the questions and answers had been carefully scripted and committed to memory.

He corroborated every event related by Rose, Webber, and Vallon. Yes, he had attended the Harlem conference; yes, he rode with Rose and Webber in the gray touring car when it picked up Dago Frank and brought him to the murder rendezvous at Bridgey's poker room; he heard them speaking but was unaware of what they were saying; he was there when Webber left to look for

Rosenthal and when he returned to announce that Rosenthal was in the Metropole; he had seen the four gunmen rush for the door when they learned of his whereabouts; he was with Rose when the thousand-dollar payment was made to Lefty Louie; he was at Pollock's house when Rose signed the affidavit, and had served as a lobbygow, carrying messages back and forth between Becker and Rose. Yet he had fathomed nothing about a plot to kill Rosenthal. This street-wise, angle-playing sharpie who knew when to hold 'em and when to fold 'em, when to leave for Arkansas and under precisely which circumstances to return, now asked the world to believe that nothing he had seen or heard had caused him to be at all suspicious that Rosenthal was in harm's way.

Given the degree of trust necessary to accept Schepps's story as fact, McIntyre appeared to relish the opportunity to get at the witness. It did not take long for him to learn that he was headed for a collision with a man who was ready and eager to go mano-a-mano with anyone in the room. Schepps's body language said all that was needed. He sat squarely in the witness chair, both feet flat on the floor, leaning slightly forward as if prepared for confrontation. Unlike the witnesses who came before him—the cool, emotionally restrained Rose; the fidgety, calculating Webber—Schepps gave every indication that he disdained being placed on the defensive; aggressive by nature, he was more comfortable on the attack.

He acknowledged that he had gone on the Sam Paul outing with Rose, Vallon, and Webber and that he heard a lot of talk about the "Rosenthal squeal," but he insisted he never heard any talk about murder. The first of many heated exchanges came when McIntyre asked, in an angry tone, "Are you trying to conceal anything?" "No, I am not," Schepps shot back and then stole a glance in the direction of the prosecution table. "Don't look at the district attorney, look at me," McIntyre shouted, then shifted direction and began questioning the witness about the night those on the excursion returned to town. Schepps said that he, Rose, and Vallon had gone to Luchow's for dinner but that he stepped outside when they started talking and did not know the subject of their conversation. It was then that McIntyre learned how nimble of wit Schepps could be.

Q: Have you been told to say that Rose never discussed anything with you?
A: No.

Q: I want to know what you talked about. *A:* The weather.

Schepps's voice oozed sarcasm and McIntyre went along with it.

Q: That the sun came up in the morning, and the clouds were in the sky, I suppose? *A:* Oh, no.

Q: Well, what did you say of the weather? *A:* That the day was a nice day.

The atmosphere grew even more hostile when McIntyre suggested that Schepps acted as paymaster for the murder. "If you say that, you lie," Schepps shouted. It was more than Justice Goff would abide. "The witness will use proper language in addressing the court," he said. Schepps's apology only served to stir McIntyre's resentment. "I want no apology from that thing," he said. "I would not lower myself to accept an apology from such a groveling specimen of humanity." Now, Whitman was on his feet. "He apologized to the court, not to you," he said, "and I object to the counsel's belligerent manner." "And," McIntyre countered, "I object to the insolent tone of the witness and to the insolence of the district attorney."

Looking for another line of questioning that would involve Schepps in the plot, McIntyre asked why he had accompanied Rose and Vallon on a visit to the home of Dora Gilbert, Rosenthal's ex-wife, when they were seeking to get her to sign an affidavit impugning Rosenthal's character.

"Why did you go to the house?" McIntyre wanted to know. "For the pleasure of the ride," Schepps said. McIntyre persisted, "But why did you go inside the house?" Still playing to the audience, Schepps responded, "You wouldn't expect me to stay outside, would you?" Not inclined to let the matter drop, the attorney demanded that Schepps tell the court what he heard discussed; wasn't the aim of the visit to get Rosenthal's ex-wife to discredit him? Schepps said he could not give a yes or no answer.

Q: You were there, weren't you? *A:* Yes.

Q: But you can't remember? *A:* I can remember if you'll let me answer you in my own way.

Q: I'll let you answer me according to law. Well, what did you hear Rose say to Dora Gilbert? *A:* I heard him say to her, "How much do I owe you for the wine we drank?" (Schepps was grinning.)

Q: And that is all you can remember? That is all that made any impression on you, is it? *A:* Yes, sir. (Schepps was grinning even more broadly.)

He was having his way with McIntyre, and it appeared that he was just warming up. McIntyre asked him how he became acquainted with the four gunmen. Schepps responded that he was introduced by Rose about three months before the murder. Asked under what circumstances he was introduced, Schepps said, "There were no circumstances. Rose and I were walking in Fourteenth Street near Third Avenue, and we came on the men, and he introduced us."

Unwittingly playing the straight man, McIntyre led Schepps perfectly. "How did he introduce you?" he asked.

Schepps held out his left hand, looked at it with a smile, and said, "This is Gyp." Then in similar fashion, he held out his right hand and said, "This is Mr. Schepps."

His little act drew a round of laughter, and Schepps, with the practiced timing of a comic, waited for it to die down and said, "That's how he introduced us. You know how people are introduced."

McIntyre, visibly suppressing his rage, was searching for a rejoinder. Finally, he said, "Yes, I know that, and I know a lot of other things about you." "Well, tell them," Schepps said, knowing he had gotten the better of the exchange. Feeling he was on a roll, Schepps was ready with another quip just a minute or two later when McIntyre was questioning him about the drive to the murder rendezvous with Dago Frank. "Where did you stop?" he asked. "We didn't stop," Schepps responded, "the car stopped." The line fell flat, and McIntyre abruptly picked up speed. He resumed the spitfire interrogation that served him best, and took Schepps back to Webber's poker room on the night of the murder.

Q: Did you know he [Webber] was going out to locate the victim? A: I did not.

Q: Did you hear any of the gunmen say anything during that time? A: I did not.

Q: Was anything said except that relating to refreshments? A: Nothing else.

Q: Coming down in the automobile with Dago Frank, was anything said? A: I didn't hear anything.

Q: You sat on the front seat so as you couldn't hear what was said between Rose and the others? A: I had no such intention.

Q: Didn't you hear what was said? A: Not a word.

Q: During that fifteen minutes was there anything said about the mission of Bridgey Webber? A: No.

Q: Did you hear he was going out for the purpose of looking up Rosenthal? *A:* I did not.

Q: Did you hear Webber say that Rosenthal was in the Metropole? *A:* Yes.

Q: And you were not suspicious? *A:* Suspicious of what? No.

Q: After the gunmen went out, did you ask what they were going out for? *A:* When I started out, Jack Rose stopped me.

Q: Did you ask Rose what Webber's statement about Rosenthal meant? *A:* I did not.

Q: Weren't you curious to know? *A:* I didn't think anything about the announcement.

The repeated, unequivocal denials might have satisfied the record, but McIntyre seemed to sense that each one amounted to a point scored by the defense. For no reasonable person could believe that Schepps was telling the truth, that the attorney's quick-witted antagonist could have spent the night among men who were hatching a murder plan while remaining innocent of what was transpiring. McIntyre continued to press the point, causing the witness to continue denying the obvious. Schepps admitted meeting with Vallon after the shooting and taking a message from Rose to the four gunmen the following day.

"You knew then, didn't you, that these men were the murderers and that Rose and Webber had arranged the murder?" McIntyre asked. "I did not," Schepps said. "You were as innocent as a new-born babe?" McIntyre suggested. An objection spared Schepps the need to respond.

McIntyre soon turned his attention to Schepps's leaving town and his stay in Arkansas. Schepps acknowledged that on the Thursday after the murder he went to the office of James M. Sullivan, who later became Rose's lawyer, and that one day later he left town. He said he went to Fallsburg, Kingston, Albany, and Buffalo—all in New York—and then to St. Louis and finally to Hot Springs, Arkansas. Schepps denied meeting there with a lawyer named James L. Graham or saying that "the gang could get immunity by implicating Becker." McIntyre's next question foreshadowed what many believed would be the fulcrum of the defense's case. "Did you say," he asked, "that the reason for killing Rosenthal was that he had 'peached' on the gang?"

For some weeks, the story had been making the rounds that the gamblers who were now testifying against Becker had raised a fund of five thousand dollars to be given to Rosenthal on the condition he leave town before making his disclosures to the district attorney. Rosenthal, the story went, had taken the money but had not left the city. The gamblers then decided to have Rosenthal killed and frame Becker, a two-for-one deal that would simplify business for everyone. Of course, Schepps denied the allegation, but it was now out in the open. The impact of the story was that it was as plausible as the one the state was making against Becker, it was not contradicted by any known circumstance, and it would explain why all the accomplices were testifying against Becker. Most significantly, it supplied the defense with an alternate scenario that could be presented to the jury as satisfying the standard of reasonable doubt. If McIntyre was planning to use the story in his defense, he had cleverly managed to introduce it to the jury through the testimony of a hostile witness.

Sticking to the time Schepps spent in Arkansas, McIntyre handed Goff a large sheaf of papers, documents assembled by the authorities who had held Schepps in Hot Springs, but the judge declined to open it. Since the defense had not obtained it as testimony, he said, it was not subject to cross-examination. McIntyre then put into evidence and read to the jury the letter Schepps sent to Rose from Hot Springs in which Schepps asked for guidance about what he should testify to. He asked the witness what he meant when he wrote that "we are in very bad." Schepps said he was referring to the leniency promised by the district attorney and to the "lies in the newspapers" that said he had acted as paymaster and passed one thousand dollars to the gunmen. He said that if he corroborated that statement, he would be corroborating a lie. Seizing the opportunity, McIntyre asked, "Did anybody ever ask you to corroborate a lie?" "No," Schepps said.

McIntyre seemed to be running out of lines of inquiry. Finally, he asked the sweeping question that was the crux of the case: "Did you frame-up on Becker in the West Side Prison?" Surprisingly, Schepps, who had fielded an array of more nuanced questions with remarkable ease, appeared to be caught off-guard. "I ..." he began and then turned and said something to the judge. "Answer that question," McIntyre shouted. Schepps turned back toward counsel and tried to explain, "I am asking the court ..." he said, but McIntyre, perhaps unwisely, cut him off again. "I want an answer," he roared, his voice yet louder than before. "All right, then," Schepps replied evenly, "my answer is no."

It was now past five o'clock, and, in what was becoming something of a ritual, McIntyre asked for an adjournment until the next day, and Goff denied it, insisting that the cross-examination of Schepps be concluded. Hart was permitted to take over for McIntyre, and he proceeded with a long series of questions about remarks Schepps was said to have made to the postmaster and other officials in Arkansas regarding his feelings toward Rosenthal, his reasons for leaving New York, and his relations with those involved in the conspiracy. Schepps routinely denied any implication in the planning of the crime, and, as darkness fell, he left the witness chair unbowed, having delivered the most entertaining performance of the trial.

McIntyre, however, appeared to be substantially pleased with his day's work. Though he had garnered no admissions, he believed he had exposed Schepps as a man who cynically, even cheerfully, had lied about his part in the murder conspiracy and dared the court to call it what it was. "We all know I'm lying," he seemed to be saying, "but we also know you can't prove it." McIntyre felt assured that Schepps had fooled no one and that he had convicted himself in the minds of both judge and jury. He had shown himself to be too savvy to have been at the center of the plot and remain ignorant of its nature. And if it was clear that Schepps was an accomplice, his testimony was useless to the prosecution.

The following day, its case winding down, the state brought forth a parade of sixteen witnesses starring, most notably, Rosenthal's widow. Mrs. Lillian Rosenthal, dressed in mourning with a black hat and long crepe veil, made a sympathetic figure, but she contributed nothing new to the state's case. Neither did the chauffeur who drove Becker to Madison Square Garden; the Pollocks, who housed Rose after the shooting; two waiters from the Union Square Hotel; a bookkeeper and a clerk from police headquarters; or a reporter for the *New York World*.

The only one of the prosecution's final witnesses whose testimony warranted a long cross-examination was a disbarred lawyer by the name of James E. Hallon who testified that he heard Becker admit he had orchestrated Rosenthal's assassination. The place where he heard it, however, cast some doubt upon his credibility. Hallon had occupied a cell next to Becker's in the Tombs when he overheard a conversation between the lieutenant and Detective James C. White, formerly of Becker's strong-arm squad, now under indictment for perjury in connection with the alleged planting of a revolver on the late Big Jack Zelig. Hallon read the snippet of conversation from a scrap of paper on which he said he jotted it down the day he heard it.

He first quoted White: "'I heard straight from Whitman's man that Louie had been found and that he had told Whitman everything.'" Then Becker: "'Oh, hell, I suppose he has. It's only the say-so of another crook. Now, see here, Jimmie, we have no one around us but professional criminals. No jury on earth will believe them. Sit fast. Just sit fast and deny everything. I tell you, when all this is over, the public will give me a pension for killing that damned skunk, Rosenthal.'"

The question now was whether the current jury would believe Hallon. He had come to the courthouse directly from Sing Sing, still wearing a prisoner's chains. He was a two-time loser just beginning his second prison term on a larceny charge, and there was a question of whether he had been promised anything by the district attorney in exchange for his testimony.

On Thursday, October 17, the state was ready to conclude its case with a few marginal witnesses who, as it turned out, did not help the prosecution's cause at all. The one who might have done the most damage to the defense was barred from testifying following an impassioned and stunningly crafted appeal by McIntyre. The witness was Daniel A. Ventien, a clerk in charge of the signature cards of the Franklin Savings Bank. It was Moss's intent to depict Becker as a graft-taking cop by producing bank records that would chart the growth of his wealth from the time he was put in charge of the strong-arm squad. McIntyre objected that such testimony was irrelevant to the charge of murder and would only "bias, inflame, and impassion the minds of the jury." His argument, critical to Becker's defense and built on finely honed legal distinctions, was to be his finest moment and brightest victory. In the absence of the jury, speaking directly to Goff in a booming but measured voice, he said;

"If the evidence showed that money came directly or indirectly from Rosenthal, it might furnish a motive, but the prosecution must show beyond a doubt that the money in the bank did come from Rosenthal and that Rosenthal knew it. There is no need for circumstantial evidence in this case. It is as if I should take a deadly weapon from my pocket and fire upon Mr. Moss and an instant later he should fall dead on the floor. That would be direct evidence against me. You would have no need to prove a motive. It is the same in this case. You have direct evidence here. Rose has taken the stand and sworn that Becker came to him and said he wanted Rosenthal croaked. Vallon and Webber have testified to the same facts—that Becker ordered the murder and they arranged it. That is direct evidence; there is no need for circumstantial evidence.

"Now, Your Honor, put this evidence in and what will it mean? It will make the jury believe that Becker is a grafter. It will make them believe that he is a bribe-taker, and it may make them believe that he is an extortioner. Would not that be to his detriment in his trial on the charge on which he has been indicted? If he has taken money unlawfully, it is another crime and for that he can be tried. But that crime has no bearing on, or relation to, the crime on which he is now arraigned.

"The law is as old as the hills. It goes back to the time of William the Conqueror. A defendant can be tried only on the single crime alleged against him. He cannot be tried on any other. If there is a doubt in Your Honor's mind, then that doubt must be given to the benefit of the defendant. I submit that there is not a precedent in all the books, or the books of the text writers, which allows the submission of such evidence. I ask that Your Honor bar out such testimony."

Goff sustained McIntyre's objection. He said that the issue turned on "whether or not Rosenthal knew of Becker's bank account, and Becker knew that Rosenthal knew of it." Since the state had produced no evidence to support such a claim, Ventien's testimony was barred. The judge's ruling cut short the presentation of the state's case. At about four-thirty, the prosecution rested. McIntyre, clearly exhausted and in poor health, petitioned Goff to adjourn until Friday afternoon, but the best he could get was ten-thirty. It was then that the defense would get its turn.

16

Much like a prizefighter who had taken his opponent's best punch and was still standing, McIntyre was feeling optimistic. He was convinced that the state had failed to prove its case. Aside from the questionable testimony of three jailhouse accomplices, there was little in the way of hard evidence that would tie Becker directly to the crime. The corroborating witness, Sam Schepps, had appeared to self-destruct on the witness stand. So confident was McIntyre, that for a brief period he had considered the possibility of presenting no defense at all, allowing the prosecution's case to fall of its own weight. But he decided that such a strategy might be a bit too subtle. Besides, he believed he could produce evidence that was strong enough to convict the accusers. He would demonstrate that the key witnesses for the state had at least as much motive to do away with Rosenthal as Becker had, and by their own admission, it was they who had carried out the plan. Furthermore, if Rosenthal, ready to expose their gambling enterprise to the district attorney, was their worst enemy, Becker, who shook them down and raided their places of business, was clearly number two. So the three gamblers—Rose, Webber, and Vallon—and perhaps Schepps—found themselves sitting at the edge of the kind of possibility that rarely beckoned. They would be able to rid themselves of the squealer and the shakedown artist with one bold act. They had motive, means, and opportunity, and in fact had admitted hiring the killers and helping to set up the hit. That was the scenario the defense was about to present. It was certainly as plausible as the state's case and thus raised reasonable doubt about the guilt of the defendant.

With McIntyre drained by nearly two weeks of intense courtroom conflict, stretched over long hours six days a week, Hart opened for the defense. His statement was brief—thirty minutes—and direct, shorn of the sweeping turns of oratory to which McIntyre was given. He began with a hopeful presumption:

"The case of the prosecution has been presented, and, doubtless, the minds of you jurors have been made up to the decision that the defendant has not been convicted. The defense does not want to rest here, however, but will prove beyond a doubt that the defendant was innocent."

He then went on to outline the arguments he would make to the jury. Describing Rosenthal as "the most thoroughly despised man in the gambling fraternity in New York," he said he would show "that Webber and Rose, with Vallon and Schepps, conspired to kill Herman Rosenthal entirely independent of Becker and each with his own motives." He said the defense would prove that "in order to save their own necks, these men, on the 29th of July, made up their minds to deliver Becker to the district attorney."

The first two witnesses called by McIntyre were of little help. William Travers Jerome, former New York district attorney with a spotless reputation, told the court that he had received a phone call from Hart on the day after the murder, that they met for a meal at Delmonico's, and then went to the Bar Association where they were joined by Becker. It was from there that Becker called Rose and told him there were two hundred policemen looking for him and that he had better give himself up. But the content of that conversation never made it into the record. Justice Goff excluded the testimony as hearsay, and Jerome was dismissed.

The second witness, Police Commissioner Waldo, testified that he had assigned Becker to the strong-arm squad and directed him to get evidence against Rosenthal. He also stated that it was he who had given the order for a policeman to remain in Rosenthal's gambling house. But the defense's chief reason for calling Waldo was to have him testify that Becker had asked to be relieved of his command and transferred to another squad, for that would have suggested that Becker was not so much tied to a graft-taking enterprise as had been suspected. McIntyre put the question in a variety of forms, but each time Moss objected, Goff sustained him, and he too was prematurely excused.

The first witness to offer substantive testimony was Frederick H. Hawley, the reporter for the *Evening Sun* who had telephoned Becker with the news that Rosenthal had been shot. Hawley was an important witness for the defense because if his timeline was correct, Becker could not have met with Rose and Webber at Bridgey's poker room after the killing. According to the prosecution's case, it was there that Becker reassured them that there was nothing to worry about and where it was arranged that Webber and Rose would give Lefty Louie one thousand dollars to be distributed to the gunmen. Now, Hawley was prepared to testify that the meeting could not have taken place. He gave this account of his activities on the night of the murder:

He was at police headquarters when he heard that Rosenthal had been shot. He took the subway to the Metropole, arrived there at 2:12, stayed for about fifteen minutes, then went to Child's restaurant in Forty-second Street and called his office to report the story. He then called Becker at his private home number and said, "Have you heard the news? Herman Rosenthal has been shot and killed." "What are you trying to do, kid me?" Becker said. "No, he was shot and killed in front of the Metropole. I am on the story now." Hawley said he asked if Becker had anything to say, and he replied, "I am sorry that he was killed, for I wanted to show the Jew bastard up."

On his way to the West Forty-seventh Street station, Hawley said, he met Becker coming out of the Times Building, and they walked together to the station house. At the corner of Forty-third and Broadway, Becker bought a newspaper, glanced at the headline and said, "You are right." They continued on to the station, and they remained there until about eight o'clock, Hawley said. They never went near Webber's poker room. They never saw Webber, Vallon, or anyone else connected to the case, Hawley testified, and during those four and a half hours, Becker was out of his sight for "not more than five minutes."

Hawley's testimony punched a hole in the narrative developed by the prosecution, and sensing the need for damage control, Whitman conducted the cross-examination himself. The D.A.'s assault on the witness was so unsparing that McIntyre objected more than once to Whitman's tone. It was clear that the district attorney did not believe Hawley's account of Becker's movements, and he wanted to know why the reporter had not written the story.

Q: You knew that this information would be of the greatest value to the defense and to the prosecution. You knew the district attorney was seeking only the truth. Why didn't you print it? *A:* Because it had no place in the story of Rosenthal's murder.

Q: Why didn't you tell the district attorney? *A:* Because I didn't like your attitude in the case. I didn't want you to know what I was going to testify to.

Under persistent questioning, Whitman got Hawley to admit that Becker was out of his sight for more than five minutes, perhaps as much as half an hour. The admission was something of a split decision between defense and prosecution. For while thirty minutes was technically sufficient for Becker to have gone from Forty-seventh to Forty-second Street, meet briefly with Rose and Webber, and return to the station house, it was unlikely that a meeting of that consequence would have taken place in so short a period.

In any event, Hawley's account was soon to be rebutted by an unexpected witness for the defense—District Attorney Whitman. McIntyre had made the claim that the D.A. himself would prove that Becker could not have met with Rose and Webber, because he had passed the critical hours in the captain's room at the police station. But McIntyre proved to be off the mark. While Whitman agreed that he had seen Becker at the station house at about 3:30, he said he had not seen him there after four o'clock that morning. He also testified that he had not seen Hawley at all, which contradicted the reporter's claim that he had spent more than five hours at the station in Becker's company. With Whitman already sworn, McIntyre took the opportunity to ask him whether he had entered into any stipulation with Rose, Webber, or Vallon in return for their testimony. The D.A. admitted that a stipulation had been signed but insisted that it did not include a guarantee of immunity and agreed to produce the document later in the trial. Whitman's testimony that he had never seen Hawley in the stationhouse that night might have been more damaging to Hawley than to Becker. The next day's *Sun* carried the following announcement on its editorial page: "Frederick H. Hawley is no longer a member of the staff of the *Evening Sun.*"

A clutch of other witnesses—many testifying to Becker's good character—made cameo appearances until the defense unveiled the most potent weapon in its arsenal. He was Jack Sullivan, né Jacob Reich, self-anointed King of the Newsboys. Built wide and low-to-the-ground, Sullivan, as he was called throughout the trial, had the self-assured look of a man who shied from nothing. Among the many notations on his resume, he had once served as bodyguard to William Randolph Hearst. He also had worked in the circulation departments of several city newspapers and later established a central distribution system that funneled papers to newsboys who sold them on the streets.

Now, wearing a blue suit, a cream-colored shirt, and a blue tie, he was led to the witness stand from a prison pen in the rear of the courtroom, for he was under indictment as a conspirator in the Rosenthal murder. Still, he carried himself with a swagger that seemed a declaration of his own invincibility and foreshadowed his performance on the stand. Among all the central characters in the plot, only the thirty-three-year-old Sullivan came to the scene untainted. He had been promised nothing by anyone. He had spurned offers of the same favors that the others accused in the plot had accepted eagerly. Further, his decision to testify in Becker's behalf alienated the district attorney, whose office could have assured his eventual release from custody. There was something both noble and defiant in his manner as he sat in the witness chair, leaning forward as if daring anyone to tip him off balance.

He began by accounting for his movements on the night of the murder. He said he had gone to the fights at Madison Square Garden with a newspaperman. They met Becker and he joined them for a drink at the Prince George Hotel. Becker was driving a borrowed car, and they drove to the Hudson Tube at Thirty-third Street, where the newspaperman left, then up to the Pulitzer Building, which Becker entered while Sullivan remained in the car. The witness said he did not know at the time that Becker had gone to the *World* office to get the Rosenthal affidavit. They continued uptown, and Sullivan got out at Webber's poker room.

At this point, McIntyre broke into his interrogation to note that Sullivan was under indictment for first-degree murder, and Goff informed him that he was not required to answer any questions that might incriminate him. Then McIntyre asked the witness: "Mr. Sullivan, in view of the statement made to you just now by His Honor, are you still willing to testify?" Sullivan immediately and emphatically responded, "I am."

Having assured the court that his witness was undaunted and no doubt leveraging his credibility with the jury, McIntyre proceeded to lead Sullivan through several hours of testimony that was at odds with the chronicle of events presented by the prosecution.

"When you got off the automobile, did you notice in what direction Lieutenant Becker went, and did you see him again that night?" McIntyre asked. "He went up Broadway," Sullivan said. "I didn't see him again until the next day in Mr. Hart's office."

Sullivan's testimony directly contradicted the statements of Rose, Webber, Vallon, and Schepps, who said that Becker had met them in front of Webber's place after the killing and told them not to worry, that there would be no trouble. Sullivan then accounted for his own whereabouts that night. He was heading for the Lincoln Hotel, looking for Sam Paul whom he owed $150, and he stopped at the fountain in the Cohan Theater for a soda. It was there that he heard the shots that killed Rosenthal. He started for Forty-third Street and saw crowds running in the direction of the Metropole. "I took my pin out of my tie and stuck it in my undershirt," he said. "I know the mob around that neighborhood." It was a bit of unintended comic relief, but it was greeted with laughter and contributed to the feeling that Sullivan was the most likable and, the defense hoped, the most trustworthy witness so far. At the Metropole, he said, he pushed his way through the crowd, leaned over Rosenthal and said, "Herman, who did it?" Realizing that Rosenthal was dead, he went back to Webber's place where he found Bridgey, Rose, Vallon, and Schepps standing outside the cigar store on the corner. It was 2:40 in the morning; Becker was not there.

McIntyre was approaching the critical portion of Sullivan's testimony. He wanted him to tell the court that he actually heard his three fellow prisoners plot to implicate Becker. "Did Rose, Webber, or Vallon ask you to connect this defendant at the bar with the murder of Herman Rosenthal?" Goff sustained Moss's objection as he had more than a dozen times in succession, and McIntyre tried again. "I now offer the first proof of this conspiracy," he began, but again Goff cut him off. "No, no, I don't want to hear any offers," he said. Sullivan, ready to answer any questions put to him, was growing impatient. On previous occasions, he had shouted the answer over Goff's objection, but now he was pushing for a direct confrontation. "I want to tell the story in my own way," he shouted at the judge. "You will have the opportunity," Goff said evenly.

Finally, he did, and Sullivan contradicted every critical piece of testimony offered by the state regarding the plot to frame Becker. On July 29, Sullivan recalled, he met with Rose, Webber, and Vallon in the counsel room of the Tombs, and the framing of Becker was the subject of discussion.

Q: Did Jack Rose say to you at that time, the 29th of July, that Harry Vallon, Bridgey Webber, and yourself were in bad? A: Not myself; my name wasn't mentioned.

Q: Did he say that Harry Vallon and Webber were facing the electric chair, and to save themselves they would have to implicate Becker? A: Yes, sir.

Q: Did Rose say, "The papers and the district attorney are hollering for Becker, and to save ourselves we'll have to implicate Becker?" A: Yes, he did.

Q: Did you say, "You bald-headed old bastard, are you going to frame-up on Becker?" and did he say, "That is the only way we can get out of this, by framing up on Waldo, the mayor, the city administration, or on Becker?" A: Yes. (Shouted over Moss's objection.)

Q: Did Rose say to you in the West Side Prison that "self-preservation is the first rule of nature"? A: Yes.

Q: Were you in any way implicated in the murder of Herman Rosenthal? A: Mr. Whitman knows I was not. I told Whitman I had no more to do with it than Whitman's baby.

Q: Did you enter in any conspiracy of assassination? A: No.

Q: When you were in the West Side Prison, did Webber say, "I'll give you $25,000 not to implicate me?" A: Yes, he said that in the Tombs.

Q: Did Webber say, "I am on the bandwagon and am going along; Rose, Vallon, and myself would frame-up on anybody"? A: Yes.

Q: Did Bridgey Webber say to you in the West Side Prison, "We have made arrangements with Mr. Whitman and Assistant District Attorney Smith, so that you can tell what you know, and you can get out?" A: He did.

Q: Did you ask Webber, "What is the idea of having me here?" and did he say, "The district attorney wanted you up here so we could talk to you?" A: Yes.

Q: On or about August 20, at the West Side Prison, before you were indicted, did Webber say to you, "You had better come in and get the benefit of immunity?" Did he say that to you? A: Yes, he said something that meant the same.

Q: Did Webber tell you to come in and get the benefit of immunity, and did you say, "I will tell the truth"? *A:* It was said in substance.

Q: Did Vallon say to come up and corroborate him? *A:* He did.

Q: Did Vallon say to you, "If you don't go with us you'll never get out"? *A:* Yes.

Q: Three days before the shooting, were you in the Garden Restaurant with Herman Rosenthal? *A:* Yes, and his wife and sister-in-law were there.

Sullivan and Rosenthal went back a long way. Herman was best man at Sullivan's wedding and he had remained close with the family. Questioned about their conversation that night, Sullivan quoted a remark he said Mrs. Rosenthal made to her husband during the course of dinner: "'We must put Becker out of business. I don't care if I live with you, Herman, in a furnished room and have coffee and cake to eat, we must get rid of Becker.'"

McIntyre then turned his focus back upon Webber.

Q: Did Webber say, "You stick to me, Jack, and you won't have to worry the rest of your life?" *A:* Yes, and he also said, "You testify against Becker and I will give you half in a $25,000 business and $1,000 besides."

Q: Did he say, "Name your own price?" *A:* He did.

McIntyre's last question went unanswered. "Is it a fact," he asked, "that only two weeks before the murder of Rosenthal, Bridgey Webber told you he was going to have Rosenthal murdered?" Once again, Moss's objection was sustained by Justice Goff, and Sullivan was turned over to Moss for cross-examination.

Moss was in somewhat of a bind with Sullivan. The defense witness had challenged every essential element of the state's case against Becker, and the verdict, at this point, seemed to turn on whether the jury would find him more believable than the triumvirate of Rose, Webber, and Vallon. Since it was clear that Sullivan had nothing to gain by offering his testimony while the state's witnesses had staked everything on the district attorney's largesse, there were few paths open to Moss other than to try to discredit Sullivan. It was a technique that did not find favor with the witness. Sullivan at first refused to answer Moss's questions. "Why should I answer you?" he shouted. "You don't want the truth. You won't let me tell it, you won't let me answer," he said, referring to Moss's frequent objections during direct examination.

But the D.A. persisted. He picked at Sullivan's past, in search of any activity that might taint his reputation and cast a degree of doubt on his credibility. Moss's every suggestion of impropriety on Sullivan's part—was he a steerer for Bridgey Webber, a collector for a local saloon, for any number of "disorderly houses"?—was met with an emotional outburst from Sullivan. He denied ever collecting money for anyone, and as Moss continued to introduce the possibility of other illicit connections, Sullivan's rage grew, and he began interrupting the district attorney before he had completed the question. Moss suggested that in justice to himself, Sullivan should listen attentively to the question before answering it. "Justice?" Sullivan said. "There ain't no justice. If there was I wouldn't be here." Unable to budge the witness and no doubt aware that keeping him on the stand would do nothing to advance his case, Moss summarily dismissed him. "What? No more questions? Why the court don't know nothing yet." Then, stepping down from the stand, he said, "If you had let me answer your questions in my own way I could have told you the whole story. Why don't you let the public know something about this case? I could tell it, but you won't let me."

Sullivan's performance was, in many respects, the most interesting of the trial. Rose, the consummate actor, had been more impressive; Schepps had been more entertaining; but Sullivan appeared to be the most authentic. He had withstood enormous pressure from both his fellow prisoners and the district attorney's office. He had turned down an inviting opportunity to cut a deal that, in all likelihood, would have allowed him to walk free and put the entire case behind him. Given his close relationship with Rosenthal, his apparent devotion to the defendant—his friend's antagonist—was even more perplexing.

While there was no hard evidence that the district attorney had offered him a deal for his testimony, it was on the record that early in August he had been transferred from the Tombs to the West Side Prison—sometimes referred to as Whitman's Ritz—where he joined Rose, Webber, and Vallon. It was widely presumed that the switch was made so that the other three prisoners might persuade him to join their ranks and testify against Becker. On August 12, he had received in his cell what he called "a very friendly letter" from Moss, which began: "I deem it my duty to inform you that the evidence already submitted to the grand jury would justify that body in indicting you for the Rosenthal murder." It went on to advise Sullivan to cooperate with the district attorney's office and take advantage of whatever considerations might be extended to him. Webber and Rose encouraged him to accept the offer, but he declined. "I wouldn't swear a man's life away . . ." he told them, "I'll rot in jail first." Whitman seemed ready to comply. The following day, Sullivan was sent back to the Tombs. A week later, he was indicted for first-degree murder. The irony was that, compared with the others under indictment, there was virtually no evidence linking Sullivan to the killing. Subsequent events offered no explanation for his eagerness to testify in Becker's behalf other than the one he himself offered: "I couldn't stand to see any man get such a raw deal from those lying bums."

17

There was a sense of anticlimax in the next day's testimony. It was Saturday, October 19, and Goff had prescribed an abbreviated session. Court would adjourn at one o'clock to allow the jurors to register to vote in the upcoming municipal elections.

The day began with the reading into evidence of the confession Rose signed in the West Side Prison and the stipulations between Whitman and Rose, Webber, Vallon, and Schepps. Introducing the confession was a risky proposition for McIntyre, because it contained statements about Rose's collecting graft money for Becker that had been barred by Goff during direct examination. Once entered in the record, it might have been used as a wedge to allow in testimony regarding Becker's bank accounts which the defense had struggled to keep out of evidence. McIntyre chose to take the chance, hoping that statements in the confession would contradict parts of Rose's testimony and raise new doubts about his credibility. But whatever discrepancies were found were of minor consequence and proved to be no aid to the defense. By the same token, the prosecution did not attempt to use the confession to pry loose new testimony regarding Becker's finances. The reading of the stipulations, eagerly awaited by the defense, also provided nothing noteworthy. The four documents were virtually identical. They said that the witness would not be tried for murder or any other crime included in his testimony provided he had not fired any of the shots that had killed Rosenthal and that he agreed to remain in custody until Becker was tried and the indictment disposed of.

The defense called a number of witnesses to support its contention that Becker was framed by his accusers. Each testified that at one time or another they heard Rose or Webber say they intended to kill Rosenthal. The first and most convincing of these was Louis Plitt, brother of Charles Plitt, Jr., who was often referred to as Becker's press agent. Plitt testified that he had visited Rose in the Tombs at the gambler's request and that Rose went down on his knees and said, "Plitt, by the grave of my dead mother, on the memory of my dead mother, Becker had nothing to do with this affair." He also said that about six weeks before the murder, Rose told him he intended to have Rosenthal killed. Under cross-examination, Moss got Plitt to admit that he had told neither Becker nor Rosenthal of the threat, suggesting that perhaps he did not take it seriously.

Much the same scenario was described by the next witness, Robert H. Smith, a construction contractor who knew Rose and Webber, and who testified that he heard both of them speak of plans to kill Rosenthal. It took McIntyre several questions to extract the quote he was looking for from Smith.

"Did Rose ever say to you that he was going to kill Herman Rosenthal?" he asked. "Not in that way," said Smith. McIntyre tried again: "Did Rose say to you that Rosenthal would be killed as sure as his name was Jack Rose?" "No," Smith responded, "he said that if Zelig hadn't got in trouble, he'd have had him killed a month before. That's what he said."

McIntyre next asked Smith whether he had ever heard Webber speak threateningly of Rosenthal. "Did Webber say to you that he hated Rosenthal so much he could kill him and lie down beside his body?" Smith replied: "He said he could cut his throat and then lie down and sleep with him all night. Those were his exact words."

The morning's final witness was Patrolman Joseph E. Shephard who, prior to the murder, was a member of Becker's strong-arm squad and who had sworn out some of the affidavits that authorized the raiding of Rosenthal's gambling house. Shephard's testimony countered the prosecution's contention that the raid was a fake, set up by Becker and conducted on false affidavits by men who had never entered the room.

At one o'clock, court was adjourned, and the jurors were driven to their respective polling places and then back to the Murray Hill Hotel where they had been sequestered for the past two weeks.

That night, McIntyre announced that Becker would be summoned to testify despite the risk of having the district attorney expose him as the head of a graft-taking operation within the police department. The announcement led to much speculation. Either McIntyre was placing the bet that Goff would exclude testimony regarding Becker's financial holdings as he had earlier in the trial or, some thought, Becker might expose the entire network of corruption and perhaps curry some favors with the prosecution. As it developed, the speculation was unnecessary. McIntyre wavered, and on Sunday night decided that Becker's appearance could cost more than it was worth. He would not be called.

All told, Monday, October 21, the start of the trial's third week, was not a good day for the defense. A total of twenty-two witnesses were called—five former members of Becker's strong-arm squad, four character witnesses, twelve who contradicted the testimony of state witnesses, and finally Assistant District Attorney Moss. Moss was questioned about the letter he had sent to Sullivan in the Tombs, but Goff would not allow the document to be introduced as evidence, and Moss was promptly excused. The other members of Becker's squad confirmed Shephard's contention that the raid on Rosenthal's house was legal and in good faith.

But the day's most telling testimony came from an officer at the Forty-seventh Precinct, and it badly undermined the defense. Lieutenant Ernest L. von Diezelski was summoned to confirm the testimony of Frederick Hawley that Becker had arrived at the station house on the morning of the murder at around three-thirty. McIntyre asked von Diezelski what time Becker had come in, confident that the witness's answer would correspond to Hawley's. But von Diezelski consulted the police blotter, looked up, and said "four-twenty-five." The response stunned McIntyre, for the time difference was critical. It had been established that Rose had telephoned Becker to tell him of the murder at two-twenty-seven. Now, two hours were unaccounted for, more than enough time for Becker to have met with Rose, Webber, Vallon, and Schepps in front of Bridgey's poker room to discuss the payout before returning to the precinct—a meeting which the defense contended never took place.

Hawley's testimony had limited the time gap to at most one hour. The extra hour was therefore decisive. It allowed for precisely the sequence of events described by the prosecution. Clearly jarred by von Diezelski's testimony, McIntyre conferred with his assistants, but there was nothing to be salvaged. Moss, who had been given an unexpected gift by the defense, knew to keep his cross-examination brief. He asked the witness if he had made the entry in the blotter and whether it had been made on the morning of July 16. Von Diezelski replied "yes" to both questions, and Moss, smiling, said, "That's all."

During the afternoon session, McIntyre turned his attention to the corroborating evidence of Sam Schepps, attempting to show that Schepps knew too much about the crime to have been on the outside. He read into the record testimony from the Hot Springs commission, which included depositions from Thomas Pettit, the acting mayor of Hot Springs; Douglas Hotchkiss, a newspaper reporter; and Postmaster Frederick E. Johnston.

Pettit's testimony reprised Schepps's claim that he had something to sell, which Whitman wanted to buy, and that it was up to him to make the best bargain he could. Johnston stated that Schepps had boasted that his testimony would send Becker to the electric chair. Most damning of all was the quote offered by Hotchkiss, who said Schepps told him that he was the key to the whole situation in New York: "I don't want you to think that we killed a man who was worth anything. That man was a cur. I'll tell you the kind of fellow he was. He'd steal another fellow's girl or his bank roll. He'd declare a chap in if they were losing and out of they were winning. I don't want you to think I'm a common murderer, but I'm here and I never expected to be in this position."

There was nothing entirely new in the Arkansas depositions, since they had already been entered as evidence. But McIntyre appeared to be running out of both witnesses and energy. Suffering from a heart condition that had only recently been diagnosed, he had slept poorly throughout the two weeks of the trial, and he was visibly exhausted. Now, about to close the case for the defense, he tried to muster what little strength he had left.

In a curious turn of events, the most important witnesses of the last day of testimony, Tuesday, October 22, were not called by the defense. In a move that was unorthodox, if not unprecedented, Justice Goff recalled two defense witnesses—Jack Sullivan and Louis Plitt. In making the announcement, Goff said that he was looking to complete the record. He noted that Sullivan's intemperate behavior on the stand might have prevented him from answering some questions completely and that Plitt was cut short, perhaps prematurely, when McIntyre said he was not well enough to continue. However, the defense believed the judge might have had other motives. It was possible that Goff wanted to allow the witnesses to answer questions that had been excluded on their first appearance and to correct flaws in the record that might form the basis of an appeal. Suspecting such a tactic, Hart declined to question them, and Goff, determined to plug any holes in the trial transcript, ordered the district attorney to put to both witnesses prepared questions that previously had gone unanswered. Moss was eager enough to comply. Reading directly from the record, he asked Sullivan if anything had been omitted in his account of how he had been invited to cut a deal with the D.A.'s office and testify against Becker. "Have you stated everything that took place?" Moss asked. "No," said Sullivan.

Q: What else was said? A: On Friday, August 9, a messenger came from the district attorney's office and handed Jack Rose a note. He read it and said to me: "You had better tell what you know and corroborate us or you will be indicted. The district attorney says so."

Q: Did you speak to him? A: Yes.

Q: Did he answer? A: He said, "You'll be indicted. You'll have to see Whitman or Moss or you'll be indicted." I said, "I don't give a damn for all the money in the world. I have an attorney to look out for me. I don't care to have any advice from you."

McIntyre then took over the questioning of his own witness:

Q: Did you say anything to Webber? A: Yes. When he asked me to lie, I said I wouldn't do it, and he said, "Just wait until Schepps talks. He will corroborate anything." I said to Webber, "He is only a lobbygow. He'll do anything he is asked to."

Q: Was it at the time you would not corroborate him that he told you those things? A: Yes.

Q: And notwithstanding that you refused to join them, they told you these things every day? A: Sure, every day. When one stopped, the other started. I told them I wouldn't have it on my conscience for anything in the world.

Again reading his questions directly from the record, Moss had Plitt repeat and elaborate on his testimony that Rose had sworn to him on his mother's grave that Becker had nothing to do with the murder of Rosenthal.

The most explosive testimony of the day came from William Shapiro, the driver of the murder car who was still under indictment for the slaying of Rosenthal. Shapiro was to have been a witness for the defense and was expected to testify that both Vallon and Schepps were riding in his car when he sped from the murder scene. Such a contention would have been a crippling blow to the prosecution, as it would have made Schepps an accomplice whose corroboration of the story told by Rose, Webber, and Vallon would have been worthless. However, between the morning and afternoon sessions, Shapiro apparently had a change of heart. He signed an affidavit saying that neither Schepps nor Vallon were in his car when it left the Metropole, and testified for the state as a rebuttal witness. The concluding paragraph of his hastily drawn affidavit also tried to discredit Sullivan and cast doubt on his testimony for the defense. It read:

"Since I have been in the Tombs prison, Jack Sullivan has urged and begged me to say that Harry Vallon and Sam Schepps ordered me away from the Metropole with a pistol in Harry Vallon's hand to my head. Neither Sam Schepps or Harry Vallon were in my car, nor did I see them on the night after I left Forty-second Street and Sixth Avenue to go to Forty-third Street."

The last of the day's testimony was taken at about three o'clock. Closing arguments were to begin right then, with McIntyre summing up the case for the defense, but he was physically unable to proceed. He pleaded with Justice Goff: "I have not had a chance to prepare for the summing up of my case. I have been busy preparing testimony and preparing questions in cross-examination, and I am all worn out. I ask the indulgence of Your Honor until tomorrow morning at ten o'clock, when I will be up here ready to go ahead with my summing up. I throw myself on Your Honor's mercy, for, in all sincerity, I am physically and mentally unfit to go on."

Goff was amenable, but he insisted that both closings be made on the same day. He asked each counsel how long he needed to make his summation. Both McIntyre and Moss said they would finish within four hours. Goff, never one to be careless with time, sealed the deal:

"Then I will adjourn court now," he ruled, "with the understanding that

Mr. McIntyre shall have from ten o'clock tomorrow morning until two o'clock in the afternoon. We will take a recess until three-thirty o'clock then, and from three-thirty o'clock until seven-thirty Mr. Moss shall be allowed for his closing address. I adjourn now with the distinct agreement that counsel for the defense shall not exceed the time thus allotted to him and that the district attorney will bring his case to a close by seven-thirty o'clock."

Thus spake Justice Goff. It was certain then that the trial of Lieutenant Becker would be over on Wednesday, October 23. Goff would give his charge to the jury the following day, and some time on Thursday the case would be handed to the jury which would decide Becker's fate. The verdict would probably come by the end of the week. That was just fine with the lieutenant, who appeared nothing but confident as he left the courtroom.

"What can they do but acquit me?" he said, responding to a reporter's question. "What evidence has been brought against me other than that of crooks and thugs? I am confident of a complete vindication."

There might be nothing more diminishing to the spirit than to sit in silence while two strangers debate the value of one's life. The question of guilt or innocence is determined in the main by mental calculations—the testimony of one side weighed against the word of the other and viewed through the prism of reasonable doubt. But the stake is higher in a capital case. In 1912, New York law mandated the death penalty for anyone convicted of first-degree murder, and so the issue to be resolved was not merely guilt or innocence, but whether the defendant deserved to continue living or, in the interest of the community, he should be put to death. Police Lieutenant Charles Becker now sat stolidly, expressionless, as John F. McIntyre and Frank Moss each engaged the twelve men who would decide his future.

McIntyre went first. He began by invoking every defense attorney's most potent weapon. He explained to the jury, in detail, that it was their legal obligation to accord the defendant the benefit of every doubt. He noted specifically that in those instances where the evidence on each side is equally persuasive the construction most favorable to the defendant is the one that must be followed. The burden of proof was on the prosecution, he emphasized; Becker was innocent until the state proved otherwise.

Anticipating a backlash that might follow a calculated attack upon the district attorney, McIntyre cautioned the jury: "I will call things and persons by their right names. I will deal harsh blows and, after a full and candid discussion of this case, I will not then fear that I will bring down upon myself the censure of this jury. By your verdict this defendant will live or die. No other determination can be made."

McIntyre followed with an appeal to the call of patriotism and provincial loyalty. Becker, an officer of the law, was being accused by four men who had spent all their lives on the other side; gamblers and con artists, they had, after all, admitted to planning and implementing the crime for which the defendant was being tried. He said:

"I am defending an American, not a murderer. His accusers are vile, not lovers of the flag or the institutions under which we live, but a lawless and degenerate set reeking in filth and infamy. They have tarnished the fair name of a great city, a city more philanthropic and generous than any other in the world. . . . The district attorney has been misled, perhaps deceived, maybe actuated by ambition, and ambition often beclouds good judgment, to the end that he has fathered a prosecution framed-up by crooks. This trial had its birth in the hearts of four murderers—Rose, Webber, Vallon, and Schepps—self-confessed assassins, all of whom, when it is over, will be free men again in this city to again murder if they please."

The swipe at Whitman did not go unnoticed, nor would it go unanswered. McIntyre had warned at the start that he would "call things and persons by their right names," and he was as good as his word. Hardly a beat later, he leveled another broadside at the D.A.'s office. "The public mind had been inflamed," he said, by the accusations against Becker and the wanton slaying of Rosenthal. "Hysteria prevailed. Public clamor was rampant. The evidence shows that the district attorney didn't want small fry but big fish. Rose saw his opportunity, and the framing-up on Becker then starts."

McIntyre segued smoothly to the most critical holes in the state's case— the actual killers had not yet been tried or convicted, and the accusations of Becker's three presumed accomplices were corroborated by a man who himself was a co-conspirator.

"Remember," he told the jury, "there were four gunmen who killed Herman Rosenthal, that the four gunmen at the bar were the actual murderers. . . . Is it not extraordinary that we find Charles Becker here today and the four gunmen still untried? [If] three months from now the four gunmen will be arraigned and found not guilty, the case against Becker falls under the theory advanced by the prosecution. You've got Becker in the death house awaiting execution and the four men who did the shooting walking the streets of New York. Isn't the situation strange? Why weren't they tried first? Of course the district attorney had the right to nominate who was to be tried first, but why was it done as it is? Is it because the district attorney and his aides believe that if the four gunmen were tried first and acquitted he could not try Charles Becker?

"Isn't there a bit of legal juggling and jockeying in this case? Take that into consideration when you consider the guilt or innocence of this defendant. Before you can convict you must find that the four gunmen, all or one of them, must have committed the murder. How do you attempt to establish the gunmen as the murderers? There is no contention that Becker ever saw one of these gunmen in his life. There is not one scintilla of evidence that he knew anything of these gunmen."

In capsule fashion, McIntyre proceeded to discredit the state's key witnesses—Rose, "a self-confessed murderer"; Morris Luban, "a forger and a thief"; James Hallon, "an ex-convict again in Sing Sing." Noted for his soaring oratory and high emotion, McIntyre did not disappoint. He seemed to gain momentum as he went on, his voice rising and falling, his arms splayed at one point, drawn together at another. The members of the jury were as quiet and attentive as a choir during the pastor's sermon. But as morning turned to afternoon, McIntyre began to weaken. He had been on his feet and at full throttle for nearly three hours when he was forced to pause and catch his breath. He turned pale and drew his hands to his chest. He staggered for a moment and appeared about to collapse. Hart rushed to his side to steady him. McIntyre took a sip of water from the glass at the defense table, drew a deep breath, and resumed with no loss of vigor.

He soon turned his attention to Schepps, the state's corroborator, and reprised the defense testimony that pointed to his complicity. He read again Rose's letter to Schepps and Schepps's reply, which, he told the jury, showed how the conspiracy was being hatched by Rose, Webber, and Vallon in the West Side Prison and how they insisted that Schepps's help was needed and could buy him his freedom. He cited once more Schepps's statement to Acting Mayor Pettit of Hot Springs: "It is up to me to make the best bargain I can. One man confessed, another corroborates him, but it takes a third man to convict a fourth."

Now, approaching his finish, McIntyre reached back for whatever he had left. His voice trembling with passion, he pointed at Becker and roared in the direction of the jury: "Who is that fourth man? There he sits now. There is the man they framed-up at the instigation of Jack Rose . . ."

His voice growing somber and dramatic, sometimes not much louder than a whisper, he concluded: "Shall this man soon lie in his grave and these others walk the streets? Where is the corroborated evidence? It is only Luban and the men they brought from jail. Now, gentlemen, you have a grave and solemn duty, one of the most solemn duties that comes to any man. A man's life is in your hands. It means life or death to this defendant. The charge against him is murder, not graft, not bribery, and not extortion. When the time comes for him to answer he will defend himself against those charges. Don't confuse grafting, don't confuse bribery, and don't confuse extortion with this charge. I ask you to separate the various elements of this case. Look at this evidence they allege connects directly with murder. This is the last time that this defendant will be heard in his own behalf. It is the last time that I may speak to you, and I ask you to weigh the evidence as it has been produced."

It was a few minutes shy of two o'clock when McIntyre's summation came to an end. He was near exhaustion, physically and mentally. Court was adjourned until three-thirty. The jurors, their service approaching its end, retired to the jury room where their lunch would be served. The judge and the attorneys each went their own way. Becker would have his own lunch in the prisoner's pen on the second floor. He could not be looking forward to the afternoon session when he would listen as the district attorney called for his execution.

Unlike opening statements, closing arguments—or summations—can sometimes turn a jury in favor of one side or the other. Summations are heard after all the evidence has been presented and therefore are fresh in the minds of the jurors as they begin deliberations. Though far from perfect, McIntyre's closing was sound enough. He made certain that the jury understood that the burden of proof rested with the prosecution, that the defendant was being tried for murder and allegations of graft or extortion were not to be considered, and, in an emotional plea, he freighted the conscience of each juror with the awareness that a guilty verdict was the equal of a death sentence.

District Attorney Moss, for his part, was not much impressed with McIntyre's remarks. "The defense had been the usual defense to such cases," he told the jury. "But I should not say that it was an orderly or a good defense. Where the case is hard, the defense frequently consists largely in vilifying the prosecutor. This, in my experience, is always done when there seems to be no other way." He then proceeded with a point-by-point rebuttal of the defense's argument.

Clearly stung by McIntyre's charges that the district attorney had been feeding his personal ambition by pressing the case against Becker, Moss responded in angry but carefully measured tones: "Not once but half a dozen times, Mr. Whitman has been accused of such practice as would make him unfit for the office he holds were he guilty of it. He needs no defender, but in their relation to this trial, Mr. McIntyre's remarks are worthy of notice."

Addressing the inference that Whitman's true ambition was being elected governor, Moss noted that the D.A. did not attend the recently held Republican State Convention. "When men were gathered together there to strive for the prizes within the gift of the people," he said, "Mr. Whitman was here looking after this case."

As for the character of the state's witnesses, Moss asked, "Can we go into the reeking cesspool where this defendant lived and moved and get good people for witnesses? Do we not have to take them where the case sends us? . . . Are we to be blamed for the character of the witnesses? They were his associates— Jacob Rose, with whom he ate and to whose house he took his wife to eat." Were it not for the acceptance of Rose, Webber, and Vallon as witnesses under the stipulations offered by the state, Moss said, "there would have been no case against Becker and the murder would have remained a mystery."

The defense had made much of the fact that there was no hard evidence tying Becker to the crime, that he was twice removed from the men who had fired the shots. Moss pointed out that the law made no distinction between those who committed the murder and those who planned and orchestrated it. Under the blanket indictment, he said, it made no difference who fired the shots that killed Rosenthal, as "the hands of every one of the seven men in the indictment fired the shots . . . the men behind the guns were the four gunmen. The men behind the gunmen were Rose, Webber, and Vallon. But the will, the brain behind the whole conspiracy was Charles Becker, and he is as guilty, more guilty, than the men who fired the fatal shots, for it was he who directed the shots. . . . We should convict the will behind the brain behind the gunmen. . . . We need not worry about the gunmen. They will have their day in court. We shall go to the conspiracy.

"You cannot have forgotten the opening address of counsel. Again and again he alleged conspiracy. . . . Suppose Rose and Webber did have a murderous feeling toward Rosenthal, and Becker knew it. He looked over the city and found that they had that feeling for three years. Rose testified that he was uncertain and that Becker urged him on by saying horrible things supposed to be from Rosenthal's own mouth. But suppose that those men did hate Rosenthal, does that let Becker out?"

Having attempted to ease any doubts the jury might have had about convicting a man who had not played a direct part in the murder, about trusting the word of witnesses of doubtful character, Moss tackled the issue of corroboration. McIntyre had driven home the point that Becker could not be convicted without the corroboration of a witness who was not an accomplice in the commission of the crime. Moss spelled out the prosecution's contention that Schepps was such a witness.

"The three accomplices," he said, "must be corroborated, not in every detail, but by some evidence which tends to connect the defendant with the conspiracy which is charged. I do not say that Schepps was not a part of this situation. Schepps knew after the murder that Rosenthal had been killed as a result of a conspiracy in which his friend Rose was involved and of which Becker was at the head. Therefore, Schepps was an accessory after the fact. But this is a separate and distinct crime, altogether removed from murder and punishable in an entirely different way. It has nothing to do with the murder charge which rests against Becker. Murder in the first degree requires premonition. Schepps never thought of the murder of Herman Rosenthal, never desired the murder of Herman Rosenthal. Schepps did not know that the murder was to be committed. He knew it afterward, and this is where he becomes a criminal; he hid Rose after the murder."

Dusk had long ago settled over the city. The lights in the courtroom appeared to grow brighter. It was almost nine hours since court was convened. Moss's allotted time was nearly gone, and he closed with an appeal to the jury aimed at softening McIntyre's admonition about sending a man to his death.

"Although Lefty, Gyp, Whitey, and Dago Frank fired the shots; although Rose, Webber, and Vallon are participants, the man who is responsible is the man who urged the murder, the man who prostituted himself as a policeman is the man to be tried first and not the gunmen. To get a verdict we must have all of you twelve men. If we lose one, if you, through sympathy, through some idea of fraternalizing, hold out, you block the administration of law and order. If, when a crime is proved, a jury breaks down through temptation, pressure, or any circumstance, all the work of the police, the judge, and the prosecution is for nothing.

"Do not shirk that duty to render a verdict as you find it, but take the manly stand. If you acquit, that is your prerogative. If you think that it is proper to hold him accountable for this awful crime, in God's name, in the country's name, do your duty. The district attorney submits this case to you, asking a verdict of murder in the first degree."

Moss had concluded on time. It was just about seven-thirty. Court was adjourned until ten-thirty the following morning. When it reconvened, on Thursday, October 24, Justice Goff would instruct the jury on the law as it must be applied. The case would then become the property of the jury.

Goff could not help but know that his charge to the jury had to be pitch-perfect. He had appeared antagonistic to the defense early in the trial. His peremptory manner was by nature at odds with the flame and flourish of McIntyre's style, feeding the widely held notion that he favored the prosecution. On the last day of testimony, he had tried to compensate by recalling two defense witnesses and allowing them to respond to questions that had been barred during their first appearance. Now, measuring his words carefully, he spoke for more than three hours. He began with a generic explanation of a juror's duty as defined by the law, often echoing the admonitions in McIntyre's opening remarks:

"Under the law, a presumption of innocence remains with the defendant throughout the case until he be proved guilty. The defendant is not called upon to prove his innocence. It is for the prosecution to prove his guilt. The burden of this proof lies with the state. When all the evidence is in, if there be any reasonable doubt, it must be given to the defendant. You jurors are the exclusive judges of the evidence. The judge is the one who rules on all points of law, and you must abide by his ruling. The arguments of counsel not supported by evidence should not be given any weight.... The credibility of witnesses must be judged entirely and solely by you."

The judge then proceeded to comment on the specifics of the case at hand and to define the charge: "The defendant was at liberty to take the stand in his own defense, but the fact that he did not elect to do so must not be construed by you as testimony either of his guilt or of his innocence. . . . The charge against the defendant," he went on, "is murder in the first degree . . . which states that a crime must be planned deliberately and with premeditation. . . . If the evidence shows that there was time to consider the crime, then it shows that there was time for premeditation." So far as the degree of the crime was concerned, Goff told the jury specifically that if Becker was guilty, he was guilty of first-degree murder. If they believed the state's testimony, he said, "premeditation has been clearly shown."

As for the operative question of whether Becker was guilty as charged, Goff embarked on a lengthy, step-by-step re-creation of the crime, as presented by the prosecution. He noted that the state's case rested almost entirely on the testimony of Bald Jack Rose, and it was the story Rose told during his long hours of testimony that the judge recounted. It might have seemed, as Goff proceeded, that by repeating Rose's testimony the judge was validating its credibility. At the very least, he was refreshing the recollection of some jurors on details that might have grown hazy. Goff had, however, made his purpose explicit before beginning: "In view of the great length of this trial and the tremendous amount of testimony," he said, "I will relate to you a skeleton of the evidence, that evidence on which the state bases its case, the story of Jack Rose. . . . If you believe this story, you must bring in a verdict of guilty against the defendant."

But for ballast, Goff instructed the jury that if they found Rose's story unworthy of credence, Becker must be acquitted. He went on to call the jury's attention to the unseemly environment in which Rose lived and worked as a professional gambler and noted that his background must be taken into account when weighing his truthfulness. He also counseled that even if the jury believed that Becker had given instructions to the men who carried out the murder, he must be found not guilty if it was deemed possible that those directly responsible might have acted for their own purposes, independent of Becker's urging.

Goff then turned to the matter of corroboration. In painstaking detail, he explained the law that required the testimony of an accomplice to be

THE SUMMER OF 1912 was one of the hottest in New York City's history. Here, (top) children cool off by licking blocks of ice in front of a grocery store on the Lower East Side. [Bottom] Free shower baths were offered for horses, which outnumbered automobiles on the streets of the city. It was not unusual to see heat-stricken horses lying prostrate on the cobble-stoned streets.

THE LOWER EAST SIDE, its streets clogged with newly arrived immigrants, was the most densely populated area of the world in the early 1900s. Peddlers lined the streets while children searched for room to play.

(OPPOSITE PAGE) TIMES SQUARE, so named in 1904 when the Times Building opened, was known informally as the Tenderloin District. [Top] Already called the Great White Way, Broadway was lit brightly at night, with crowds gathered to see films projected outdoors from the top of the Times Building. At the near-left bottom is the New York Theatre. At the rear left (photo 1) is the Hotel Cadillac (43rd Street and Broadway), just a short distance from the Metropole, the site of the killing. It was from in front of the Cadillac that police set out in pursuit of the getaway car.

GETTING ON BROADWAY CAR

BIG JACK ZELIG, who some thought might testify for the state, was shot dead on a streetcar such as this two days before Becker's trial was to begin.

THE TOMBS, (opposite left side) on Centre Street in Lower Manhattan, was a forbidding, fortress-like structure that provided maximum security and minimal comfort for prisoners. It was connected to the Criminal Courts Building (right inset) by a second-story enclosed corridor called the Bridge of Sighs. Here (bottom) onlookers gather, hoping to catch a glimpse of Becker as he crosses over from the court-house to the prison.

THE TENDERLOIN POLICE STATION, at West 47th Street, was the headquarters from which Becker ran his graft-collection operation, known as the System. Here, a prisoner is booked at the front desk.

THE CITY'S DAILY NEWSPAPERS, more than a dozen in those days, covered the Becker case in great detail, competing with one another for any edge. Newsboys hawked the papers on the streets, shouting out current headlines or on occasion the long-since-forgotten cry of "Extra, Extra, read all about it."

CHARLES BECKER (center, marked by small "x") is ushered into Sing Sing by Sheriff Julius Harburger (center, with white moustache) and a cluster of deputies.

EFTY LOUIE AND GYP

e Blood led police on a
erry chase for two
onths, with reports
at they had been
potted everywhere
om Upstate New York
Colorado. They were
nally arrested in an
partment above a hand
undry in the Glendale
ection of Queens, just
ver the Brooklyn line.

THE FOUR GUNMEN are led to Sing Sing following their conviction and death sentences. The two men covering their faces are Whitey Lewis (right) and Dago Frank.

corroborated by the testimony of one who was not an accomplice and who could connect the defendant to the commission of the crime. He then stated specifically:

"I charge you that Rose, Webber, and Vallon are accomplices on their own confessions. About Schepps," he said, "I am in doubt." He acknowledged that "there is no question that after the murder Schepps had equal knowledge of the crime with the others. He knew the men concerned in it, and he was present at the payment of the money. He had guilty knowledge, but that does not make him an accomplice in the eyes of the law, and so I cannot thus charge. You must decide that for yourselves."

Goff concluded his charge by stating: "I have instructed you as to the rights of the defendant, and they must be observed. This defendant is on trial for murder and not for anything else. Whatever you find your duty to be, you must discharge it. If you believe his is innocent, your duty is to acquit him. If you believe he is guilty, it is your duty to so find. I charge you as sworn men to do your duty and do it as you feel it should be done."

The jury now had the case. The trial had lasted seventeen days. Ninety-eight witnesses had been heard; their testimony covered 2,745 pages. At two-thirty the jurors were taken to the Murray Hill Hotel for lunch. They returned around four o'clock and were locked in the jury room in back of the Supreme Court on the White Street side of the Criminal Courts Building. The streets around the courthouse soon filled with legions of the curious. A squad of police from the Elizabeth Street Station was needed to keep them from entering the building. White Street was the gathering place of choice, as the silhouettes of jurors could occasionally be seen through the four large, opaque glass windows, and now and again the voices of jurors could be heard in heated discussion. Becker waited in the sheriff's office on the fourth floor. Helen Becker, now thirty-eight years old and five months pregnant, waited with him.

The jury was out barely half an hour when they asked to see the documents from Hot Springs relating to Schepps's statements; they also requested Rose's confession. At six o'clock, word came that the jury wanted to review the stipulations between the district attorney and Rose, Webber, and Vallon. Speculation was that the requests favored acquittal. The jury, it seemed, was scrutinizing closely Schepps's role as corroborator and was giving careful consideration to the concessions made by the state in exchange for the testimony of the accomplices.

At eight o'clock, the jurors were served dinner by waiters who arrived in automobiles from the Murray Hill Hotel. The Beckers ate lightly—chicken sandwiches with coffee for the lieutenant and tea for Mrs. Becker. The wait continued. The heat in the building had been turned off, and many of those who remained donned overcoats against the chill of late October. As the hours passed, those who favored the defense grew optimistic. It was judged that long deliberations favored acquittal. But optimism was mixed with anxiety, and few were more anxious than Shapiro, Reich, and the four accused gunmen, all of whom waited in the Tombs. Warden Hanley told the press that these men would know the verdict just a shade later than Becker would hear it himself; it would travel through the prison, he said, faster than it could be transmitted by telegraph.

Justice Goff had spent the early evening at the Museum of Natural History listening to a lecture by Rodman Wanamaker, son of the merchandise prince John Wanamaker and celebrated aesthete and aviation pioneer. At about eleven-thirty, he returned to the courthouse and went directly to his chambers. Goff's arrival was a signal to the crowd waiting outside that a verdict might be at hand, and there ensued a mad rush to get inside the room. Ten minutes later, District Attorney Whitman entered the courtroom, followed almost immediately by the twelve jurors who filed in deliberately and took their seats in the jury box. Becker, escorted by two deputy sheriffs to the counsel table, took his place alongside McIntyre and the defense team. The court secretary rapped loudly on the rail to signal the judge's approach. Goff mounted the bench, bowed to the jury, and took his seat. The court clerk called the roll. After each man answered to his name, the clerk turned to the jury and asked, "You have found a verdict, gentlemen?" Foreman Harold Skinner said, "We have." "How do you find?" the clerk asked. Skinner hesitated for an instant, and it seemed as if time had stopped. Then Skinner announced, in a tone that exuded conviction, "We find the defendant guilty as charged in the indictment."

Becker was plainly stunned. He looked like a man who had been struck by a sucker punch. He had been confident of acquittal, and now he did not know how to react. He swallowed hard, and his mouth opened as if he were about to cry out. He made a visible effort to steady himself. He fixed a hard gaze at the jury as each member responded "It is" to the question "Is that your verdict?" But his body betrayed him. He appeared to be sagging slowly. He grabbed the rail behind him to steady himself. Two court attendants approached from either side, and each took hold of an arm. Still resolute, still defiant, Becker stiffened and hung on for the next few minutes until Goff announced that court was adjourned.

Helen Becker was among the last to get the news. She had remained outside when her husband was summoned to the courtroom and then found herself locked out. The stampeding crowd had filled the room to capacity, and the doors were bolted before she could enter. Police from the local precinct pounded on the door but got no response. They brought her a chair, and there she sat, her head pressed against the wall. Her sister and brother-in-law waited with her. She learned of the verdict when the doors flew open and she heard a shout of "Guilty" as reporters rushed for the telephones. She rose from her chair, swayed for an instant, and then fell to the ground. When she revived, she was taken to the prison floor where she rested on a bench until she regained her composure. She then gave a statement to the press: "I was so shocked. I could not believe it. To think that this thing has happened to my husband. It seems impossible." McIntyre offered words of encouragement: "There is not the slightest doubt that there will be a reversal of this verdict in a higher court. I cannot and will not say anything more."

Sentencing was scheduled for Wednesday, October 30. It would simply be a matter of form; New York State law mandated a penalty of death for murder in the first degree. Still, the courtroom could not hold the number of people who crowded to get in. The court attendants were unable to close the doors. When the court secretary signaled the approach of the judge, those seated were squeezed so tight they had difficulty rising. Outside the courtroom, the corridors were jammed, and those who could get no closer climbed the stairs to the sheriff's office on the floor above.

Though the outcome was known, the inevitable held its own degree of fascination. Not every day did one have the opportunity to observe at close hand the reaction of a man who was to be told when, where, and how he was to die. Becker, for his part, gave them little to take with them. He had prepared himself well for the moment. The verdict had taken him by surprise, but now he knew what to expect, and he stood unflinching and erect as the district attorney, without ever looking directly at him, rose and said, "I move that the court pronounce sentence upon the defendant in accordance with the verdict." Becker remained silent when asked if he had anything to say about why the sentence of the court should not be carried out. He stood equally unbowed and without apparent emotion as Justice Goff, in solemn tones, read the death penalty statute from the volume before him.

With no further business before it, court was adjourned. Two deputies led Becker across the Bridge of Sighs to his cell in the Tombs. There he would gather up some personal items and prepare for the trip upstate. He was headed for the death house at Sing Sing.

The Appeal:

Retrial and

Execution

Sing Sing was among a generation of prisons that became part of America's folklore. Their names alone—Alcatraz, Dannemora, Attica, San Quentin— were enough to conjure visions of leather-tough wardens and defiantly resourceful inmates. No one called them correctional institutions; they were designed to punish, and no one pretended otherwise. In the argot of the time, they were referred to as the Big House, the pen, the slammer, the lock-up. Sing Sing, which opened in 1828, was among the oldest of these fortress-like structures. It was located on the banks of the Hudson River, about fifty miles north of New York City, in the municipalities of Sing Sing, named after an Indian tribe called the Sint Sinck. The name of the town was changed to Ossining in 1901; the prison's name remained unchanged.

From early on, Sing Sing had been associated with the electric chair.

The "chair," as it was called colloquially, had replaced hanging as the prevailing form of execution in 1890. It was invented by Edwin R. Davis, an electrician at Auburn Prison in Upstate New York and was used for the first time—on August 6, 1890—on a convicted axe-murderer named William Kemmler. By the time Becker arrived, Davis had left Auburn for Sing Sing and attained the lofty position of official executioner.

Becker found his new accommodations even less inviting than those at the Tombs. His cell was seven feet long; three feet, three inches wide; and six feet, seven inches high. His cot was three feet wide and six feet long, several inches shorter than his body. Perhaps even more disquieting was his cell's location, only a few feet from the entrance to the execution chamber. Those who occupied such cells could not help but hear the sounds of the macabre ritual of death from beginning to end. One convict, who was exonerated and freed after spending many years in the death house, said those sounds had never stopped troubling his sleep.

Becker arrived at his new home at about one-twenty in the afternoon on Wednesday, October 30. It was just a few hours since he had been sentenced. A prison van had been waiting for him when he left the Tombs. He was escorted by Sheriff Julius Harburger and four of his deputies. A throng of onlookers watched as the van passed through the iron gates of the Tombs and headed north on Lafayette Street. It continued uptown on Fourth Avenue, turned left on Forty-third Street to Lexington Avenue, and finally pulled up at the Forty-fifth Street entrance to Grand Central Station. Becker was led into the baggage room and taken by freight elevator to the train level. A combination baggage and smoking car had been reserved for the prisoner and his cortege on train 83, which was known as the Peekskill local. Already on board were Becker's wife, Helen, and his brother John and his wife.

Becker took a window seat six rows from the front of the car; Helen sat next to him. Deputy Sheriff Carroll, to whom Becker was handcuffed, flipped the back of the seat in front of Becker so that the two men faced each other. Helen asked if the manacles could be removed. Becker pleaded his case to Carroll: "Please take these off," he said. "It's all right, I won't try to run away." With Harburger's consent, Carroll obliged. His left arm now free, Becker draped it over his wife's shoulders, and they rode that way until the train neared its destination. Helen had appeared stalwart throughout the trip, but as the train passed through the tunnel that led to the edge of the prison grounds, she began to break down. She was sobbing freely. Becker pulled her to him. "Little woman," he said, "keep up your spirits. We'll beat this case yet, and then we'll go far away and begin things all over again."

When the train came to a stop, the deputies drew Becker away from his wife, gently. Together with her brother- and sister-in-law, Helen took a cab to the prison, arriving well ahead of her husband. Becker was again shackled to Carroll who flanked him on one side and, with Harburger on the other, they started walking toward the prison, about two hundred yards away. They climbed four flights of wooden stairs leading to the upper roadway which ran into Sing Sing. Becker's step was quick, almost jaunty. He offered no outward sign that he was heading for a cell in death row that might be his final destination.

At the prison door, he was met by the warden, John Kennedy, who led him down four stone steps into the prison. Still cuffed to Carroll, he was then ushered through four doors, which, in succession, clanged shut behind him and were immediately locked. Finally, they arrived at the office of Head Keeper Connaughton, where custody was transferred from the sheriff to the prison guards.

"Well," Harburger said, "goodbye and good luck. I've tried to do my duty as gently as possible."

"I know that," Becker said, "and some day I hope I'll have the chance to reciprocate."

The sheriff handed Connaughton the death certificate and was given a receipt in return. One of the deputies nodded in the direction of Connaughton and said, "He'll treat you all right, Charley."

"I know that, old man," Becker said.

Connaughton started to speak: "I'm sorry," he said, but Becker cut him off. "No one is more sorry than I am," he said.

Next, Becker was taken to the bathroom where he was stripped, bathed, and dressed in the dark-colored suit that was standard issue for men in the death house. On the way to his cell, he passed the warden's office where Helen had been waiting. The door was half open and, catching a glimpse of her husband as he went by, Helen cried out, "Charley, Charley! Oh, please let me see him." But it was too late. His wife's words echoing in his head, Becker was taken to his cell. Her cries were drowned out by the sound of the door slamming shut behind him.

Although his execution was to be scheduled for the week of December 9, Becker would be granted an automatic six-month stay to allow him to appeal his conviction. McIntyre, though in failing health, had started preparing the appeal immediately after the verdict was handed down. Just one day later, he cited ten major grounds on which the appeal would be based:

The testimony of Rose, Webber, Vallon, and Schepps had not been corroborated by credible evidence. In a capital case, he pointed out, the Court of Appeals reviews the facts as well as the law and will decide whether or not the accomplices were lying.

If a conspiracy to kill Rosenthal existed, it ended with the commission of the crime; therefore, any discussion of such a conspiracy that took place after the fact should have been barred. The Court of Appeals, he said, previously had ruled that conspirators cannot testify about a conspiracy after its consummation.

Justice Goff had refused to charge the jury that before they could convict Becker it must be proved beyond a doubt that the four gunmen, or one or all of them, did the killing.

The "conspiracy meetings" between Becker and Rose at the Union Square Hotel and in Rose's house should not have been allowed in as evidence since the testimony regarding them was circumstantial and not sufficient to corroborate a conspiracy charge.

The jury should have been instructed that according to the evidence Schepps was an accomplice, not a corroborator.

The trial judge read a skeleton of the state's evidence to the jury while excluding testimony given by witnesses for the defense.

The judge should not have instructed the jury that the hostility that Rose and Webber felt toward Rosenthal did not in any way exculpate Becker.

There were discrepancies between Rose's written confession and the testimony he gave from the witness stand.

The state's offer of immunity through stipulations was motive enough for the accomplices to testify against Becker.

The "public clamor and hysteria" influenced the jury, making it impossible for Becker to get a fair trial.

McIntyre also maintained that the jury had given short shrift to consideration of the evidence. "Taking out the time spent at meals and traveling back and forth," he said, "the jury did not put more than four hours into consideration of the evidence contained in the 4,500 pages of typewritten record. It stands to reason that that time was not sufficient."

The jury, it was learned later, had taken three ballots. The first vote was eight-to-four for murder in the first degree, with the minority voting for a second-degree murder conviction. The second ballot was ten-to-two and the third was unanimous in favor of murder-one. At no time did any juror vote for acquittal.

While outlining his case for appeal, McIntyre stated for the record that he had great respect for Goff and was not accusing the justice of conducting an unfair trial. "I do not mean to reflect on the actions or rulings of Justice Goff," he told the press, "for whom personally I have always cherished pleasant feelings. I regret if the newspapers made me appear to be bullying or discourteous to him, but I was only trying to safeguard to the utmost every interest of my client. If Justice Goff's rulings are in any way open to criticism, it is for the Court of Appeals to say so, not for me."

Whatever respect McIntyre might have harbored for Goff personally, it certainly did not extend to the judge's conduct on the bench. He had taken more than four thousand exceptions to Goff's rulings, and they were part of the record that would be submitted to the Court of Appeals. McIntyre's remarks, it was safe to say, were more a bow to prudence than an expression of respect, for the trial judge plays no small part in the tortuous appeal process that could take a year or more before ever reaching the court. Goff would review the whole case before it was placed on file, and while he could hardly be expected to view the appeal with favor, McIntyre understood that it was best not to invite his hostility.

The trial judge was in a compromised position when it came to an appeal, for appeals are, in most instances, a referendum on the way in which the judge conducted the trial. The appeals court considers no new evidence; it determines whether the defendant had a fair trial by searching the record for reversible error. It is understandable, then, if the judge, a presumed pillar of neutrality, becomes something of a partisan during the appeal process; a reversal of the trial court's verdict suggests that he had somehow failed in his trust to administer justice in equal measure to both sides.

Becker's appeal would be heard by the full court since it was a capital case, and the outcome would be decided by majority vote. If the appeal was upheld, the guilty verdict would be overturned and Becker granted a new trial. McIntyre sounded a note of optimism. "The Court of Appeals," he said, "more than any jury, is jealous in its guarding of a man's rights." It is unaffected, he said, by the public fervor that could not have helped but influence the conduct of the trial and the judgment of the jury.

Becker, too, appeared confident. "They have convicted an innocent man," he told newspaper reporters. "I can prove this, and I will do it when I get another chance. . . . I am not through yet, the case is not over. I will get out and show the people of this city that there is not the slightest truth in the charge of which I have been convicted. My vindication will be complete. I feel certain that there will be a new trial and a different verdict."

His new trial was more than a year in the future, and Becker would have to face down many difficulties until then, not the least of which was his depleted bank account. The original trial had been costly. According to McIntyre, it had cost Becker about $23,000, which was all he and his wife had. McIntyre said that his and his colleagues' fees had been modest but that other expenses, such as independent investigations, stenographers' fees, and travel expenses had been enough to make it necessary for Becker to take out a mortgage on his home. The accounting of Becker's finances was more than incidental, for it raised the question: If he had been raking in large sums from illegal gambling operations, where had the money gone?

The cost of an appeal and the prospect of a new trial would further strain Becker's resources, but it was an issue that was not likely to affect McIntyre. The head of Becker's defense team was ailing, and the emotional and physical strain of the trial had pushed him close to the edge. Shortly after Becker's conviction, McIntyre laid the ground for his withdrawal from the case. Looking gaunt, and clearly exhausted, he announced that he might never try another case. "I myself am completely broken down under the stress of this trial and my physician orders me to leave the city at once. I cannot sleep, and the weakness of my heart, of which I have only now been apprised, makes it impossible for me to take any drugs to bring sleep artificially." In any event, Becker was reluctant to entrust his fate to a man who might not have the stamina to endure a protracted struggle; the search for new counsel was begun.

Hart, who had been Becker's attorney of record, withdrew from the case just days after its conclusion and left to practice law in California. McIntyre denied reports that he too would be retiring, but on Saturday, November 2, Supreme Court Justice Samuel Seabury signed an order making Joseph A. Shay Becker's attorney of record. Shay, who was predominantly a negligence lawyer, had worked briefly with McIntyre on a well-publicized murder case before returning to his accident practice. His professional record was not spotless. He had been suspended for a year after he admitted paying ambulance chasers to bring him clients. At first take, Shay seemed an odd choice to formulate an appeal in a murder case, but McIntyre, apparently having regained some vigor after a week's rest, assured all who would listen that he was still at the helm and that he would be working closely with Shay.

"The report that I am out of the case," he said, "did not emanate from Becker, any member of his family, myself, or anyone else identified with the Becker defense. It emanated from a hostile source and is entirely false. I am still in charge of the defense and will be back in my office working on the appeal papers Monday."

While the defense was preparing its appeal, there was still some legal business pending that could influence the outcome of Becker's case: The four accused gunmen were yet to be tried. Immediately after Becker's conviction, they had sent their attorney, Charles G. F. Wahle, to the district attorney to sound him out regarding a plea bargain. But Whitman, flushed with victory in a grueling and far more difficult case, was of no mind to compromise. Rumors that one or more of the gunmen was ready to turn state's evidence in exchange for leniency were denied by Wahle's law partner, H. L. Kringel, who would be second-chair at the defense table.

"There will be no confession from any of these men," Kringel said, "and the story that they are in mortal fear and all that is utter rot. They are still confident, and when the time comes they will present a defense that will surprise a lot of people."

The trial was set to begin on Friday, November 8. At the request of their attorneys, the four men were to be tried individually, with either Whitey Lewis or Lefty Louie to go first. The defense obviously felt that the case against those two was weakest, and if one of them could win an acquittal it would accrue to the benefit of the others.

The prosecution, appearing indifferent to the tactics of the defense, focused its attention on William Shapiro, the driver of the gray murder car. About a week before the trial was to start, Whitman met separately with Shapiro and his attorney, Aaron J. Levy. Shapiro was brought to the D.A.'s office from his cell in the West Side Prison, and spent two hours discussing the case with Whitman. As he had done before, Shapiro corroborated the stories told by Rose, Webber, Vallon, and Schepps, but he also added something of great value to the state; he identified the four defendants as the men he chauffeured from Bridgey Webber's poker room to the Metropole and then whisked away from the murder scene. Also for the first time, he confirmed the contentions of Vallon and Schepps that they had not entered the car after the murder and that neither of them was the man who held a gun to his head and told him to speed their departure from the Metropole. Shapiro's testimony would be critical, for he was the only prosecution witness who could identify all four men.

Despite the difficulty of his position, Wahle exuded confidence. While he declined to elaborate, he hinted that developments at the trial would provide surprising new details and that the murder would be shown in an entirely new light. As for the defendants, they offered their own views in a joint statement:

"There is no truth in the stories published in the evening papers that we are going to confess. We have nothing to confess. We are innocent. We had nothing to do with the Rosenthal murder, and that will be proved to the satisfaction of any twelve men who are selected to decide our fate. We did not know Becker and do not know Becker, and had nothing to do with him in any way, shape or manner.

"Our innocence will be established by the testimony of law-abiding people and not by self-confessed criminals. We are not looking for any pleas. There is no need of it. We want to go to trial because we can prove our innocence and will be free men at the end of the trial. There are no differences between us and we are all in entire harmony."

Whitman, for his part, paid little heed to the defendants' declarations of innocence. He was certain he had what he needed to win convictions, and his future never seemed brighter. He was being honored and praised and heralded as a political force whose options were without limit. Good fortune seemed to come his way from every direction, sometimes in shapes that would not reveal themselves until much later. Three days before the start of the trial, on Tuesday, November 5, Woodrow Wilson was elected president in a landslide. He received 409 electoral votes to 107 for Teddy Roosevelt, who ran on the Bull Moose party line. The incumbent, President William Howard Taft, won only 15. In the Democratic sweep, William Sulzer, Tammany's candidate, was elected governor of New York. Though he did not know it at the time, Sulzer's election would help shape Whitman's future.

20

On the day before the trial was to start, the defense team for the four gunmen announced a fundamental change in strategy: the men would be tried together rather than in separate trials. The switch was urged by Wahle, accepted by the defendants, and welcomed by the prosecution. Wahle said he had several good reasons for making the change but declined to elaborate. Whitman, on the other hand, could not have been more pleased. A single trial simplified matters for the state; it eliminated the possibility that a defendant might alter his story if it proved ineffective in an earlier trial, and it nullified the uncertainty that attends the seating of each new jury. Perhaps the greatest benefit to the prosecution was the critical matter of eyewitness identification. The testimony of the informers—all of whom had denied being present at the time of the shooting—would not, on its own, have been sufficient to win convictions. The state was obliged to produce witnesses who could place the defendants at the scene, and only Shapiro was able to identify all four of them. Whitman felt that the cumulative effect of having Shapiro testify that he had driven them all to and from the murder scene would have a greater impact than naming each individually; in separate trials, he would have been allowed to identify only the defendant. Furthermore, by putting the four men on trial together, the defense had acknowledged an umbilical connection among them—they were all either guilty or innocent.

As a consequence, testimony by a witness who could identify only one of the men would indirectly implicate the others. So the decision to try them all together appeared to offer a distinct advantage to the district attorney with no tangible benefit to the defense.

From the very beginning, there was something mechanically precise about the way the trial played out. There was little contention between prosecution and defense. It was as if they had agreed that it was in the best interest of all concerned to move forward expeditiously and with minimal rancor. Aside from the facts of the case as presented to they jury, what suited one side was often good enough for the other. The first five jurors, selected from a special panel of two hundred, were chosen in a matter of hours. The state used only six of its peremptory challenges; the defense used five. Things moved a bit more deliberately on the second day, but when it was done a full jury—consisting mostly of men beyond middle age—had been seated. The defendants had taken an active part in the selection, often conferring with their attorneys. They were pleased with the results and seemed confident of the outcome. When court adjourned, they gave every appearance of having already been acquitted. They were laughing and chatting lightly with the press. Gyp the Blood and Lefty Louie, speaking for all of them, offered this statement for publication:

"All we want is a square deal. Any reasonable jury will have to acquit us on the testimony that will be brought out. We are sure of acquittal." They asked the reporters for their cooperation. "For the sake of the effect on the public, we hope sincerely that the newspapers will give a good showing to our side of the case. It will be worth it." And they closed with an invitation: "We'll be out of here by Thanksgiving. Come and have a drink with us then. We'll be ready for one by that time."

On the first day of testimony, Tuesday, November 12, the defendants sauntered into the courtroom with the ease of men who had come to pay their respects and were now preparing for a celebration. Their air of assurance contrasted oddly with the attitude of the prosecution, which was one of quiet, almost casual resolve. The district attorney had made no secret of the fact that he believed the gunmen's trial would be little more than a victory parade after the trench warfare needed to convict Becker.

In his brief opening statement, Moss outlined much the same case that the state had presented against Becker. The routine witnesses—the policemen on the scene who testified there was a shooting and the coroner who assured the jury that the victim was Rosenthal and that we was indeed dead—were followed by the marginal ones—Louis Krause, the waiter who had happened on the scene and Jacob Hecht, the waiter at the Metropole—who again made their identifications of one or more of the gunmen. But they were no more than bit players who warmed up the jury for the introduction of the state's star witness. To emphasize the importance of the testimony to be given, District Attorney Whitman, who had not appeared at the trial since the selection of the jury, came forward to conduct the direct examination.

William Shapiro, still under indictment for murder, had not testified at Becker's trial, but he was ready now. Built like an NFL nose guard, low to the ground but wide and hard, he looked far more intimidating than any of the men he had been fearful of identifying. As he leaned forward on the witness stand, his forearms, resting on his knees, seemed to pulse with power, and his hands looked strong enough to crush the skull of any of the defendants without thought or effort. Yet he still appeared nervous and tentative. His voice was thin, his eyes filled with dread, as if he had glimpsed the specter of an unhappy ending and did not know how to turn it away. He freely admitted that he would not be testifying if Big Jack Zelig were alive. "These are his boys," he said. "I'd be killed as sure as I say a word," he told the D.A. "My life wouldn't be worth a cent when I leave prison." But Zelig was safely dead, and Whitman led him gently through his whole story, from the first call for his car through the flight from the murder scene.

Shapiro told the court that his night began when he was summoned from his stand at the Café Boulevard and told to go to Sharkey's on Fourteenth Street. There, he picked up Rose, Vallon, and Schepps and drove them to Seventh Avenue and 145th Street. Schepps got out, rang a doorbell, and returned to the car with Dago Frank, whom he identified for the jury. With Frank aboard, he drove to Bridgey Webber's poker room on Forty-second and Sixth. The passengers exited the car, and about twenty minutes later, "Dago Frank came back down with Gyp, Lefty, and Whitey and told me Rose wanted me to drive them to Forty-third Street." At this point, Whitman asked the witness if he could identify the other men. With the district attorney beside him, Shapiro rose, walked to the defense table, and pointed to each as he named them: "Gyp, Lefty, Whitey, Dago."

When he returned to the stand, Shapiro continued: "Frank told me to drive around the corner, and I turned into Sixth Avenue, driving north to Forty-third Street and then turned westward and drove almost to Broadway."

Whitman asked, "Did you hear any conversation among the men after they entered the car?"

"Yes," Shapiro said, "I heard Dago Frank say, 'Everything is all right. There are no cops around. Becker said so.'"

The four men left the car and crossed the street to the Metropole, Shapiro said. He waited there for fifteen to twenty minutes and then heard several shots. "I looked around and I saw the four men running toward the car. Two of them had revolvers in their hands. Two got in one side of the car and two got in at the other. Gyp the Blood stuck a gun against my head and said, 'Drive on, you boob. Get out of here.'" Shapiro said he drove back up to Harlem where the gunmen abandoned the car and went their own way.

There was little Wahle could do under cross-examination except try to impair the credibility of the witness. But Shapiro dulled the impact of the attorney's attack by volunteering that he had lied to Deputy Commissioner Dougherty when he said he did not know who his passengers were. "I was afraid to tell," he said, but Wahle objected, and the remark was stricken from the record. Whitman, however, understood that Shapiro's reason for lying was critical, and he waited for the opportunity to redirect. Then he asked, "You said you didn't identify these men before. Why?"

"I was afraid I would be killed," Shapiro said. He explained that it was at his mother's urging that he finally decided to identify his passengers.

The prosecution had almost finished presenting its case, but it was late in the day, and the testimony of Jack Rose had yet to be heard. He would be the state's lead witness the following day, telling largely the same story he told at Becker's trial, but with far less emotion. He appeared entirely detached as he repeated his lines in staccato fashion, like an actor giving his second performance of the day, weary of his part and working now just for the paycheck. Wahle had no more luck shaking him from his story than McIntyre had had. He was not even rewarded by Rose with a show of temper. The witness was on the stand until after four P.M., and it was past six when the state rested and Wahle opened his defense.

His first priority was to strip from his clients the image of bloodless killers that had been projected at Becker's trial. They were, after all, young men, still in their early twenties, and they did not have about them the look of menace that might have warned of trouble ahead. Of course, the names they were known by did not suggest choirboy backgrounds, and Wahle made it a point to use their legal names throughout the proceedings: Gyp the Blood was referred to as Harry Horowitz; Dago Frank was Frank Cirofici; Lefty Louie was Louis Rosenberg; and Whitey Lewis, legally Jacob Seidenschner, had enough aliases to make choosing one difficult, but Wahle settled on Lewis Muller. In a subdued tone, earnest and at times pleading, he told the jury:

"It is fitting that you should hear that these men are not monsters in human shape, but are simply four young men, one of them scarcely more than a boy (Lefty Louie had just turned twenty-one), bad without question of a doubt, wicked without question of a doubt, each of them, but far, very far from such depths of crime as might culminate in the commission of murder."

Wahle offered brief profiles of each of them and then outlined the defense's version of Beansie Rosenthal's murder which concluded with Webber, Vallon, and a shadowy figure called Itzky doing the shooting while the defendants watched from close range. The tale would be told in detail by Gyp and corroborated by his three co-defendants.

Twenty-four years old and a bit more polished than the others, Gyp assumed his role as narrator with an ease of manner that surprised many observers. Slight of build and dressed in a brown suit and high collar, he looked as natty as Jack Rose when he took the stand, and his looks were no deception. He was composed and cool during direct examination and unflappable under the aggressive cross of the district attorney.

Wahle led him through his story step by step, careful to omit no pertinent detail. Gyp testified that he had known Zelig for about three months before Big Jack was killed, that he had known Rose, Webber, and Schepps for about a month before the Rosenthal murder, and that he had not met Vallon until the morning that Rosenthal was shot. On the night of the murder, Gyp said, he, Whitey, and Lefty were at the International Café on Second Avenue, the same café where Zelig had been arrested, when Lefty received a phone call. The caller, whom Gyp did not name, asked them to come to Webber's poker room. They arrived at about eleven o'clock. Already there were Rose, Dago Frank, Schepps, Vallon, and Itzky, the nebulous stranger who was becoming an increasingly significant presence. According to Gyp, Rose called them over and said:

"Listen here, boys, I brought you here because you accused me of framing up Zelig. I am going to prove to you that I had no hand in it. I am going to introduce you to the officers that arrested Zelig to show you that they are [Police Inspector Edward] Hughes's men, not Becker's."

Then, Gyp said, Webber told him, Lefty, and Whitey to order any refreshments they liked, and the rest of them went outside. About fifteen minutes later, Itzky returned and asked them to come with him to the Metropole. He said Detectives Steinert and White would be there and would assure them that Rose had nothing to do with Zelig's arrest. Itzky left them in front of the nearby Cadillac Hotel and walked over to where Rose, Webber, Vallon, and Schepps were waiting. Dago Frank had gone home. Here's what Gyp said happened next:

"They walked over toward us. Webber and Vallon walked in front and Schepps and Rose walked behind. The stranger was on one side. They got near the Metropole when all of a sudden I heard shots and saw Webber and Vallon and the stranger firing from revolvers."

Then, Gyp said, he, Lefty, and Whitey fled the scene. They ran to the Times Square subway station, took a train to Ninety-sixth Street, transferred to a Lenox Avenue train and continued uptown to Dago Frank's Harlem apartment. After giving his description of the murder, Gyp went on to deny virtually every statement made by Rose—he had not met with him at the Lafayette Baths, he had not gone with him to the Garden Restaurant on the night of the aborted murder attempt, he had never discussed with him plans to kill Rosenthal. In fact, Gyp said, he had not seen or spoken with Rose from the first night he met him, on June 3, until the night Rosenthal was slain. Clearly pleased with Gyp's testimony and the manner in which he delivered it, Wahle turned the witness over to Moss for cross-examination. He would be no less satisfied when Moss was done with him, for Gyp was quick enough to parry most of the Assistant D.A.'s thrusts.

Asked about his flight after the shooting, Gyp said that he and Lefty had gone to Kingston, then to Monticello and Parkville before returning to

Brooklyn and finally to the Queens apartment where they were arrested. He said they had considered giving themselves up but then thought better of it. Moss asked if they had learned of Dago Frank's arrest when they returned to New York. Gyp seemed to relish the opportunity to respond: "That's just the point," he said laughing. "He wasn't arrested until we got back. That's one reason we didn't give ourselves up. He wasn't even at the shooting, and still they arrested him." Moss bit again. If he and Lefty knew Frank was innocent, why didn't they come to his defense? Because, Gyp explained, Frank could not get himself freed and there was less evidence against him than there was against him and Lefty. What chance did they have?

Moss got him to admit that he had lied to Deputy Police Commissioner Dougherty when he was arrested, but Gyp had more to say on the subject, and it caught Moss off guard. Dougherty, Gyp said, had urged him to "squeal" before the others did. Then, looking directly at Moss, he added: "You offered me immunity if I confessed." Moss was stunned. "Stop that now," he said. "Not another word. Stop that." But Gyp persisted: "Yes, you did, you know you did." Moss appealed to Justice Goff to quiet the witness, and Gyp, savoring the moment, smiled and apologized.

Finally, Moss asked if Gyp and the others had suspected that they were being lured to the Metropole so they could be framed. "No," Gyp said. "When they began to shoot I thought they were shooting at us. It wasn't until we read in the papers that Rosenthal had been killed that we realized what the shooting had meant."

The three other defendants followed Gyp to the stand and told the same story without variation. Wahle then called fifteen corroborative witnesses who, as a group, damaged the defense's case as much as they helped it. For their recollection of events and identification of faces varied one from the other, and Moss found it easy enough to discredit much of their testimony. Still, Wahle felt that the story the defendants told and the manner in which they told it had been convincing. The last of them to testify, Dago Frank, had in many respects been the most impressive. He was polite at all times and gave the impression of being cooperative, attentive and, above all, truthful. Wahle watched the jury intently, and he believed he detected a note of trust in their expressions while the defendants were on the stand. He rested his case on Friday, November 15, certain that things had gone as well as one might have hoped.

The story advanced by the defense was no less plausible than the one it was designed to counter. In effect, the accused had accused the accusers, and the accusers—Rose, Webber, Vallon, and Schepps—had all confessed to playing a part in the murder of Rosenthal. It did not strain the imagination to think that, together with a professional gunman named Itzky, they might have done the job themselves, rather than hire four killers connected to an underworld figure as imposing as Big Jack Zelig. Itzky, consistently referred to in the press as "the mysterious stranger," had been mentioned several times during Becker's trial, but now he had become a central figure. He was, it was soon learned, a real person. The *Times* carried a story citing him as a confederate of Lefty and one of a nine-man band of robbers who had been cited in a court record kept by General Sessions Judge Edward Swann. He was described as being about twenty-six years old, five-feet-ten, with thick curly hair, a straight nose, and an exceptional chest expansion. The court record included an address on Humboldt Street in Brooklyn, but he was never named, nor was he arrested or even picked up for questioning. Not for nothing was he called the mysterious stranger.

But with or without Itzky, the defense had spun a scenario that was as credible as the one offered by the state. There was, however, one question that had not been addressed: If Rose had planned to have Itzky, Webber, and Vallon do the shooting, why would he have invited the four defendants to the Metropole to witness the murder? It was a question that might have eluded the district attorney, but Justice Goff had taken note, and the issue would be raised later, with telling effect.

Though obviously pleased with his clients' performance, Wahle would see his case tipped off balance before it ended. On the final day of testimony, the prosecution called thirteen rebuttal witnesses to refute the evidence offered by the defense. They included Deputy Commissioner Dougherty and Alva Johnston, a reporter for the *Times,* both of whom testified that the gunmen had contradicted statements they had made earlier, as well as the four informers, who emphatically repeated the story they had told earlier. There was little Wahle could do by way of salvage. He called no witnesses in sur-rebuttal. When Moss announced that the prosecution rested, Wahle simply echoed him: "The defense rests," he said.

A total of forty-three witnesses—twenty-four for the prosecution—had been called in five days of testimony which ended on Saturday, November 16. Wahle spent all day Sunday preparing a review of the defense for Goff to read to the jury. McIntyre had not provided the judge with such a review in Becker's behalf, and Goff's instructions to the jury focused almost exclusively on the case presented by the state. Many critics, most prominently Becker himself, had ascribed his conviction largely to what they believed was a one-sided charge to the jury. Some reasoned that the defense's omission might have been calculated for future advantage; that an appeal could be based, at least in part, on a slanted jury-charge. However, the gunmen's trial had been much shorter and less contentious than Becker's, and Wahle presumed there was less likelihood of the kind of judicial error that could prompt an appeal. He decided to place his bet on an acquittal at the trial level.

In summing up to the jury, Wahle had made Rose the center of the murder conspiracy. "He is the crux of the issue here," he said. "His is the brain which conceived this diabolical plot which, he asks you to believe, resulted in the killing by these four men of a man they had never seen. He was the guiding hand, the hand which pulled the triggers of whatever weapons may have discharged into the body of Herman Rosenthal the bullets which killed him."

Goff, too, saw Rose as the pivot on which the case turned. The problem for the defense was that the judge believed what Rose had asked him to believe, and he made it plain in his instructions to the jury. He, seemed, in fact, to suggest that Rose's credibility should be the determining factor in reaching a verdict.

"Take the testimony of Rose," he said. "He admitted that he was an agent and had got the men who performed the murder. Gentlemen, that is a remarkable situation. Take Rose's manner and carefully examine him. Do you believe Rose was the man who actually shot Rosenthal? Do you believe there is any foundation but truth in his charge against these defendants? Bear in mind, gentlemen, that Rose did not say he saw these men shoot Rosenthal. He testified he laid down on a couch in Webber's poker parlor. He did not see the shooting. Would he have stopped short before the culmination of the plot by lying down and failing to take a position where he could see the prisoners actually do the shooting? These comments are made without any prejudice on either side of the case."

Goff then introduced the question that had not been raised at trial: "If the defendants' contention is true that Rose and his companions shot Rosenthal, would Rose have invited them around to the Metropole to see the shooting? Is it reasonable? Is it conceivable?"

It was a question that went directly to the heart of the defense's case. Why lure the gunmen to the murder scene, creating four witnesses who would be able to identify the killers? Presumably, Rose was bringing them there so they could be told by Detectives Steinert and White that Rose had nothing to do with framing their boss, Big Jack Zelig. But neither Steinert nor White was there and no mention was made of their absence. The matter of squaring things with Zelig was never raised again, while the defendants, according to their testimony, just stood aside and watched while Rosenthal was shot by the men who brought them there.

"Are these statements true or the result of pre-arrangement?" Goff asked before sending the jury off to the consultation room. It was then past one-thirty, and when the jurors asked to begin their deliberations without going to lunch, the defendants knew they were in trouble. On the first ballot, in just twenty minutes, the jury found the four men guilty of murder in the first degree. The defendants appeared stunned but not surprised. They had entered the courtroom in the morning with a spring in their step, looking confident, almost cocky, but their mood shifted with Goff's charge to the jury. Back in his cell in the Tombs, Whitey spoke for all of them:

"When we heard Goff we knew it was all off. We were certain we would be acquitted before that, but when we got back here after listening to him we threw up our hands. He ordered our conviction, and the jury obeyed orders. We knew that they would. . . . The jury would have convicted a priest after listening to that charge."

Two days after the gunmen were convicted, on Thursday, November 21, Bald Jack Rose, Bridgey Webber, Harry Vallon, and Sam Schepps were released from the West Side Prison. Whitman explained that he was bound to free them by the stipulation that had induced them to testify for the state. The vagrancy charge that was pending against Schepps was dismissed. Shapiro was released a day later, as he had to appear in court to have the murder indictment against him dismissed.

The four informers all had plans to leave the city and enough money to fund future ventures. Rose said he was writing a book called *Twenty Years in the Underworld*. Webber, who was suffering from sciatic rheumatism, said he would head for a warmer climate for the winter months, but he planned to return to New York. He was said to have amassed a fortune of more than $100,000 running his poker establishment, and he was not about to give it up. Schepps said that after spending a few weeks in Hot Springs he would go into vaudeville; he had already received offers of more than $200 a week. His act would be a monologue based no doubt on his experiences in New York's underworld. Vallon's plans were not yet certain, but he told his lawyer he would not be spending the winter in the city. All four had pledged to return to New York if they were needed in connection with future legal proceedings.

On Tuesday, November 26, Goff sentenced the four gunmen to die in the electric chair some time during the week of January 6. Minutes after the sentencing, they left the Tombs on their way to Sing Sing, where they would join Becker in the death house. A crowd of more than two thousand clogged Lafayette Street to get a look at the condemned men. It took the police several minutes to cut a path through the mass of people to the van that would take them to Grand Central Station, where a throng that was almost as large was waiting. Scores of onlookers eager for a closer look bought train tickets that got them to the platform from which the Peekskill local would leave for Ossining. Crowds also had gathered at every station, looking through the windows of the train for a glimpse of the four young men. At Ossining, the station was so packed that it took the police ten minutes to move the prisoners no more than one hundred yards. One might suppose that it was more than curiosity regarding the looks of the young men that drew people to get within sight of them. There was perhaps a certain allure about being in the presence of men who had become a part of the dark side of history. Cold-blooded killers never lacked for attention.

While the four convicts were taking up residence on death row, their opposite numbers—the informers whose testimony sent them away—were embarking on more pleasant journeys. Bridgey Webber in particular had wasted no time in embracing the good life. Impatient, as he put it, to get his nerve back and traveling under an assumed name, he embarked on a cruise to Havana aboard the Ward liner *Saratoga*. If his nerve had left him, it apparently had not gone very far. He spent the days at sea playing poker with those passengers ready to take their chances, and, by all reports, he picked them all clean. He was well set up for Havana's winter thoroughbred race meeting when he arrived on Wednesday, December 4. Together with his wife, he had planned on an extended stay, but Cuban authorities were not thrilled to play host to a professional gambler and a self-confessed accomplice to murder. He was asked to curtail his stay, and he returned to New York less than a week later but not without fanfare. Webber had a story to tell that was vastly different from the one he told in court and one that no one had heard before. He now told a cluster of reporters that Becker had not instigated the murder of Rosenthal, that it was not part of a conspiracy at all but was carried out by two drunken gunmen who had disobeyed orders. As Webber now told it, the gunmen had been sent to "throw a fright into Rosenthal," but two of them had gotten drunk and shot him instead.

"Now, I want to say right here," Webber said, "that there was never any intention to have Rosenthal killed. The idea was to buy him off or scare him away. . . . As for Becker, he knew that a lot of people were sore on him, and he was afraid of the effect on his career if Rosenthal went to Whitman and told him what he knew. Becker wanted Rosenthal bribed or scared off, and he would come to me and talk about it.

"I would tell Becker that everything was all right. I never had anything to do with hiring any gunmen. Rose attended to that. Becker would go to Rose and ask him what was being done about Rosenthal, and he would tell Rose how strong he was in the department, and Rose, believing him, would tell the gunmen that Becker's pull was so great they could even croak Rosenthal and get away with it. But nothing was said about killing Rosenthal.

"When I was arrested I intended to keep quiet, and I stood pat until the morning of the day that Jack Rose came over with his confession. That morning I sent my wife with ten thousand dollars to the office of Max D. Steuer and she gave him the money in his office and not on the street, as the papers stated at the time. The next thing I knew, Rose had confessed. What was I to do? I got in line."

The reaction to Webber's statement was immediate, and, as might be expected, everyone reacted in a manner that best suited his own ends. McIntyre declared that it meant a new trial for Becker. He said he would make such a motion in the State Supreme Court, and if it was denied he would take the issue to the Court of Appeals, which is the highest court in New York State.

"What has happened," he said, "is exactly what I have been expecting ever since the conviction of Becker. I have known all along that the truth in this case would ultimately come out, and the story that Webber told today is the same story that was communicated to me when I was first retained in Becker's defense. Circumstances were such, however, that I never could get the verification that would stand the test on the stand, but I have never doubted in my own mind that eventually the truth would appear in the case and that the public would learn, before it is too late, that Becker was the victim of a diabolical frame-up."

Rose, who gets scuffed up in Webber's new version of events, returned the favor when questioned by reporters at his home in Far Rockaway. He accused Webber of lying and said that Rosenthal had been murdered precisely because Becker had placed Bridgey in charge of making arrangements.

"When Webber makes the statement that there was no intention on the part of the gang to kill Rosenthal, he deliberately lies," he said. "As a matter of fact, Webber had murder in his heart for a week before Herman Rosenthal was killed. For two whole months I held off that murder. I did not want to see Rosenthal killed, and I took no stock in Becker's assurance that he could fix matters up if Herman was killed. Only a few days before the murder, Becker cast me aside and put Webber in charge of negotiations for the croaking of Rosenthal. If Webber says that two members of the gang were drunk when they left his place, he tells what is not true. I saw them leave and they were sober.

"After Webber was placed in charge of the negotiations I pleaded with him to go slow and not to go so far as to commit murder. As a matter of fact, Webber hated Rosenthal just as much as did Becker, and that is proved by the fact that only a week passed after he was placed in charge before the murder was committed."

Asked why Webber would come forth with his new story, Rose had a response immediately at hand: "Why, he wants to get in with the gang again and get back into the gambling business. I remember now that while in the West Side Prison he was in the habit of sending messages to the gamblers in which he said he had not squealed and that he would explain everything when he got out of jail."

Whitman, in his statement, had the final word on the matter. He said simply that Webber had called him on the phone and denied ever having made those remarks, and Whitman believed him.

"Webber assures me," the D.A. said, "that the interview credited to him today is false in every particular, and he said he will make an affidavit to that effect if I so desire. However, as long as he did not make the statements he is quoted as having made I see no occasion for an affidavit on his part and will not ask him for one. Webber told me that he realized he would go to jail if he said what the newspapers said he did [presumably for perjury] and he added that he had no desire to return to a cell. I do not see how he could possibly have made those statements, and I must take his word that he did not."

Whitman, one must conclude, could more easily see how a number of reporters would choose to get together, fabricate an interview with Webber, and then carry identical versions in their respective papers. But Whitman was in a position to believe whatever he chose to believe. With Becker and the four gunmen convicted, he declared "the beginning of the end of the rule of gangsters and gunmen in certain parts of the city. The murder of Herman Rosenthal, in all its attendant circumstances, protected as it was by a man high in police affairs, was a direct challenge to law and order and to every decent man in this city and state."

Charles Seymour Whitman had met the challenge and was now ready for whatever came next. He had become one of the brightest stars on the political horizon. The office of mayor was being dangled before him, but while he expressed interest in being the Republican candidate, it was clear that his reach extended as far as the governor's mansion and perhaps even beyond. As 1912 ebbed away, the Becker case too seemed to slide into the past. For half a year it had been the biggest story in town, front-page news nearly every day. Legally, the case was far from dead. Motions were being made, an appeal was being prepared, but it was no longer the focus of public attention. Other events had begun to overtake it, both locally and nationally. The next few years would mark a turning that would transform the country forever. The United States was on its way to becoming the headquarters of the world, and New York City was its capital.

21

Nineteen-thirteen would be the last year of its kind. The following sum-mer war would sweep across Europe, and nothing would ever be the same again. The entire world seemed to have crossed the threshold into a time of fast-track acceleration, and just a few years later, life in 1913 would appear to be quaintly out of date. But in retrospect, the transformation that took root and flourished after the war had already begun. It was in 1913 that a new man-ufacturing concept, the Ford assembly line, was introduced, cutting the time it took to produce a car from twelve and a half to one and a half hours. The labor movement, driven largely by Big Bill Haywood and Elizabeth Gurley Flynn, had mustered new strength following its victory in the lengthy tex-tile mills strike in Lawrence, Massachusetts. Suffragettes were on the march, and Congress was beginning to listen; ground had been laid for the passage of the Nineteenth Amendment, giving women the right to vote.

In New York, already the fulcrum of change, the new Grand Central Ter-minal opened in February. Two months later, the sixty-story, 792-foot-high Woolworth Building became the tallest in the country; it was called the Cathe-dral of Commerce. At around the same time, the nation's largest general post office opened at Eighth Avenue, between Thirty-first and Thirty-third Streets. It was a time—that last year before the big guns fired—when it seemed pos-sible to dream great dreams and appropriate a future of endless promise.

The convictions of Becker and the four gunmen had raised the issue of police graft to public consciousness, and District Attorney Whitman seized the opportunity to ride it as far as he could. He addressed the situation at public gatherings all over town, emphasizing his belief that while the New York City police department was second to none, there was a strain of cops, ranging from patrolmen to inspectors, who were on the take, and he was determined to root them out. He backed up his commitment early in the year, launching an investigation that led to the dismissal of dozens of beat policemen and higher officials. No fewer than four inspectors were convicted and sentenced to terms at Blackwell's Island penitentiary.

Mayor Gaynor, too, was optimistic. In an address before the Forum of New York University, he offered high praise for Commissioner Waldo and expressed confidence that the force was in the process of being thoroughly cleansed.

"I came in as mayor determined to stop police grafting," he said. "There are grafters still left from the old regime. They are being retired one after another, and every chance we get we dismiss one. But the process of purification and education takes some time. We have made much progress in the last three years, and I hope by the end of my term to be able to say that all graft has been cut off from the police force."

Then he turned specifically to the Becker case. "You ask me if I think Becker represents a type of police official? . . . I cannot say that Becker is a type. If what was testified against him is in all respects true, he is one of the greatest criminals of the age and not a type. He was known in the force as what they call a 'good' policeman. That is to say, he did things, he got results. But if the evidence of Rose and the others must be taken as true in all respects, as it is given to me, he must have been without any moral sense whatever. But I do not wish to say anything to hurt him. He is now struggling for his life, and I do not wish to say anything about him."

Gaynor was by no means exaggerating. Becker was now in the snare of the judicial machinery and was indeed struggling for his life. The new year had not begun well for him. Helen was near term, and her pregnancy was a difficult one. When she was two weeks past due, the doctors at Women's Hospital decided on a Caesarian section. They warned her that they could not ensure the survival of both mother and baby. If it came to that, she told them, they had better save her because the newborn could not be of much help to her husband. A girl, to be called Ruth, was born on February 1, but she did not survive her first day. Helen needed several weeks to recuperate, but later that month she resumed the weekly ritual of visiting her husband every Saturday for the ninety minutes allowed by regulations. She wrote to him daily and shared her views with the legal team that was working to get him a new trial.

The appeal of Becker's conviction was not scheduled to be heard by the Court of Appeals until later in the year, but his new attorney, Joseph Shay, notified the district attorney that he was going to petition the court for a new trial. His motion would be based on four grounds: new evidence had been discovered; the verdict was contrary to the law and to the weight of the testimony; one of the jurors had separated himself from the others during the course of the trial; and finally, the interests of justice would be advanced by a new trial.

Armed with twenty-four affidavits, Shay made his plea before Justice Goff on June 5. He argued enthusiastically and at length, but his case seemed thin, even a bit desperate. The most significant item of "new evidence" was contained in an affidavit stating that Sam Schepps was among the men who had ridden away in the murder car. That, Shay argued, would make Schepps an accomplice and disqualify him from corroborating the story told by the three informers. Other affidavits were based on the story told by Bridgey Webber on his return from Cuba that there had never been a conspiracy to kill Rosenthal. Yet others contended that Mayor Gaynor had made remarks prejudicial to the defendant and that the overall atmosphere had made it impossible to conduct a fair trial. It turned out that the juryman who had separated himself from the rest of the jury was Samuel S. Haas who had twice been given leave by the judge to visit a dentist to relieve the discomfort of a toothache.

The prosecution did not require much time to counter the defense's arguments. There was really no new evidence, the D.A. said, and nothing had been introduced that could not have been entered into evidence at the first trial. Objections now attributed to the defendant could have been placed on the record if Becker had testified in his own defense. Whitman dismissed the grounds for a new trial as inconsequential. Goff agreed. On July 12, he denied the defense motion, explicitly citing the criteria that must be satisfied to order a new trial:

The new evidence "must be such as will probably change the result of a new trial; it must have been discovered since the trial; it must be such as could not have been discovered before the trial by the exercise of reasonable diligence; it must be material to the issue; it must not be cumulative to the former issue; and it must not be merely impeaching or contradicting the former evidence. None of the affidavits submitted complies with all these requirements."

Goff's rejection of his plea did not mark the end of the line for Becker. Issues regarding judicial errors in his trial were still undecided. They would form the substance of his appeal, which was still pending. Arguments before the Court of Appeals, originally scheduled for May 20, had been postponed several times, first at the request of the defense and later on petition of the state. Whitman, it seemed, had other concerns that required his attention.

He had announced early in June that he "would be willing to run for mayor" at the municipal election in November. It was the kind of announcement made by a coquettish candidate who thought the nomination would be his for the asking. In fact, Whitman tacked on a proviso to his availability. He said he would accept the nomination only if it was offered by an "organization properly constituted." No one knew exactly what that meant, but it sounded as if he were reluctant to campaign actively against other candidates and felt certain that the Republican Party was ready to nominate him by acclamation. He might indeed have been correct, for no more than one week later all five Republican county organizations offered him their support. The problem was that in solidly Democratic New York City no Republican had ever won election unless he was a Fusion candidate or had the support of another political organization. Whitman's options in that regard were limited. The Bull Moose Party offered little hope as its leader, Teddy Roosevelt, regarded Whitman as a political opportunist who had little respect for the truth. The Progressive Party was considering nominating Gaynor for reelection but preferred that its candidate be chosen in an open primary rather than by the party's leadership. The Republicans, unanimous in their support of Whitman, said they were ready to work with the Fusionists to defeat whichever candidate Tammany Hall might place on the Democratic ticket.

The Fusion nominating committee met on July 9, and by that time two new candidates had emerged. They were Manhattan Borough President George McAneny, and John Purroy Mitchel, former chairman of the Board of Aldermen who had resigned that post to become Collector of the Port of New York. Although Whitman was the favorite, there was strong support for McAneny, who many regarded as better suited for the position of mayor. Mitchel, who had briefly filled in for Gaynor after he had been shot, was also held in high regard by the Fusion Committee.

Almost lost in the shuffle was Gaynor himself, the Democratic mayor who enjoyed whatever advantage incumbency conferred. Gaynor's disadvantage was that he had run as a reformer and governed as a reformer, and Tammany wanted no part of him. He was a man without a party and he knew it. In an interview with the *Evening Mail*, he said he believed he should be the natural candidate of the Fusionists since they shared the same ideals, and he had put into effect many of their programs. The Fusion Committee advised him that they could not consider nominating him unless he pledged not to accept a Tammany nomination or endorsement. Of course he had, during his term as mayor, alienated Tammany Hall beyond any likelihood of receiving its blessing in any form whatever. But that was not the Fusionists' chief concern. Though widely respected, Gaynor was viewed as a wounded warrior who had served well but whose time was up. He came close to admitting as much himself. In his interview with the *Mail,* he had said:

"I did not ask to be nominated for mayor. The nomination was offered to me twice in former years. How I came to accept it four years ago I can hardly tell you. Something led me into it. I have been through a pretty tough time since. I bear the marks of physical and moral assassins on me, and I am perfectly content to go out carrying them with me to the end."

His remarks, as it turned out, were prophetic.

At its nominating convention, on the last day of July, the Fusion Committee named Borough President Mitchel its candidate for mayor in a meeting that took eight ballots and lasted more than four hours. The first ballot was relatively even, but McAneny's support began to dissolve on subsequent votes, and his backers started to defect to Mitchel and Whitman. In the final tally, Mitchel received forty-four votes to Whitman's forty-three, with McAneny retaining one token vote.

Whitman, by all accounts, had expected the nomination to be handed to him with the party's gratitude. He had left for Canada on July 20 for his first vacation since the trials of Becker and the gunmen, and returned in time for the meeting with the Fusion Committee. Apparently he reacted at first like a jilted lover. He refused to make any comment, and left the city for Bretton Woods, a mountain resort in New Hampshire. When he returned, he expressed doubt that Mitchel could defeat the Tammany candidate, ex-Justice Edward E. McCall, and word began to circulate that Whitman might oppose the Fusion candidate and run as a Republican. In the end, however, he chose unity. He endorsed Mitchel and agreed to join the Fusion slate and seek reelection as district attorney. It was essential, he said, that they stand together to defeat Tammany. McAneny, who also might have been suffering the pangs of abandonment, was courted by Gaynor's supporters to replace the ailing mayor and run as an independent. But he, too, finally succumbed and enlisted as the Fusion candidate for president of the Board of Alderman, putting him next in line to the mayor.

Gaynor, whom history would honor as one of the city's most distinguished leaders, was still planning to run, but his fragile condition raised concern even among his most ardent followers. His health had been failing ever since he was shot three years earlier, and the demands of the mayor's office appeared now to be too great a burden. On Thursday, September 4, he and his family sailed aboard the White Star liner *Baltic* for a vacation in Ireland. He was hoping to regain strength for what he expected would be an arduous campaign. The ship was nearing the Irish coast six days later when his son, Rufus, found Gaynor slumped over in a deck chair, dead of a sudden heart attack. He was sixty-four years old. The news reached New York two days later, via Liverpool.

Sworn in as acting mayor was Ardolph L. Kline, a Republican from Brooklyn's Fifty-first Aldermanic District. Ironically enough, Kline had become chairman of the Board of Aldermen when Mitchel resigned the post to take the job of Collector of the Port of New York. In just a few months, Kline would be neither mayor nor chairman of the board.

The November election was a complete sweep for the Fusion party. Mitchel defeated McCall by more than 20 percent of the vote; the rest of the ticket did nearly as well. Tammany did not win a single seat on the Board of Estimate, and its obituary was being written by almost every publication in the city. It had not been a good season for Tammany in other respects as well. Two months earlier, it had lost its patron saint. Big Tim Sullivan, the heart and muscle of the organization for nearly three decades, was struck and killed by a freight train on the tracks of the New York, New Haven & Hartford Railroad about three hundred feet north of Pelham Parkway in the Bronx. His body went unrecognized and unclaimed for almost two weeks. One of the city's most celebrated presences—loved and feared in equal measure—state senator, U.S. congressmen, Tammany boss, and King of the Tenderloin—had somehow found anonymity in death.

Not yet fifty years old, Sullivan had been experiencing mental lapses since early in the summer of 1912, even before the Rosenthal murder. Tammany leaders understood that Big Tim was not sound enough to return to the State Senate, but he was deemed perfectly fit to serve in Congress. He ran in the Sixteenth District and was easily elected, although he did no campaigning. But he never made it to Washington. In January 1913, a court declared him formally incompetent. That summer his family took him to Europe, hoping that the change of scene would rejuvenate him. It didn't. When they returned, Sullivan was put in the care of three male nurses at his brother Patrick's home in the Eastchester section of the Bronx. Early on the morning of August 31, after spending Saturday night playing pinochle with his caretakers, he waited until they were asleep and walked out. He was reported missing, and a citywide search ensued; it continued for thirteen days.

Later on the day he disappeared, a railroad worker discovered a body on the tracks near Pelham Parkway. Although it was plain that the deceased was not a hobo—he was dressed well and wearing gold cufflinks set with diamonds—it apparently did not waken the interest of the three detectives assigned to investigate. (All were later stripped of their rank and returned to uniform.) The body was taken first to the Westchester morgue, then to the morgue in Harlem, and finally to the main morgue, in Bellevue Hospital, where it arrived thirteen days after it had been discovered. From there, it was ticketed for burial in an unmarked grave in Potter's Field until Peter Purfield, a patrolman who worked at the morgue, recognized the body. Purfield had looked once and started to walk away. Then, struck by a sense of familiarity, he turned back and took a longer look. "Why, it's Tim," he shouted, "Big Tim. God rest him!"

Big Tim was laid to rest on September 15 in what some observers described as the largest funeral ever held in New York. A crowd estimated at 75,000 clogged the streets as the funeral procession wound its way from the lower Bowery to the old St. Patrick's Cathedral on Mott Street. Among the mourners were five Supreme Court justices, four United States senators, and sixteen members of the House of Representatives. Yet, but for the last-minute identification by a morgue attendant, the most recognizable figure in New York City politics during the decades that bridged the turn of the century, would have had a pauper's burial. His disappearance would have remained as deep and lingering a mystery as that of Judge Crater.

It was no doubt coincidental that Big Tim's demise was followed two months later by Tammany's total defeat at the polls. The Becker case certainly played a part, as it turned the light on a city that seemed to be nourished by police graft and political corruption. But those who believed Tammany had been buried as surely as Big Tim Sullivan would soon learn that reports of its death were greatly exaggerated. It would take back political power after Mitchel's four-year term as mayor, despite an administration few could fault. With Police Commissioner Waldo pushed into retirement, Mitchel appointed Arthur Wood in his place, and Wood introduced widespread reforms that did not endear him to Tammany. Run by Charles Francis Murphy, who had succeeded Sullivan, Tammany attacked the new mayor at every turn. Often referred to as the Boy Mayor of New York, Mitchel, at thirty-five, was the youngest ever to hold the office. He was also the youngest to leave it. In 1917, he was defeated by Democrat John F. Hylan, and the Tammany powers were back in control. After failing to get reelected, Mitchel enlisted in the Army Air Signal Corps just months after the United States entered World War I. On July 18, 1918, thirteen days short of his thirty-ninth birthday, he was killed when he fell from an airplane during a training session in Louisiana. He was honored that same year when Mitchel Field on Long Island was named for him. (Contrary to popular belief, the air field was not named for Billy Mitchell, the renowned "Father of the Air Force," a misapprehension that often leads to the misspelling of the field's name.)

Whitman, for his part, was comfortable enough with the new administration. The drive to reform police practices did nothing but enhance his own image; he was, after all, still district attorney. Besides, the prize he had coveted had been the office of governor, not mayor, and he was positioned as well as one could be. Henry Clay Sulzer, elected governor in 1912, did not hold that office very long. Early in his term, he clashed with Tammany, and he soon discovered that Murphy and his crew still had plenty of muscle to flex when they chose to use it. After a bruising battle, Sulzer was impeached and removed from office less than a year after he assumed it. He was replaced by Lieutenant Governor Martin H. Glynn, who would be Whitman's opponent in the next election. Given his running start, Whitman was feeling confident.

22

The Court of Appeals heard Becker's case in Albany on December 1, 1913. Joseph Shay's defense brief, 60,000 words long and citing thousands of points of law, offered twenty-five reasons why Becker's conviction should be overturned and a new trial ordered. The reasons were familiar enough to anyone who had followed the case even casually. Most centered on the manner in which the trial was conducted and the judicial indiscretions committed by the judge. But Shay had the foresight to raise an issue that would turn out to be the core of the appeal and the basis for requesting a new trial. He questioned the reliability of the testimony concerning the Harlem conference at which Becker was said to have met with Rose, Webber, and Vallon to plan Rosenthal's murder. For if the meeting had not occurred, there would be no direct evidence connecting Becker to the murder conspiracy. And while all three accomplices testified to having taken part in the meeting, they could not agree on when it had been held.

The decision of the court was unequivocal. On Tuesday, February 24, Becker's conviction was reversed in a blistering, seventy-seven-page ruling that denounced Goff's conduct of the trial both on matters of discretion and on points of law. Writing for the six-to-one majority, Judge Frank H. Hiscock said that Becker "did not have the manner of trial which the law guarantees to him. His counsel was hampered and embarrassed; his case was discredited and weakened; full and impartial consideration by the jury was impeded and prevented. He never had a fair chance to defend his life, and it would be a lasting reproach to the state if under those circumstances it should exact its forfeiture." Hiscock also noted that Justice Goff "created an atmosphere of hostility to the defendant Backer which must have impressed the jury, entirely aside from his erroneous rulings." In a separate concurring opinion, Judge Nathan I. Miller described the lower court's verdict as "shockingly against the weight of evidence" and said the trial "was so conducted as to insure a verdict of guilty, regardless of the evidence."

Other citations of judicial misconduct included the haste with which the trial was conducted; Goff's repeated refusals to grant appeals by the defense counsel for adjournment; his denial of permission for the defense to reopen cross-examination of witnesses; his exclusion of evidence on cross-examination; the opportunity for Rose, Webber, and Vallon to communicate while they were imprisoned and Goff's refusal to allow them to be cross-examined regarding their prison communications; and the judge's insistence that defense counsel conclude his cross-examination of Rose despite his plea that he was mentally and physically exhausted.

The citations of judicial misconduct were sufficient to overturn the lower court's conviction, but they would be of little use to the defense in a new trial. The point on which a future trial was likely to turn was the Harlem confer- ence, and the Appeals Court made it clear that it considered the testimony regarding that meeting to be at best dubious. The decision stated directly that "if the existence of the conference is not established, the case against the defen- dant falls in utter collapse. If the Harlem conference ever occurred, as claimed by the people, it is urged that two other witnesses could have testified to it."

The two witnesses were the chauffeurs, known colloquially as Moe and Itch, who the prosecution contended had driven the conspirators to the vacant lot in Harlem where the conference was said to have been held. The two men had signed affidavits stating that they had never made such a trip, but they had not been called as witnesses. Becker's fate in a future trial would rest on whether the state could prove that the Harlem conference had taken place. But no one connected with the defense thought that Becker would be retried. "They will never put him on trial again," Shay said, "for [the Court of Appeals] decision is not only a reversal, it's an absolute vindication."

Helen Becker was elated. Her mother had died the day before the court overturned her husband's conviction, and she was making preparations for the funeral when she learned of the court's ruling. "I knew all along that he was innocent," she said, "and I felt certain that the Court of Appeals would be just and take Charlie out of that awful death house. . . . I was always certain that truth would triumph in the end."

So far as Becker was concerned, he was out of danger. "I feel like a free man already," he said. "I knew the decision would be in my favor . . . I had thought that the Court of Appeals would throw the trial record into the sewer." He was already planning his future. "When I am free," he said, "the first work that I am going to take up is that of hunting down the murderers of Herman Rosenthal. They are still at large. The man who actually committed the murder, I am convinced, was Harry Vallon. The immunity contracts of Vallon, Rose, Schepps, and Webber are void, because they lied and I will be able to prove it. The district attorney gave them those life-insurance policies on the condition that their testimony should be the truth, and I will prove that it was perjured. This may take six months or a year, but no matter how long it takes I will show who the murderers really were. I mean to do this to vindicate myself, not for the sake of revenge by sending those fellows to the place where I was. I wouldn't want a dog to go through what I have gone through. I wouldn't even want the men who framed me up to suffer as I have.

"During the sixteen months that I was in the death house I saw twelve men go to the electric chair. The keeper came each time to the man's cell and said, 'They are waiting for you.' The man walked out and that was the last of him. Everyone in the death house knew what it meant. Twelve times that happened. You can imagine what torture that was. The law never meant that doomed men had to undergo such cruelty as that, and one of the first prison reforms ought to be the abolishing of the death house."

There was just one obstacle to Becker's vision of the future, to Shay's optimism, and Helen Becker's assurance that her husband would soon be a free man: they were not shared by the district attorney. Whitman was already preparing for a new trial. He did not think he would need much in the way of new evidence. The reversal was based chiefly on judicial misconduct, and that could be remedied with a new judge. The critical point would be proving that the Harlem conference had really taken place, and the prosecution would set to work on that immediately. He would be ready for the new trial early in May.

While Becker was preparing to leave Sing Sing and return to a cell in the Tombs, the Court of Appeals was signing the death warrants of Gyp the Blood, Lefty Louie, Whitey Lewis, and Dago Frank. On the same day that Becker's conviction was overturned, the court affirmed the convictions of the four gunmen. Whether or not Becker had a hand in planning Rosenthal's murder, the court determined that it was the four defendants who did the shooting. They were to die in the electric chair during the week of April 13.

But for Becker and his family, it was Christmas in February. There had been a huge snowfall, and he and his party—Helen, his brother John, and Shay, with two deputy sheriffs serving as escorts—left the prison by sleigh on the way to the railroad station. Becker had been a popular inmate, and he was given an enthusiastic send off by those with cells facing the outside of the prison. He was serenaded with what was known in Sing Sing as the "prisoners' yell," which was described in the *Times* as a "mournful, piercing, uncanny" chant. Becker acknowledged their tribute by waving his black derby in their direction.

Back in the Tombs, Warden John Hanley and two keepers ushered him to Cell 117 on the first tier, three cells from the one he had occupied while awaiting trial. He was not discouraged by the news that Whitman had determined to retry him. "I am as good as acquitted now of the charge of murder," he said. Shay was equally optimistic. "It is a certainty that Becker will be acquitted, if he gets a fair chance," he said. "I have new evidence that will clear him completely."

What Shay had was ten new witnesses who, he said, would shatter the testimony of the four informers who were the heart of the prosecution's case. Principally, they would establish that Schepps was a party to the conspiracy and therefore could not corroborate the story told by Rose, Webber, and Vallon. One of the witnesses, a waiter by the name of Patrick Ryan, had already provided the defense with an affidavit swearing that just a few minutes before the murder he had seen Vallon and another man standing in front of the Metropole. On the other side of the street, he said, he saw Schepps holding open the door of the getaway car. Shay said he had several other witnesses who would place Schepps at the scene, although he declined to name them.

The two most significant additions to the defense's case were the chauffeurs that the Court of Appeals said should have been called by the state during the first trial. They presumably could have supported the prosecution's contention that Rosenthal's fate had been sealed at the Harlem conference at which Becker was an active participant. The two men had in fact been named in Schepps's testimony as the drivers who had taken him and the other three informers to the meeting site. However, they were not summoned by the prosecution to testify, and for good reason: they both denied having driven any of the state's four key witnesses to Harlem.

While on the witness stand, Schepps had said he knew the chauffeurs only as Moe Levy and Itch. Eager for evidence that would tie Becker to the fatal meeting, the district attorney pursued the lead and found that Moe Levy was legally Harry N. Cohen and Itch's real name was Isidore Schoenhaus. They were taken to the D.A.'s office where they spoke with Bridgey Webber in the presence of a deputy district attorney. Shay said that Schoenhaus, questioned first, denied Webber's statement that he had driven him to Harlem. Bridgey then asked to speak with the chauffeur alone. In private, Schoenhaus now swore in an affidavit, Webber pleaded with him to testify that he had taken him to Harlem where he met with Becker, but the chauffeur refused.

Cohen's affidavit was even more explicit. He said a detective had taken him to the Criminal Courts Building where he met with Webber and a deputy D.A. There, Webber said that Cohen had driven the three others to Harlem, while he was taken to the meeting place by Schoenhaus. Didn't he remember that, he asked Cohen? According to Shay, Cohen said, "'No, you are lying, Bridgey.'

"Webber then asked and received permission for a private interview with him. When they were alone, Cohen says that Webber fell on his knees and said, 'For God's sake, Moe, don't fall down on me like this. If you want to save my life, say that you did drive them up to Harlem.'

"'I should worry about your life,' Cohen says he replied. 'I am not going to commit perjury for anybody.'

"Now," Shay continued, "when it turned out that neither Cohen nor Schoenhaus would do as witnesses for the prosecution, they were released. The defense at the trial believed that 'Moe Levy' and 'Itch' were fake names and were unable to locate the men as witnesses."

The new defense team was more industrious. They did a quick survey of limousine services in the area and found that Moe Levy and Itch were partners in just such an enterprise. They told Shay that they did not offer their testimony to the defense the first time because they were intimidated by the furor surrounding the case. They were afraid that anyone who testified in Becker's behalf would become a target for those who were setting him up. But that was more than a year ago, and things had since quieted down.

Shay believed that his case was now virtually impregnable. He pointed out that the Court of Appeals had held that the Harlem conference between Becker and the informers was the heart of the prosecution's case and that the charge against Becker stood or fell with it. "These two witnesses utterly smash the case against Becker," Shay said.

For added measure, Shay said that twelve members of Becker's strong-arm squad would be called to testify that Becker could not have been present at the Harlem conference because they had been with him that entire night. Although the informers differed on the precise date of the meeting, it was supposed to have taken place in the last week of June 1912, one night after Becker had raided a crap game in Harlem, and the policemen were ready to swear that one or more of them had been with Becker all that night.

While Becker's spirits were buoyed by the brightening prospects of a new trial, the four gunmen could do little but wait for the curtain to fall. Warden James J. Clancy had brought them the news that their appeal had been denied. It seemed to take a while for the crushing finality of the decision to settle in. Lefty Louie, the most literate of the four and their unofficial spokesman, announced that they would take their appeal to "the greater court of honest public opinion, who, we feel, in the end will do justice." In a letter "to the public" that was signed by all of them and printed verbatim in the morning papers, Lefty laid out a sound, though not legally compelling case for sustaining their appeal, based chiefly on the lack of credibility of the state's witnesses. Their attorney, Charles G. F. Wahle, had a more practical notion. He petitioned the governor, Martin H. Glynn, for a stay of execution until there was a verdict in Becker's trial, which was to commence about six weeks later, on May 6. The petition was given added impetus as it was signed by ten of the twelve jurors who had convicted the gunmen. It also had a solid legal foundation.

With new witnesses ready to testify, it was not unreasonable to think that testimony might be produced that would accrue to the benefit of the defendants. Every day, it seemed, new witnesses were coming forth who would tell the court that someone other than the four convicted men had done the shooting, and their affidavits were attached to Wahle's petition. Samuel Kalmanson, a clerk from Buffalo, New York, swore that he was passing by when the shooting took place and saw a man whom he now knows to be Harry Vallon clinging to the running board of the murder car with a gun in his hand.

The legendary gambler William B. "Bat" Masterson, written into lore by Damon Runyon, signed an affidavit saying that a man he knew as Butch Witt told him repeatedly that he had witnessed the murder and saw Vallon and Webber fire the shots that killed Rosenthal.

Louis Libby, owner of the gray murder car, was prepared to testify that Shapiro, the driver of the car, told him that none of the gunmen had done the shooting, nor had any of them put a gun to his head and told him to speed away from the scene.

Hartford T. Marshall, counsel for Jack Sullivan/Jacob Reich, swore that Shapiro told him that after Rosenthal fell dead Vallon ran from the Metropole and jumped on the running board of the getaway car. He then struck Shapiro on the side of the head with a revolver and ordered him to speed away.

Wahle also argued that the conviction of his clients was based on the testimony of Rose, Webber, Vallon, and Schepps, all of whom the Court of Appeals found to be unworthy of belief, their statements "somewhat unsatisfactory and in some cases contradictory."

The petition was filed on March 31, two weeks before the executions were to be carried out, and early indications were that Glynn was inclined to grant the respite. He told the press that he had been getting appeals from prominent men all over the state asking him to approve the stay. He noted that delaying the execution for a few weeks could not hurt the interests of justice, but if the men were executed and Becker's trial produced evidence that might serve to exculpate them, justice would suffer a terrible loss. He was clearly troubled by the burden he was forced to carry. He said he favored a pardon board so that questions of life and death would not be left solely to the chief executive.

One week later, Glynn denied the appeal. He had no shortage of explanations for his decision. The Court of Appeals, he said, had found no reversible
error and had determined that the defendants had been given a fair trial. He
would have acted differently, he noted, if the verdict had depended on the testimony of the four informers alone. But four other witnesses had positively
identified one or more of the gunmen, and together they had identified all
four of them as participants in the shooting.

There is no way to assess to what degree Glynn was influenced by Whitman and Goff. Whitman was quick into the breach when he learned of the
petition. "There is no doubt of the gunmen's guilt," he said, adding, "I am
unalterably opposed to the application for a stay of execution."

Goff was no less emphatic. "As near as absolute certainty can be attained
by human means in a human tribunal, it was attained when these four men
were convicted of murder." The judge also addressed the issue of the relevance of Becker's trial to the fate of the gunmen. Their guilt, he said, did not
depend on the prior conviction of Becker. "The person who procures
another to commit a crime and the person who commits it are distinct enti-
ties, and the conviction of one in no sense is dependent upon the conviction
of the other. . . . Even if Becker, on his trial, should be acquitted, it might leave
to doubt and conjecture the identity of the instigator, but it would not raise
any doubt as to the identity of the men who fired the shots."

Once again, Warden Clancy was obliged to inform the four men that their
plea—their last chance at escaping the death chamber—had been turned
down. Though they had expected a favorable report, they showed little emotion when they heard the news. At a brief press conference, the warden told
reporters: "Never in my life have I seen such an exhibition of calmness. There
was not the least excitement about it; no emotion, nothing of that kind. The
boys just listened to their fate and then proceeded to act as if nothing had happened. They had their nerve all right. I was astounded." The execution was
set for sunrise on April 13, the day after Easter Sunday, and there seemed to
be nothing that could head it off, nothing at least that could be reasonably
anticipated.

Since everyone assumed the request for a reprieve would be granted, no
preparations had been made for an execution to take place on Monday. Edwin
R. Davis, Sing Sing's chief executioner, lived in Salem, Massachusetts, and he

needed to be summoned to New York for the occasion. The job of executioner was performed on a per diem basis, at the rate of $250 a day, so the state would certainly be getting its money's worth with four executions for the price of one. Davis arrived in New York on Saturday, tested the equipment, and returned home when he found everything to be in working order. Early on Sunday morning, however, it was discovered that the special dynamo that powered the electric chair had been destroyed some time the previous night. It had been hammered to pieces; a number of parts were missing altogether. Davis arranged for the delivery of an entirely new dynamo and, with several aides, spent all day Sunday installing it. At eleven o'clock that night, an extra-heavy charge of 2,500 volts was sent coursing smoothly through the system.

Late Saturday night, with little more than twenty-four hours of their lives remaining, a statement of innocence was issued signed by "Gyp," "Lefty," and "Whitey." Dago Frank's name was noticeably absent, intensifying rumors that he was going to make a full confession in exchange for his sentence being commuted. Like many another man confronting death, Frank Cirofici had turned to religion as the time of execution drew nearer, embracing Catholicism and receiving regular visits from the Reverend Father William E. Cashin, Sing Sing's Catholic chaplain. He was to receive the sacraments of the church before going to his death, and these include a full confession to a priest. Word spread that Father Cashin had brokered a deal to have Cirofici's sentence commuted in exchange for an admission of guilt and a full account of the events of that night. As it developed, the rumors were only partially correct. There would indeed be a statement, but it would not be a confession and Cirofici would share the same fate as the other three young men.

The spiritual needs of Gyp, Lefty, and Whitey—all Jewish—were attended to by Rabbi Jacob Goldstein, the Jewish chaplain at the prison, and Rabbi Mayer Kopfstein, of Temple Adath Israel in the Bronx. As the hours slipped by, the four condemned men maintained their composure, but their nerves were rubbed raw when they were visited by members of their families. Lefty Louie broke down completely when he was forced to part from his young wife; a similar scene played out in front of Gyp's cell when his wife was led away. Dago Frank's mother left on the arm of one of his brothers, and all the women received the support of Morris and Joseph Seidenschner, Whitey

Lewis's brothers. Jacob Rosenberg, Lefty's father, never got to see his son at all. He arrived at the prison Sunday evening, but was emotionally unable to go to his son's cell. His wife had never gotten even that far; she had collapsed at the railroad station and had to be taken home. Rabbi Goldstein agreed to accompany Mr. Rosenberg to visit his son, but when they arrived at the stair-case leading down to death row, Mr. Rosenberg began sobbing and shaking. "My God," he cried, "I want to see Louie but I can't, I can't go down there again." He could not keep his feet and was helped to a chair by the rabbi. "You had better go home," the rabbi told him. "Your duty is to those at home; go and be with them."

At about four o'clock on the morning of Monday, April 13, less than two hours before he would go to his death, Dago Frank Cirofici made the state-ment that everyone had been waiting for. It was not a confession. He denied having been on the scene when Rosenthal was slain, but he admitted that he knew about the plot and acknowledged that he was the leader among the four men. In the presence of Father Cashin, Superintendent of Prisons John B. Riley, Warden Clancy, his mother and his sister, Cirofici said, "The men who fired the shots were Gyp, Louie, and Vallon. I had nothing to do with the shooting, and so far as I know Becker had nothing to do with the case. It was the result of a gambler's fight that had been going on for fifteen years."

Cirofici's statement was made too late for it to have any effect. Superin-tendent Riley said that had it been made earlier, the execution would prob-ably have been postponed until the end of the week, but there were no grounds for commuting the sentence. He also said the statement would not affect Becker's upcoming trial. He pointed out that no one had claimed that Becker had dealt directly with the gunmen, so the fact that Frank knew noth-ing of his involvement would have been of no use to the defense. He also noted that Cirofici's statement had not been made under oath, nor had any notes been taken. Riley, who appeared sympathetic to the condemned men as preparations were made for their execution, took the opportunity to declare his opposition to capital punishment.

"There are fifteen other prisoners in the state prisons," he said, "eleven of whom are in Sing Sing, awaiting decisions on appeals from death sentences." He said he wished there would be no more executions in New York State, but he expected that many more would follow. In fact, the number of executions would increase dramatically as the electric chair came to be judged an efficient and humane instrument for invoking the "ultimate sanction," and Sing Sing would become its most prolific user.

The four executions that would be carried out beginning at sunrise were testimony to the mechanical precision with which "the chair," as it would soon be known, could carry out its mission. It took just thirty-nine minutes—less than ten minutes each—to dispatch all four. They had been prepared the night before, dressed in loose black jump suits. The trousers were slit to allow an electrode to be attached to their legs. They would wear no shoes or socks; they would go to their deaths barefoot. In keeping with Clancy's orders, the men were kept busy all day Sunday. When no visitors were present, guards saw to it that they were occupied. Personal items that were taken from them when they entered Sing Sing sixteen months earlier were returned to them and were distributed among their relatives. Copies of photographs that had been taken during their stay were signed and given to the visitors. Those who would witness the executions arrived long before sunrise. New York State law required executions to be witnessed by at least twelve observers. The warden was to be assisted by seven deputy sheriffs. Each condemned man was permitted to be attended by no more than two clergymen. Physicians would be present to pronounce the men dead and perform autopsies. The remaining seats in the death chamber would be given to newspaper reporters, men of science, and criminologists who had a professional interest in observing the executions at first hand. The warden made his selections from among hundreds of applications he received.

The order in which the men were to be executed was determined by the physicians. They were instructed to watch the four men closely and arrange the succession on the basis of which of them appeared best able to endure waiting while the others were ushered to the death chamber. The weakest would go first. That man, they decided was Dago Frank Cirofici.

At just past five-thirty, he was taken from his cell, physically supported by Father Cashin. "Good-bye, boys, God bless you," he shouted as he passed the cells of the other condemned men. He entered the death chamber at 5:38. When he was strapped into the chair, he began mumbling, almost inaudibly, "God have mercy, God have mercy ..." He was cut off summarily when Davis threw the switch, sending 1,920 volts of current racing through his body.

Moments later, Jacob (Whitey Lewis) Seidenschner entered, attended by Rabbi Goldstein. When he saw the electric chair, he paused, and his nerves seemed to take over. He brushed aside the two keepers on either side of him and began prattling, incoherently at first, then at a pace so rapid that each word seemed to fold upon the next. "Gentlemen," he said, "Gentlemen, I want to make a statement before I go. Gentlemen, for the sake of justice I want to make a statement. Gentlemen, them people who were on the stand, who said they see me, they were perjurers. I swear by God I didn't fire a shot at Rosenthal . . ." When it appeared he was about to start mentioning names, Rabbi Goldstein stepped in front of him, cut him off and began chanting the Hebraic *Sh'mah* in English: "Hear, O Israel, the Lord is our God, our Lord is one." Two quick jolts of electric current ended the ordeal.

Harry (Gyp the Blood) Horowitz, also accompanied by Rabbi Goldstein, made no statement. As the rabbi read from the prayer book, Gyp, the least literate of the men, was unable to read the responses. The rabbi read them, and Gyp repeated them mechanically. He seemed dazed as he was led to the chair. Some said he might have been sedated. He displayed no emotion as he was fastened to the chair and hooked up to the electrodes. He went quietly.

Louis (Lefty Louie) Rosenberg confirmed the doctors' judgment in holding him for last. He appeared entirely unmoved as he entered the chamber. He pushed the keepers away forcefully, with obvious disdain, and went to the chair unattended. Although he was the smallest of the men and had about him a boyish quality, he showed himself to be the toughest. It took four jolts to put him away. At 6:17 in the morning the last of the gunmen was pronounced dead.

The physicians performed autopsies on each of the corpses. Their brain cells were preserved to be studied for the benefit of science. Their bodies were claimed by their next of kin.

23

ecker seemed to welcome the prospect of a new trial. He felt that all the stars were aligned in his favor this time. The judges on the Court of Appeals had deemed the key witnesses against him to be untrustworthy; they believed that the trial judge had acted as an ally of the prosecution. Had he had the benefit of a fair trial, Becker clearly would have been acquitted. Now, he had a new defense team and a judge who was celebrated for his even-handed application of the law. Even history appeared to be on his side: No one convicted of murder in New York County had ever been convicted in a retrial.

Becker's new attorneys had come on board just weeks before the trial was scheduled to begin and a matter of hours after Shay had announced his withdrawal. The day after the four gunmen were executed, Shay met with Becker in the Tombs and emerged with a written statement that he was withdrawing from the case. His explanation was explicit. Shay said that Becker's brother, Lieutenant John Becker, had been busy soliciting perjured testimony that would aid his brother's defense. He was said to have been seeking the same kind of tainted evidence on behalf of the gunmen. Shay said that, shortly before the hearing on his motion for a new trial, he had received an anonymous call in which the caller suggested they meet to discuss the possibility of obtaining manufactured evidence. Shay said he never met with the man

242

and did not know his name. In an interview at his Far Rockaway home on the eve of Becker's second trial, Shay said: "I am glad I retired from the case when I did. I should have retired sooner. As I said in my statement on retirement, I did not want to be associated with a case in which John Becker had a part. He meant to help his brother, of course, but he hurt his case."

Becker's new attorneys were ready to step in immediately. Martin T. Manton, of the firm of Cockran & Manton, had met with Becker a week before Shay announced his retirement and agreed to take the case. Manton, like Shay, was principally a negligence lawyer and had not been involved in many criminal cases. He had become Cockran's junior partner about a year earlier, and what the thirty-four-year-old Manton lacked in recognition and experience was more than compensated for by the senior partner. Former Congressman W. Bourke Cockran, at age sixty, was a formidable presence whose reputation as an orator reached across the Atlantic. In 1895, a young Winston Churchill had visited the United States and was smitten by the manner in which Cockran projected his voice and framed his words. Speaking one-on-one or before a large group, he was able to mesmerize his audience by the manner of his speech, regardless of what it was he was saying. Churchill later wrote: "I must record the strong impression this remarkable man made upon my untutored mind. I have never seen his like, or in some respects, his equal." He was impressed on sight by Cockran's imposing stature—a tall, burly man "with an enormous head, gleaming eyes and flexible countenance," but it was his voice, thundering yet modulated, that captured his imagination. When Churchill, half the older man's age, asked him how he could learn to keep an audience of thousands spellbound, Cockran told him to speak as if his voice were an organ, to use strong words and enunciate clearly in wavelike rhythm.

Adlai Stevenson, the eloquent but unsuccessful Democratic candidate for president in 1952 and 1956, discussed his last meeting with Churchill in the early 1950s. "I asked him," Stevenson recalled, "on whom or what he had based his oratorical style. Churchill replied: 'It was an American statesman who inspired me and taught me how to use every note of the human voice like an organ.' Winston then, to my amazement, started to quote long excerpts from Bourke Cockran's speeches of sixty years before. 'He was my model,' Churchill said. 'I learned from him how to hold thousands in thrall.'"

Cockran had never reserved his oratorical gifts exclusively for the courtroom. He was a celebrated Tammany Hall politician with a reputation as a renegade who did not hesitate to turn his back on the party's power structure and go his own way. Born in Ireland and educated there and in France, Cockran came to the United States in 1871 at the age of seventeen. He taught in a private academy and became principal of a public school in Westchester County, New York. He studied law, was admitted to the bar in 1876, and practiced in New York until he was elected to the House of Representatives as a Democrat in 1887. He delivered rousing speeches at the Democratic national conventions in 1884 and 1892, opposing the nomination of Grover Cleveland. In 1896, as an advocate of the gold standard, he jumped the party and supported the Republican William McKinley against William Jennings Bryan, the Democratic candidate. But Cockran did not remain allied with the Republicans for very long. He took issue with the imperialism of the McKinley administration, which led to the Spanish-American War, and he campaigned for Bryan in 1900.

Never shy about taking on a world-class opponent, Cockran did not blink when he found himself on opposite sides of a scientific issue with no less an eminence than Thomas Alva Edison. Their difference involved the use of the newly invented electric chair in 1889 when William Kemmler was sentenced to become its first victim. Representing the condemned man, Cockran obtained a stay of execution on the ground that the new device violated the Eighth Amendment's prohibition of cruel and unusual punishment. Cockran argued that electricity was inherently unpredictable and would act differently from one situation to another. He based his argument on the nature of resistance—the ability of a substance or thing to impede the flow of electrical current. Cockran maintained that resistance differed vastly from person to person, and there was no sure way of knowing whether a man would be killed instantly or would suffer through increasingly high charges until they proved fatal. Edison, the chief witness for the state, demurred; in fact, he called Cockran's argument "nonsense." The chair would work quickly and humanely, he insisted, if sufficient voltages were used. The trick, of course, was to know whether "sufficient voltages" would vary depending on the object to which they were being applied. The judge who heard the arguments ruled in favor of the state. Cockran appealed and the case went all the way to the United States Supreme Court, which also denied the appeal. Kemmler thus became the first man executed in the electric chair on August 6, 1890, in Auburn Prison in Upstate New York. As far as anyone could tell, he died quickly and painlessly. But future circumstances would show that Cockran was correct; the effectiveness of the voltage depended on its object. Ironically, the thesis would be validated at the painful expense of his own client.

Perhaps the most significant change in Becker's favor was the appointment of Samuel Seabury to serve as judge at the retrial. Seabury was a patrician New Yorker whose prematurely white hair and somber, dignified demeanor made him appear older than his forty-one years. His career had begun inauspiciously in 1899 when he lost a bid for the City Court running as an anti-Tammany candidate. Six years later, with Tammany's support, he was elected to the State Supreme Court. He achieved a measure of notice for the manner in which he conducted the trials of several police inspectors who had run aground following Becker's first trial. Mainly on that record, he had been named to preside over the lieutenant's new trial.

Seabury's salad years were still far in the future. More than a decade later, he helped topple the corrupt regime of Mayor Jimmy Walker, was instrumental in the election of Fiorello H. LaGuardia who became New York's most popular mayor, and championed Governor Franklin Delano Roosevelt's campaign for president. He is best remembered as the leader of the eponymous Seabury Commission whose relentless investigation of corruption in city government drained much of the power from Tammany Hall.

In the spring of 1914, Seabury's immediate objective was winning the Democratic nomination for the Court of Appeals in the November election. Sitting as judge in a high-profile trial could be a stepping stone in that direction. Becker, for his part, was relieved to have escaped the capricious, unbending atmosphere of Goff's court in favor of what promised to be a more orderly courtroom and a judge who had earned a reputation for being scrupulously impartial.

Despite Becker's optimism, the initial round of judicial sparring did not go well for the defense. Becker was arraigned on April 15, and Justice Seabury set May 6, exactly three weeks later, for the start of the trial. Shay, serving the defense in transition, objected strenuously. Three weeks was not nearly enough time for Manton to prepare the case, he told the judge. He noted that there were more than three thousand typewritten pages of the trial record alone. There also would be about sixty witnesses to examine. "The defendant does not seek a delay," he told the court. "He wants to go on with the case as soon as possible, but it is a physical impossibility to be ready by May 6."

Seabury didn't agree. "In my judgment," he said, "the trial should go on then, and you should stay in the case until other counsel can take it up."

The day before the trial was to begin, Tuesday, May 5, the defense was jarred by a turn of events that was entirely unforeseen. One of the new witnesses who was expected to turn the case in Becker's favor had decided to switch sides. Harry Cohen, the chauffeur also known as Moe Levy, walked into the office of Assistant District Attorney Frederick J. Groehl and told him he was prepared to turn state's evidence. He would testify that he had driven Schepps and Webber to the Harlem conference at the corner of Seventh Avenue and 124th Street. He would appear for the state as a non-accomplice and corroborate in every detail the story Schepps had told on the witness stand.

Cohen, of course, had signed an affidavit in which he swore that he had not taken Webber and Schepps to the site at which Becker was said to have met with the accomplices and planned Rosenthal's assassination. The absence of evidence regarding the Harlem conference had been cited in the Court of Appeals decision as sufficient on its own to reverse Becker's conviction. Confirmation that the meeting had indeed taken place could be enough to doom any prospect of an acquittal. There was no easy explanation for Cohen's decision to flip. Asked about the conversion, Whitman said, "I can't answer that now." Shay was totally mystified. He offered a full account of Cohen's offer to cooperate with the defense:

"I searched for the chauffeur whom Schepps called 'Moe Levy,' and I found him after the trial. He came to me with a number of his friends and made out an affidavit which was submitted as a part of the application for a new trial. There were five witnesses present when the affidavit was signed, and three of them were strangers to me. I considered the affidavit very strong and was glad to see that the Court of Appeals also considered it so.

"Cohen impressed me as a man of more than average intelligence. He made a very good impression, spoke well, and seemed refined. He admitted that he knew all the informers against Becker and that he had taken them out in his automobile many times, but he swore that he had never taken any of them to 124th Street and Seventh Avenue. He did say that he carried two of them up Seventh Avenue on July 13, 1912, but that had nothing to do with the case, for the alleged Harlem conference, according to Rose and Webber, took place in the latter part of June, 1912."

J. Robert Rubin, second deputy police commissioner, reinforced Shay's account of the story. Rubin, who was an assistant district attorney at the time of the first trial, acknowledged that Cohen and Schoenhaus had told him before the trial that they did not recall driving any of the informers to the site of the Harlem conference. There was no immediate accounting for what caused Cohen to switch sides on the eve of the trial. Nor would there ever be, for he was not called to testify by either side. He had been unexpectedly lost to the defense, and as the trial unwound, it developed that the prosecution did not need him. There were other, more reliable witnesses, who would place Becker at the Harlem conference.

The trial opened on May 6, a Wednesday, and there were fireworks right from the start. Cockran opened with a series of perfunctory motions, all of which would be denied, but the one that got the juices flowing was a motion that Justice Seabury hold Whitman in contempt for circulating stories to the press that were detrimental to the defendant. Cockran was in full roar, his face red with emotion, his fist clenched at one moment, then thrusting a finger in the direction of the district attorney. Whitman remained composed and visibly indifferent. He smiled back at his assailant, which fed Cockran's rage until finally he stormed from the courtroom declaring, "I am through with the Becker case, through with it. This is assassination."

Cockran of course would be back with a flourish, but the grunt work, the voir dire of prospective jurors and the interrogation of witnesses would, for the most part, be conducted by the firm's more methodical junior partner. The prosecution too had a change in personnel. Moss, who had carried much of the load in the first trial, had left the D.A.'s office, presumably over differences with Whitman, and was working for an organization called the Society for the Prevention of Crime. In his place were Assistant District Attorneys Frederick J. Groehl and John Delehanty.

The selection of the jury, which got off to a good start when five panelists were seated on the first day, subsequently unraveled; jurors that were accepted by both sides one day were found unacceptable the next. On Friday, it appeared that the jury box had been filled, but a day later three jurors were released, with serious consequences. An early edition of the *New York Globe* announced that the selection process had been completed but, more critically, that assumption led the paper to publish Whitman's opening address. Following a procedure that was not uncommon, the D.A.'s office had distributed advance copies of his remarks to the press. Trusting that the jury had been chosen and that the state would open its case the following morning, editors at the *Globe* decided to carry Whitman's statement. However, with three new panelists still to be selected, it meant that prospective jurors had the opportunity to read Whitman's statement prior to being examined. The defense asked for a mistrial, but that motion too was denied. Seabury fined four members of the *Globe* staff $250 each, and the matter was considered closed.

The jury was finally filled on Monday after four and a half days during which 331 prospective talesmen—144 more than for the first trial—were examined. In the aggregate, this jury was somewhat younger than the first, and not all of the men were married, a condition that Becker had insisted on nineteen months earlier. With all the pieces in place now, District Attorney Whitman stepped forth to address the jury. Becker, looking more robust than he had the first time, settled back to listen. He knew what to expect this time; he had heard it all before.

24

District Attorney Whitman's opening was largely a reprise of his earlier performance, but this time he was more direct. There was no longer any need to explore the nuances of the case, to acquaint the jury with the subtleties of guilt by implication. Everyone hearing the case at this point, no matter how closely vetted, would be acquainted with the basic facts that led Becker to be charged with first-degree murder. So Whitman came at the jury straight ahead.

He named all those involved in the conspiracy and described the defendant as "the worst murderer of them all." The case, he told the jury, was a simple one. Their task was to weed out all the underlings who had been hired to commit the act and get to "the man behind them all, the man with the motive for murder in his heart." To clarify matters, Whitman placed the cast of characters in three categories. In the first were the four men who did the shooting and had since been executed. The second group was made up of the informers whom the D.A. described as "middlemen" and as the "brokers of human life." In the third division, said the prosecutor, was "just one man. He was a police lieutenant, the most sinister influence behind the murder plot, the only one of them all in whose breast there was a real motive for the murder of Rosenthal, the only man who could profit by his death, to whom it would be of most vital interest to have Rosenthal's tongue forever silenced.... I believe that all the others were his instruments, just as much as the pistols which shot

Rosenthal down. Gentlemen of the jury, I believe that you have before you now the real murderer of Herman Rosenthal."

Following his opening remarks, Whitman called five witnesses who offered much the same testimony that had been placed in evidence at the first trial: Patrolman, John J. Brady, who was stationed near the murder scene and heard the five pistol shots; Detective Edward G. Frye, who led the chase of the murder car; Sergeant William J. File, who named those he saw in the Metropole just before Rosenthal was shot; the ex-coroner's physician who showed where the shots had struck the victim; and Louis Krause, the waiter who happened to be passing by and witnessed the shooting.

The first of the heavy hitters called to the stand was William Shapiro, the chauffeur of the murder car, who had driven the gunmen to the scene of the crime. Shapiro had ducked testifying at the first trial because he feared for his life, but he was an uneasy witness for the state at the trial of the gunmen. Now, he described in great detail his flight from the Metropole, but some of the details differed from his earlier testimony. At the gunmen's trial, he said that Dago Frank had leaned over the driver's seat "and told me that there were no cops, that Becker had fixed that." This time he said that he did not know which of the gunmen had told him that Becker had the cops fixed.

Manton tried to make the most of the discrepancy on cross-examination. He asked the witness if he remembered naming Frank at the trial of the gunmen. "I don't remember what I said at the trial," Shapiro responded. "How is that?" asked Manton. "If you cannot remember what happened a few months ago at the trial, how can you remember the night of the murder?" The question remained unanswered. The defense had scored a point, but it was a small one. Shapiro's testimony had clearly benefited the prosecution.

The court was bulging with spectators later that day for the encore appearance of Bald Jack Rose. He came to the stand as well-groomed and polished as he had been the first time, but it was not the same Jack Rose. Like many another lifetime criminal, once freed from the specter of prosecution he had found religion. The voice of retribution had whispered in Rose's ear, and he had followed its guidance diligently. Since being sprung from prison, he had been writing and lecturing at churches and YMCAs all over the city, confessing the sins of his "Life in the Underworld" and expounding on the virtues of clean living. His transformation was proof enough. During the first trial, he had come to court from a cell in the West Side Prison. This time, he motored in from his own country home in Norwalk, Connecticut.

He had described his new life to the press just two months earlier. He explained that he earned barely thirty dollars a week on the lecture circuit, having turned down a four-figure salary for theater engagements because he wanted "to carry a message to young men to shun dissolute companions and gambling. I and my companions in the Rosenthal affair are horrible examples of what dissolute companionship and gambling can lead to," he said.

But now, as he settled in for two days on the witness stand, it was the lives of his dissolute companions that formed the focus of his examination. Rose went over the same ground he had covered more than a year and a half ago, sounding even more detached than in his first appearance. Clearly, he had grown weary of telling the same story and answering the same questions, but it was the price he had agreed to pay for his freedom. Theatrical man that he was, he played the part that was given him. There was, however, a new twist or two to the original narrative. One of the most compelling was Rose's contention that Rosenthal acted as a spy for Becker, checking out gambling houses and gathering evidence that would facilitate a raid. Rose quoted Rosenthal directly:

"'You don't know what I've done for that fellow Becker. I've been doing things for him I wouldn't have done for anybody else on earth. It was me that made it possible for him to raid practically every place along the avenue so as to help him make a show. If Becker couldn't get the goods on a place I would go in for him and get the layout . . .'"

Casting Rosenthal in the role of Becker's stool pigeon appeared to be of some service for the defense, as it gave weight to the argument that the murder was the result of a feud within the gambling fraternity. For if owners of casinos raided by the strong-arm squad believed they had been set up by Rosenthal, they would have motive enough to plan his assassination.

In another bit of new testimony, Rose said that Becker was not responsible for stationing a patrolman in Rosenthal's place after the so-called friendly raid. It was officials of higher rank who had made that decision, he said, and Becker did not have the authority to have him removed. But Rosenthal held Becker responsible, and it was the continued presence of the policeman that provoked Rosenthal to go to the district attorney with his story of police corruption and Becker in control of the System.

There were a few other revelations of minor consequence and shades of difference in Rose's testimony at the two trials, but none seemed significant enough to turn the jury in Becker's favor. All the same, Manton did his best under cross-examination to puncture holes in the witness's story. He also tried to refashion the plot to create the suspicion that it might have been Rose himself who sponsored the murder. The scenario Manton created went this way:

Rosenthal, Rose's bitter rival in the gambling trade, had spread the word that Rose had framed Jack Zelig on the gun charge, hoping that Zelig's boys would avenge their leader by killing Rose. Rose, in turn, got wind of the plan and decided to turn things around. He set up the assassination of Rosenthal, and conspired with his cohorts to frame Becker, an easy target whose disappearance from the scene would benefit everyone involved. It was a credible enough story, given the fragile network of conflicting interests that ran through the gambling industry. What it lacked was the first suggestion of evidence and the likelihood that any could be produced. Zelig and the four gunmen were dead, and so was Rosenthal. Rose and his accomplices were forever bound together by the tale that freed them from a charge of murder.

Nevertheless, Manton was nothing if not determined. He kept Rose on the stand for five hours, the questions often coming faster than the witness could answer them. But in the last analysis, the cross-examination went nowhere. Rose parried every thrust calmly and routinely, and finally left the stand as unruffled as if he had spent the time chatting with members of one of his adoring church gatherings. There was, however, one remark made by Rose, not noted at the time, whose significance would grow in succeeding days. For the first time in either trial, the name of James Marshall was mentioned. He was the "little colored boy" who Vallon had testified was at the scene of the Harlem conference and who had spoken to Becker. His name would come up again, and he would soon be heard from.

Both Webber and Vallon testified the following day. Webber, thirty-seven years old, was now a businessman with an interest in a paper box manufacturing firm in Passaic, New Jersey, and he looked every bit the part. He had, he said, given up gambling forever. The new Webber told much the same story as the old one except for a slight change regarding the Harlem conference. It had begun, he now recalled, two hours earlier than he had testified at the first trial—at nine-thirty rather than eleven-thirty. That, he said, was the first time he had become involved in the plot, summoned there by Becker to orchestrate the slaying of Rosenthal. During the course of his cross-examination, Manton said he had a dictograph recording that would show that Webber had admitted after the first trial that Becker had nothing to do with the killing. The recording also would prove that Webber, whom Manton described as "the captain of the murder army," said Becker was framed by Rose to deflect the guilt of the real killers.

Like the two witnesses who preceded him, Vallon echoed his previous testimony almost verbatim. But once again, there was a new emphasis on the meeting in Harlem. Vallon described the scene at the vacant lot off the corner of 124th Street and Seventh Avenue. Becker was sitting on a plank that spanned two barrels while the others stood. At one point, Becker called the "colored boy" over and spoke with him briefly. After the boy had left, Becker said, "'That's a little stool pigeon of mine. I'm going to raid a crap game just a block from here, but he tells me there are only two people in the place. I've got to wait.'"

Ten days into the trial, the prosecution's case seemed to be less persuasive than it had been the first time. There was little in the way of new testimony and, as yet, nothing but the word of the informers that would link Becker to the crime. The session on Friday, May 15, began inauspiciously with a procession of minor witnesses who affirmed details of time and place that were largely uncontested. But late in the day the whole tenor of the trial shifted with the appearance of an unexpected witness.

At about four o'clock, Mrs. Lillian Rosenberg, the young widow of Lefty Louie Rosenberg, took the stand for the state, and in just seven minutes of testimony she did more damage to the defense's case than the prosecution had managed in the previous week and a half. She provided the uncontested corroboration the district attorney had been seeking since the murder charge was lodged against Becker. Lefty Lillie, as she was called by her husband's friends, told the court that Rose was telling the truth when he said he had hired Lefty and the other gunmen. She said that Rose had come up to her apartment on Southern Boulevard when word was making the rounds that Rosenthal was going to tell all to the district attorney and warned her husband that he and his pals would be framed by Becker unless they arranged to have Rosenthal killed.

"Will you state the conversation which you heard?" Whitman asked.

She said: "Rose came up one day and says, 'Becker sent me to tell you and the other boys that he was going to frame you up with a gun,' and Louie says, 'We don't carry no gun.' Rose says, 'That don't make no difference if you carry any or not. As soon as you step out on the street Becker is going to frame you up.' So then Louie says, 'Can't I fix it up any way with Becker?' Rose says, 'Yes, you know that Rosenthal is squealing on Becker, and the only way you can fix it up with Becker is by you getting the other boys to kill Rosenthal.'" Then, Lillie said, "Louie pulled Jack Rose by the sleeve, not to say anymore."

Whitman then asked Lillie what she had seen on the night of July 16. She said she had seen the four gunmen at six P.M. in the apartment on Seventh Avenue. Louie "had a package of money," she said. "It was wound around with about an inch of paper, tied around, pasted around, like. And in about twenty minutes, ten or twenty minutes, Frank came after him and they went into a little room. They went into a little room, and when they came out I seen Whitey have a few bills in his hand."

Mrs. Rosenberg's testimony was devastating, and Manton did what he could to deflect it. Reading from the record of the gunmen's trial, he asked the witness:

"At the trial of your husband in November 1912, do you remember this question being asked you and your giving this answer: 'Q.—While you were in the apartment, in your presence, did you hear Jack Rose say anything to your husband or to any other men about the killing or the croaking of Herman Rosenthal? A.—No.' Do you remember that?"

Lillie remembered, and she had the answer: "I lied to save my husband at that time."

Who could doubt the statement or quarrel with the response? Lillian Rosenberg was the perfect collaborator. She was not an accomplice, and she had no motive to lie on behalf of the state. She detested the district attorney for the relentless manner in which he had prosecuted her husband and campaigned against his appeal. She had said that she felt humiliated and was ashamed to appear in public. On the other hand, she bore no animosity toward Becker. She had told a friend that she decided to offer her testimony "in the interest of justice."

At one point during direct examination, Mrs. Rosenberg had said: "Jack

Rose did not tell me to say that I had lied at the first trial to save my husband. I promised my husband ..."At that point, Manton's objection was sustained by Justice Seabury, and no one learned what she had promised her husband. Not surprisingly, reporters covering the trial suspected that the best of what she had to say was still unspoken. The following day, a number of them gathered at her mother's apartment in Lower Manhattan hoping to fill in the blanks. At first, she was reluctant. "Oh, please don't ask me any more questions," she said. "I don't want to say any more about the case." But the newsmen persuaded her that this was her opportunity to keep the promise she had made to her husband. Finally, she agreed.

"I went to the death house on Easter Sunday," she said, "the day before Louie and the others were put to death. It was on that day that Louie made me promise that I would tell the whole truth. 'Now, girlie,' he said to me, 'there is no chance of my escaping. I'm ready for my punishment. I don't want you to tell no lies for me or about me. You tell nothing but the truth. You tell whatever you know.' On that Easter Sunday, only a few hours before the boys were to die, my husband said to me, 'Rose and Becker are responsible for all of this.' My husband never fired a shot," she said. "Only two men fired the shots. They were Harry (Gyp the Blood) and (Dago) Frank." In his last-minute confession, Frank had said that he was miles away when the crime was committed. "Are you sure that Frank was there?" a reporter asked. "Yes, Frank was there," she said.

Lillie explained her reluctance to testify. "I was hoping that I would not have to tell this," she said. "I was thinking about it all the time. Although Louie told me to tell the whole truth, I thought of what he had to suffer in the death house and hesitated. I had no hatred for Becker, and I didn't want Mrs. Becker to suffer as I had suffered. Then the district attorney sent for me, but I still hoped I wouldn't have to testify. I begged not to be placed on the stand."

She then told of a chance meeting she had with Mrs. Becker and the high regard she had for her. "I met Mrs. Becker in the subway on the same day that the reprieve for my husband and the others was denied by Governor Glynn. Mrs. Becker is a mighty fine woman. She said to me, 'I feel terribly sorry for you, but don't lose hope.' She asked me up to her home. The next day I went up to Albany to see Governor Glynn, and on the way back I went to Mrs. Becker's house. I told her it looked very bad and that it didn't look as if I could save my husband.

Mrs. Becker said to me, 'Don't despair. My husband's lawyers are doing every-thing to help you and the other boys.'"

Mrs. Rosenberg's interview provided the newsmen with more interesting copy than they had gotten during most of the trial, and they wrote it fully, and their papers were generous with the space they allotted her story. But it was not evidence; most of what she had to say would have been legally char-acterized as either hearsay or lacking relevance and would not have been admitted at trial. Still and all, if the news fraternity was feeling somewhat list-less at the lack of fireworks being offered, they just needed a bit more patience. There were better days ahead.

The state was preparing to close on Monday, May 18. It was nearly two weeks since the trial opened, and thus far the prosecution's case did not appear very strong. Mrs. Rosenberg's testimony was compelling, but it certainly was not enough to convict the defendant. The objection raised by the Court of Appeals had not been satisfied. There was still no hard evidence that would tie Becker to the murder conspiracy, nothing that would place him in direct contact with the killers, no corroboration of the story told by the inform-ers. Not yet. The final day of the state's case would be all that was needed to gain a conviction. Sam Schepps, the sole corroborating witness at the first trial, was nowhere to be seen this time. His testimony had been branded suspect by the Court of Appeals, and the prosecution now considered him a liabil-ity. He was replaced by five new witnesses who would corroborate the story told by Rose, Webber, and Vallon, and what they had to say would send Becker to the electric chair.

The first was Charles B. Plitt, Jr., once Becker's press agent who did the police lieutenant's bidding and conveyed his legend to all who would listen. Although he did not testify at the first trial, Plitt was considered a possible witness for the defense. After Becker's conviction, he had tried to persuade reporters that the lieutenant had been railroaded, the victim of a relentless campaign by the *New York World* and the district attorney's office, which, he said, bribed witnesses to testify for the prosecution. But somewhere between the two trials, Plitt switched sides and delivered some of the state's most dam-aging testimony against the defendant. He was, however, not the most con-vincing of witnesses. He was young—in his midtwenties—slight of build, and hesitant in his responses even under direct examination. He also came to the stand with some unusually heavy baggage for a witness: he had recently served time on a charge of perjury.

Curiously, Plitt was the indirect cause of the first break that occurred between Becker and Rosenthal. It was Rosenthal's refusal to contribute to Plitt's murder defense that had roused Becker's ire and placed Rosenthal's Hesper Club squarely in the lieutenant's sights. Plitt was subsequently acquitted, but a civil suit was brought against him in connection with the murder case, and it was his testimony during that proceeding that resulted in his perjury conviction.

Now, Plitt was an instrument of the state in trying to establish that Becker knew in advance that Rosenthal was to be killed late on the night of July 15, 1912. Earlier that day, Plitt testified, Becker had instructed him to keep a memorandum of his movements "'so that you can have an alibi. You may need it,'" he said. "'And above all things, keep away from Times Square tonight. Keep that under your lid, too.' I asked him why I should prepare an alibi and why I should keep away from Times Square. 'Is anything coming off?' I asked, and he replied, 'Never mind, you just do what you are told and no harm will come to you.'" The following day, Plitt said, he met Becker in the police station, and they discussed the murder. Becker asked him, "'What in the hell was the matter with that bunch? Were they all cockeyed drunk? From the way they acted in pulling off that trick, you would think they were setting the stage for a moving picture show.'"

Plitt said he saw Becker regularly during the weeks following the murder. On one occasion, after Rose's arrest, Becker told him "'to get in touch with Rose and tell him to sit tight. Tell him that I will take care of him.'" Becker became increasingly fearful that Rose might open up to the district attorney. Plitt quoted him as saying, "'I wonder if those bastards will squeal on me or stick. Tell Rose that I am doing all I can for him. I wonder how he is fixed down there in the Tombs.'"

After Becker was convicted, Plitt rode with him in the train to Sing Sing. At one point during the trip, Plitt testified, when they were alone in the washroom, Becker instructed him, "'If anything happens to me, I want you to kill that squealing bastard Rose.'"

Plitt had taken the stand at 11:55, and Whitman turned him over to the defense in less than an hour. It was the most destructive testimony that had been elicited thus far. Manton understood that it was essential for the defense to cast doubt on Plitt's story, and after a break for lunch he began to hammer away at his credibility. He got him to admit that he did not know the date of his birth. He asked Plitt if he had ever been in an institution for the feeble-minded, and he responded, "Not that I can remember." He got Plitt to give the same response, "I don't remember," to a series of questions concerning his relations with Becker. Finally, he arrived at the core of the matter, which was Plitt's dealings with the district attorney's office. Plitt said he met with Assistant District Attorney Groehl ten to twelve times, including one meeting about a month earlier in Atlantic City.

"Why did you go to Atlantic City?" Manton asked. "For my health," Plitt said.

"Who paid your expenses?" "The district attorney's office."

"The district attorney's office sent you to Atlantic City for your health?" "Yes."

Plitt testified that he had been in Atlantic City for three months, with the D.A.'s office paying all expenses. Since returning, he had been paid a salary of thirty dollars a week.

Manton then asked the question to which everything else had been prelude:

"Now, isn't it a fact that you struck a bargain with Mr. Groehl in which it was agreed that if you turned state's evidence the charges of perjury against you should be dismissed?"

"No," Plitt responded.

Manton next read a long letter Plitt had written to John Becker offering an account of the testimony he had given to the grand jury that indicted Becker. In it, Plitt denied having been Becker's press agent or ever having given him information regarding future raids. He also said that Becker had never admitted having played a part in planning Rosenthal's murder. He told the grand jury that Becker had been framed by the district attorney's office, and was finally ordered out of the grand jury room for making statements that accused Whitman and Moss of framing Becker.

Before dismissing Plitt, Manton had one more weapon in his arsenal—a letter Plitt had sent to the editor of the *Summit Record* in New Jersey. The letter was dated December 5, 1912, less than two months after Becker was convicted, and it said, "If you only knew the real truth of Becker's case it would open your eyes. Becker has gone to the death house an innocent man." The letter laid the blame for Becker's conviction on the district attorney's office, which Plitt called a "carload of murderers," and said Whitman was seeking political fame and would do anything to win higher office.

It was clear that Manton was pleased with the product of his interrogation. He told reporters that he believed Plitt's testimony had helped the defense. "Who would believe a man who was so discredited?" he asked. "He has cracked the state's case."

But the state's case was not yet concluded. There were four other witnesses who would offer new lines of corroboration.

Former Deputy Commissioner George Dougherty testified that Becker had lied to him when, on the morning Rose turned himself in, he said he had not seen Rose in at least a month. Dougherty said Becker knew where Rose was when he was wanted by the police but did not share the information with them.

Harry Pollock, who had provided Rose with shelter when he was in hiding, told the court that Becker knew Rose was at his home and had instructed him, "'Tell Rose to stay there until I communicate with him, and tell him not to worry.'"

Mrs. Lillian Rosenthal corroborated Rose's statement that her husband was Becker's personal representative in his gambling house and that Becker had been there every night until the raid.

And finally there was James Marshall. Substituting as a prosecution witness for Harry Cohen, the reversible chauffeur, Marshall would be the state's most potent witness. He had come to the district attorney's attention by way of an off-hand remark made by Harry Vallon when he testified at the first trial. Vallon had followed Rose and Webber to the stand and repeated the same story they had told before volunteering a new piece of information. Questioned about the Harlem conference, he said, "There was a little colored boy on the other side of the street, and [Becker] called him over and spoke to him." The "little colored boy," now twenty-two years old, was James Marshall. He had been found in the Washington, D.C., area working as a vaudeville dancer, and now, at four o'clock on a Monday afternoon, he stepped to the witness stand, and in just thirty minutes of testimony he provided the state with the critical evidence that would seal Becker's fate.

Marshall said he first met Becker when the Strong-arm Squad raided his brother's Eighth Street café in the spring of 1912. He said that Charles Steinert, a member of the squad, asked him if he ever gambled. Marshall said he did, and Steinert gave him ten dollars and told him to go out and gamble. Becker was standing nearby and thought that Marshall—neat, polite, and with an inclination to risk a few bucks here and there—would make a fine stool pigeon. From then on, Marshall said, Becker often gave him money which he used to get evidence on Negro gambling houses that Becker wanted to raid. It did not take Whitman long to get to the point at issue. He determined that on the night of June 27 Becker had given Marshall money to gamble in a house on West 124th Street. Marshall later made out an affidavit that was the basis for a warrant being issued to raid the premises. Whitman produced the affidavit, establishing the date of the raid. He then led the witness through a series of questions that would tie Becker to the conspiracy:

Q. Had you seen Becker before, at 124th Street and Seventh Avenue? *A.* Yes, on the northwest corner.

Q. Was he alone? *A.* No, sir.

Q. Where were you? *A.* On the south side of 124th Street.

Q. Where was he? *A.* Across the street. Mr. Becker called me over. He said, "Jimmy, why don't you hurry up?" I told him there were only a few men in the place, and he decided to wait until more came.

Q. Was he alone? *A.* No.

Q. Who was with him? *A.* There was a man speaking with him and a man standing a little bit away.

Q. Do you know any of them? *A.* Yes, sir.

Q. Who are they? *A.* One of them was Mr. Rose.

Thus the prosecution had gotten what it was looking for, the third-party corroboration that Becker had met with Rose and the other informers to plan Rosenthal's murder. It was the piece of the puzzle that the Court of Appeals said had been missing, and now the picture appeared to be complete.

Manton pressed hard on cross-examination, but he had no place to go. He tried first to put into question the accuracy of Marshall's identification:

Q. You say you saw some men with Becker? *A.* Yes, sir.

Q. Were they policemen? *A.* No, sir.

Q. When did you find out that one of the men was Rose? *A.* After I saw his picture in the newspapers.

Q. Who took you downtown to the office where you saw Rose recently? *A.* Mr. Maxwell, from Mr. Whitman's office.

Q. You have only seen Rose once before in your life, that night in Harlem? *A.* Yes, sir.

Manton's last thrust was an attempt to taint Marshall's motive for coming to New York to testify. "Were you promised any money for your testimony?" he asked. Marshall responded, "They told me they would pay me for the time I lost in my regular work as an actor. I expect to get that."

On redirect examination, Marshall said that he had been under contract to perform in Pittsburgh that week and Whitman had agreed to reimburse him only for the salary he would lose. There was no suggestion that Marshall had been paid anything more than the money he forfeited by not appearing in Pittsburgh, and to all appearances he had made the trip to New York reluctantly at the urging of the district attorney.

It was late in the day when the state rested. The defense had a mountain to climb.

25

Throughout most of the state's presentation, Manton had considered the possibility of offering no defense and proceeding right to summation. The prosecution's case, he insisted, was weaker than it had been during the first trial. It rested almost exclusively on the testimony of the three accomplices, which already had been branded untrustworthy by the Court of Appeals. Nothing new had been added, and therefore there was nothing the defense felt compelled to respond to. But all that changed at the very end of the state's case, with the testimony regarding the Harlem conference. Even Becker, who had oozed confidence from the start, now appeared worried. He tried to convince his attorneys to allow him to testify in his own behalf, but, as in the first trial, they were reluctant to open the way to the introduction of evidence that would taint Becker as a crooked cop in the minds of the jury. It was a reasonable enough concern, but in all likelihood, the wrong decision. For the defense had little of consequence to offer in rebuttal.

In his opening statement, Manton made it clear that the core of his defense would be the lack of credibility of the state's witnesses. "There isn't any cause of action in this case," he told the jury. "It's all just words, words, words," he said, quoting Hamlet. "We have self-confessed perjurers, like that fellow Plitt, coming up here and telling of conversations which cannot be substantiated. We have men who admit that they have been lying all their lives come into the district attorney's office and sign instruments obligating them to tell the truth. Can you believe them? All I want in this trial is the truth. Bring me the true facts in this case and this man Becker will walk out of here a free man."

That, as it developed, was the best Manton had to offer, and it would not be enough. Once again, Reich, or Sullivan, as he was referred to by both attorneys, was the chief witness for the defense, and he told much the same story he had the first time: how Rose, Webber, and Vallon hatched the murder plot in the Tombs; how Rose encouraged him to join with them in the conspiracy; and how, when he refused, Webber offered him $25,000 to go along. He expanded a bit on Webber's relations with Rosenthal. When they walked up Broadway shortly after the murder was committed, Reich said, Webber pinched him on the cheek and said, "Jack, this is the happiest moment of my life. I can go home now and see my wife and walk about the streets without fear. You know that son-of-a-bitch Rosenthal was going to have me croaked, but I thank God he got it first."

Reich added yet another fillip with regard to Webber. He said he did not see Webber again until about a year after Becker's first trial. The Court of Appeals had not yet ruled, and Becker was still in Sing Sing under the sentence of death. Webber told him, Reich said, that Becker's conviction weighed heavily on his conscience and he could not sleep. He said he would be willing to serve five years in prison if that would help to free Becker. Reich suggested that he swear out an affidavit that he lied during his testimony, and Webber at first agreed but later said his attorney told him that as a confessed murderer his affidavit would be worthless. The two of them then concocted a plan to try to get Becker exonerated through the testimony of Sam Schepps. They would ask Schepps to meet them at the home of a mutual friend, Isidore Fischman, and Webber would install a dictograph and get Schepps to talk about the murder in a way that would show him to be an accomplice rather than a corroborator. The meeting never was held, and the dictograph recording that Manton had promised to produce when he was cross-examining Webber never was mentioned again.

Under cross-examination, Reich was as belligerent as he had been during the first trial, but Whitman was ready for him. He appeared at times to challenge and goad the witness whose spontaneous outbursts, often coated with self-righteousness, created the image of a man who was too quick to proclaim his virtue and so could not be entirely trusted. There were moments when Whitman moved up close and leaned in toward the witness, and Reich came forward as if to meet him nose to nose, roaring his response and giving every indication that he was ready to pounce at the district attorney.

Whitman seemed to relish every opportunity to tip Reich off guard and show him to the jury as something other than what he represented himself to be. At one point he asked the witness if he had ever made a living by posting bail for ladies of the night. Reich replied that he had only furnished bail for one woman and that she was totally respectable.

"Didn't you bail Lillian Wolfe?" Whitman asked.

"I don't remember," Reich said.

The trap was being set. "What?" Whitman said, "you say you bailed only one woman and yet you don't remember her name? Isn't it true that you have bailed so many women that you can't remember their names?"

Reich threw his head back and laughed. Whitman baited the trap. "Didn't you furnish bail for Lillian Wolfe on June 13, 1906, and wasn't she fined ten dollars for soliciting?"

Reich said he had never bailed a woman charged with soliciting. Whitman sprang the trap: "Don't you know that I was the magistrate in that case?"

None of the remaining twenty-six defense witnesses had Reich's star quality, but the cumulative effect of their testimony was nonetheless helpful.

Following Reich to the stand was Isidore Fischman, a long-time friend of Rose, Webber, Vallon, and Rosenthal, who repeatedly said he heard one or another of them say they had framed Becker to save themselves. Webber in particular, he said, told him again and again that the three of them had agreed to deliver Becker to Whitman. He also said that he now regretted the part he had played in the conspiracy. "I will try to save Becker some day," Fischman quoted Webber as saying. "I will make an affidavit if Max Steuer, my lawyer, says that that will do any good."

The parade of witnesses supporting Reich's contention that the three informers had framed Becker continued. Morris Beecher, an attorney, corroborated Reich and Fischman regarding Webber's remorse. Two newspaper reporters—Roslyn D. Whitock of the *World* and Richard H. Rooney of the *Globe*—told of their shipboard interview with Webber, shortly after Becker's conviction, in which Webber said there had never been a plan to kill Rosenthal; they had intended only to scare him, and there would have been no murder "if a couple of the kids had not got drunk." Charles Reich, Jacob's brother, backed his brother's testimony in every detail. And Frederick H. Hawley, former reporter for the *Sun* who had called Becker and informed him of Rosenthal's murder, repeated the testimony that had gotten him fired after the first trial; to wit, that Becker had never been out of his sight that morning and therefore could not have met with Rose and Webber. Hawley was the last witness of the day. Twenty new witnesses came forth the next day to testify in Becker's behalf.

Three members of his strong-arm squad affirmed that they were with Becker on June 27, the night the Harlem gambling room was raided, but they swore there had been no conference with the conspirators. They had seen Becker speak briefly with Marshall, but Rose and the others were nowhere in sight.

Police Inspector Hughes said he had met Becker in the station house shortly after the murder, and Becker had said, "I'm sorry they killed him. I wish they had waited. I have something in my pocket that would have shown him up."

Thomas F. McInerny, the head keeper at Sing Sing, tried to introduce into the record Dago Frank's "death bed" confession in which he said Becker was not involved in the murder plan, but Justice Seabury ruled that since it had not been sworn to or recorded, it was hearsay evidence and thus inadmissible.

Detective Sergeant James D. White testified that Becker's raid on Rosenthal's gambling house was not a fake but part of an effort to clean up gambling operations in the area. White's story was backed by four other members of the strong-arm squad.

Two deputy sheriffs who had accompanied Becker on his ride to Sing Sing contradicted Plitt's testimony that when he and Becker were alone in the washroom Becker told him to kill Jack Rose "if anything happens to me." The deputies said they had been with Becker throughout the trip, and he was never alone with Plitt.

Whitman alertly raised doubts about some of the testimony, but all told it was a good day for Becker. While nothing altogether new or substantial had emerged, the sheer repetition by twenty witnesses that Becker could not have participated in the murder plan created an atmosphere that was of benefit to the defendant.

Each side called a witness of little consequence the following day, which was the last day before the case would be given to the jury. The summations of the defense and prosecution attracted the largest crowds of the trial. The courtroom could not hold half of those who tried to squeeze in. Would-be spectators spilled into the hallways, blocking the elevators and staircases so completely that the building was cleared of all those who could not show tickets of admission. When Becker entered the courtroom, he had to push his way through a cluster of people who clogged the aisle. With polite apologies, he gently moved aside one person after another until he reached the defense table. He sat stolidly as Manton rose to plead his case to the jury. Some expected Cockran to make the summation, but Manton led the defense day by day and if he lacked Cockran's passion and eloquence, he offered by way of compensation an even-tempered, clinical approach that was respectful of detail and calculated to neither enflame nor alienate judge or the jury.

Manton's summation was reflective of the case he had put on. Methodically and relentlessly, he attacked the character and credibility of the state's witnesses. He described Rose, Webber, and Vallon as "products of the scum of the earth." Who, he asks, "does the prosecution pick out to prove the connection of Becker with this crime? Through three certain men, self-confessed assassins, the prosecution asks you, gentlemen of the jury, to determine this most important case. Do these three men come with open hearts, remorseful? No, they come with signed stipulations which protected them from trial for murder and every other crime on the calendar. They were glib men, evasive, defensive."

By contrast, Manton called his own chief witness, Jack Sullivan/Jacob Reich "the greatest character the city has ever produced." Unlike the informers who testified for the prosecution, Manton said, Sullivan "has the fervent desire to tell the truth and to see justice done" even if it meant going to jail on trumped-up charges. "Why was he locked up?" Manton asked. "Because he drank soda water when the shots were fired? Was he locked up because he was a murderer? Oh, no; only because he wasn't a collaborator.... He didn't come across, and he was indicted, and he went to prison for nine months. That is why I say he is the greatest character ever produced. This boy, crude as he is, should have the admiration of the jury. He could not be tempted; he could not be bribed.

He was willing to spend a life in prison to preserve the truth. It is a compliment to the human race that such a man can be found in life. Oh, men of men, will this defendant go to the electric chair on the testimony of perjurers, or will he be saved by this man who speaks with rugged honesty?"

Manton looked up at the clock. It was five P.M., and he noted that his three-hour time allotment was just about over. Though he was not a man given to theatrics, Manton decided to make the most of his last chance, and he went for the dramatic finish. He leaned in close to the front row of jurors and in lowered voice said:

"This man is charged with murder in the first degree. I want you, gentlemen of the jury, to understand that I want no compromise verdict. I want this man's life spared for God's free air, or else I want him sent to the electric chair. If he is guilty, that will be a merciful death for him." Then, by way of explaining why Becker was not called to testify, he continued, "I didn't believe, and I do not believe now, that it was necessary for him to deny the accusations of perjurers and thus, perhaps, bring in other things foreign to the case. He is either innocent or guilty of murder in the first degree and nothing else.

"I do not come to you with requests for sympathy; I don't want sympathy. I ask you to do your duty so that your conscience won't bother you when you go back to your homes. But think of those cells in the death house from which the light of heaven is barred. Think of these things, gentlemen of the jury, and all I ask of you is to give him an impartial verdict. I say now that he has had a fair and impartial trial, and it is for you to give him a fair and impartial verdict."

The jury, which had appeared somewhat impassive during much of Manton's summation, was clearly captivated by his closing. Yet, unaccustomed as he was to courtroom dramatics, Manton might have twice overstepped the interests of his client. Proclaiming that Becker had had a "fair and impartial trial" might have limited the defense's options if the verdict was appealed. And insisting that a conviction be for nothing less than first-degree murder with its mandatory death sentence conceivably swayed some jurors in the wrong direction. Lesser charges—second-degree murder and manslaughter—were available and would have spared Becker's life. In fact, it was later revealed that some jurors initially favored convicting him on a reduced charge.

All the same, both Manton and Becker seemed optimistic when the trial broke for dinner. The district attorney would offer his summation when court resumed. With the trial in its final hours, it seemed apparent that the verdict would turn on which witnesses the jury believed to be more credible. Becker's entire defense had placed its bet on the notion that his accusers could not be trusted because they were confessed murderers who would be on trial themselves if they had not plotted to frame Becker. It was no surprise then that Whitman addressed the issue right from the start.

"A man is not necessarily lying because he is a thief," he said; "he is not necessarily lying because he is a criminal; he is not necessarily lying because he is a gambler; he is not necessarily lying because he is the lowest of the low. If he can be made through hope or through fear or through any reason or any motive to tell the truth, you have no right to discredit the statement because it comes from a tainted source. If you want to know about murders or crimes you don't go to the altar or lyceum. I am not responsible for the fact that I can't put gentlemen on the stand to testify to the conditions of the underworld. If you want to know the truth of the matter and the dealings that have been had between the gambler and the police officer, to whom do you have to go to get it? There are only two people on earth that can tell you the truth; one of them is the officer and the other is from a tainted source and poisoned, but that is the only person that can tell you.

"Mr. Manton has told you that we have gone down to the slums, that we have gone down into the underworld, and it is perfectly true that we have put on the stand witnesses who, under ordinary conditions, are never to associate with the people that you and I know and love, and it is perfectly true. If I held any brief for these men, why did I go and arrest them? I pounded and pounded and pounded them—Rose and Webber and Vallon over there in the city prison—and held them there in jail before the coroner day after day, and day after day, convinced as I was that they had the truth, and determined as I was that it was my duty to get it if I could. Don't you suppose I knew during those days, when I had those three, that I had the men who knew the truth? They did fight well. Rose did stand, and so did Webber stand, and so did Vallon stand for hours and days of examination and pounding, just as Mr. Manton says, and they did try to protect the man who had compelled them to be what they were.

"They are not my witnesses; they are not Whitman's men. They are your witnesses and the people's witnesses. If they are not telling the truth, has a single person taken that stand, one who has contradicted successfully any single material fact, one single word of evidence that is competent in this case? I ask you to think with me for a minute. There has not been a single denial of the essential evidence presented by Rose or presented by Webber or presented by Vallon. I am not saying they were worthy of belief. We corroborate their statements. Has any voice been raised on that stand to contradict these rats, if you please? Don't you think it would be easy to deny it if it could be? Just think that over for yourselves."

Having invested his own witnesses with a degree of credibility, Whitman turned his attention to the most important witness for the defense. He not only accused Sullivan of lying, he accused him of being Becker's accomplice in planning the murder.

"That man who sat there," he said, pointing to the witness chair, "whom Mr. Manton now calls the noblest product of the nation, but whom I call a little monster and a most notorious professional bondsman for fallen women, that man, I say, is a murderer. I believed it from the beginning, but I never was so firmly convinced of it as I am at this very moment. Of course he would protect Becker. He is another murderer on the list of murderers that we have revealed."

It was late Thursday night when Whitman concluded his remarks. On Friday morning, Seabury would charge the jury. The verdict on Lieutenant Charles Becker would be in before sundown.

Seabury understood that his instructions to the jury had to be meticulous. The Court of Appeals had cited Justice Goff's charge as favoring the state when it overturned Becker's conviction, and Seabury was careful to frame his in language that was neutral and inclusive, making certain to parse every legal nuance the jury would have to consider. He defined the two degrees of murder and one of manslaughter that could be imposed; he spelled out the difference between "certain" and "uncertain" circumstantial evidence; he explained what an accomplice was and what constituted corroborative evidence, and then outlined, in great detail, the connection between the two.

"It is not necessary," he said, "that corroborative evidence shall cover every material fact testified to by an accomplice. If the accomplice is corroborated as to some material fact or facts, the jury may infer that he speaks the truth. In weighing the testimony of Rose, Webber, and Vallon, the jury must consider that they are accomplices; that they were given immunity; and that they had an interest in shielding themselves. But the law does not say that because a witness is tainted his testimony is therefore untrue. If you gentlemen of the jury find that the testimony of these three men has been corroborated by other evidence that tends to connect the defendant with the crime, you must convict the defendant. If, on the other hand, you find that their testimony has not been corroborated sufficiently, if you believe that it is not true, you must acquit the defendant."

The judge's instructions identified the Harlem conference as the core of the case, as the Court of Appeals had ruled, making the testimony of James Marshall the critical factor in determining whether it had in fact taken place. He went on to brief the jury on the issues it was required to consider.

"Now," he said, "some question was raised upon the argument as to whether or not Marshall might be mistaken in the identification of Rose. That is an important thing for you to determine; you will determine whether you think Marshall was telling the truth; you will determine whether or not you think Marshall was accurate in his identification; you are to determine whether you think he would recognize Rose; you are to determine whether or not you think Rose was easily identifiable. Those are all circumstances in the case which the jury have a right to consider in determining the question as to whether or not this so-called 'Harlem conference' took place."

Seabury's charge took two and a half hours. The *New York Times* said it "was regarded as dealing heavy blows to the defense" and that "most who heard it agreed that Becker had been damaged by it." But it also noted that "all agreed it was a masterful effort," that the judge's review of the case from the points of view of both prosecutor and defense was the best and most balanced exposition of the case that had yet been given. All told, Seabury's charge was widely viewed as beyond reproach. If Becker was damaged by it, it was likely because the state had presented a more convincing case than the defense. Certainly, that was the way the jury felt. It took them less than two hours to convict Becker on a charge of first-degree murder. Becker listened to the verdict impassively. He showed no emotion. He did not grip the rail for support as he had the first time. A deputy ushered him back to his cell in the Tombs. The deputy carried a pair of handcuffs; he did not put them on the prisoner until they left the courtroom.

It was later learned that the jury had little trouble deciding the case. Only one formal poll was taken. Immediately after beginning deliberations, seven jurors voted for a first-degree murder conviction, three for a lesser degree of murder, one for acquittal, and there was one abstention. After a brief, informal discussion during which the testimony of the various witnesses was reviewed, they agreed to discard Plitt's testimony for the prosecution and Sullivan's for the defense as untrustworthy. By contrast, they were inclined to take James Marshall at his word. Any doubts they might have had were erased when it was noted that Vallon had mentioned at the first trial that a colored boy had spoken with Becker during the meeting at the Harlem site. It was downhill from there. After about forty minutes, the jury foreman, F. Meredith Blagden, asked if all were agreed on a murder-one conviction. Each man nodded in turn. Conscious that it might appear that they had come to a decision without sufficient deliberation, they waited about an hour in the jury room before sending word to the judge that they had reached a verdict.

On Friday, May 29, Becker was sentenced to die in the electric chair during the week of July 6. Of course, that was an artificial date. Manton had announced that a notice of appeal would be filed within a few days, which would result in an extension of at least six months. That afternoon, Becker made his second trip to Sing Sing. To avoid the circus atmosphere that attended his first trip, with crowds awaiting his arrival at railroad stations, he was given a private ride to Ossining in the sheriff's own car. With little fanfare, he donned his prison-gray uniform and was locked into Cell 17 on the gallery tier of the prison. The cells on the gallery tier, referred to by the inmates as "hot boxes," were on the second floor of the death house and, in summer, were that much hotter than the twelve cells on the ground level. When Becker checked in, there were fourteen other inmates in the death house. A prisoner by the name of Pietro Rebacci was scheduled for execution on June 23. Two others would have to go to their death before Becker would be awarded a cell on the main floor.

While Becker began adjusting again to life on death row, Rose was in Boston organizing a theater company called Humanology, with the aim of producing plays that would celebrate the possibilities of uplifting humanity.

Webber had returned to his paper-box manufacturing firm in New Jersey. Vallon had left for a short vacation before resuming his life in Brooklyn where he worked as a chandelier salesman. Whitman was at his leisure in his recently acquired summer home in Newport, Rhode Island. He was gathering energy for the run of his life. The governor's mansion loomed just around the bend.

26

Whitman was awarded the Republican nomination for governor with little opposition, but he could hardly take his election for granted. He was,
after all, running against an incumbent—Martin H. Glynn—and a former
governor—William Sulzer—whose impeachment and removal from office
had opened the door for Glynn. Whitman campaigned relentlessly through
the late summer and early fall, ascending speakers' platforms wherever they
were available—banquet halls, churches, the headquarters of fraternal
organizations—bringing the word to the converted and the uninitiate alike.
His subject was as fundamental as one could have it: good against evil; and
his position on the matter was unequivocal—he stood for the good, no matter what the consequences.

On November 3, 1914, Whitman was elected by a substantial plurality of
133,000 votes over Glynn, the Democratic incumbent. The surprise in the
race was Sulzer, the candidate of the American and Prohibition Parties, who
finished third and received more than double the vote of the Bull Moose's
Frederick Morgan Davenport, a state senator, who ran with blessing of
Teddy Roosevelt. Roosevelt had stirred some juices during the campaign
when he denounced Whitman as an opportunist whose political ambitions
colored his performance as district attorney. "The truth is not in him," Roosevelt said of Whitman.

The Becker trial also was nutrient for the career of another participant. Justice Samuel Seabury, the Democratic candidate, was easily elected to the Court of Appeals, replacing the Republican Emory Chase. The success of neither Whitman nor Seabury was good news for Becker. There could be little doubt that the prosecution of Becker had propelled Whitman to the state capital. His celebrity had soared to the point where, even before he made the trip to Albany, he was being heralded as a possible candidate for president. His popular profile was that of a man who was unrelenting when pursuing his quarry and uncompromising when it came to fitting the punishment to the crime. Though such an image resonated with the public, it did not auger well for Becker, for if he lost his appeal, his last resort would be a grant of executive clemency from the governor, an unlikely prospect from the man who had staked his future on convicting him. As for Seabury, he would be taking the seat of Justice Chase, who had voted with the majority when the court awarded Becker a new trial. It appeared that aligning oneself with the fallen police lieutenant was not a good career move.

Early in the new year, with his appeal just a few months off, Becker received the best piece of news that had come his way in many months. James Marshall, whose testimony had linked him to the Harlem conference, recanted. He swore out an affidavit saying he had lied when he placed Becker at the scene and repudiated everything he had said at trial. Since Marshall was the principal corroborator at the second trial, his recantation seemed to place the prosecution's case in jeopardy. Certainly, it might be enough to warrant the Court of Appeals overturning Becker's conviction on some of the same grounds on which it had been reversed previously.

Marshall had come to the attention of the defense from an unexpected direction. On Saturday, February 13, he was arrested for spousal abuse in Philadelphia and brought to the station house for booking. There, he was questioned by two reporters from the *Philadelphia Evening Ledger* who asked him about his part in the Becker case, and he offered to sell them what he said was a sensational story. They turned down his offer, but Marshall apparently was ready to tell his tale free of charge. The crux of what he had to say was that he had lied on the witness stand. The reporters recognized a scoop when they saw one, but they also understood the need for validation. They sent a wire to Manton's office and told him of their discovery. Manton immediately dispatched his associate, John B. Johnston, to the *Ledger's* office where U.S. Commissioner Howard Long also was waiting.

They heard Marshall swear that his testimony had been coerced by Assistant District Attorney Frederick J. Groehl under the threat of arrest. He said Groehl had produced a false affidavit signed by Marshall regarding one of Becker's gambling raids and told him he would be charged with perjury if he refused to cooperate. The D.A., he said, wanted him to testify that he had seen Becker speaking with Rose at the corner of 124th Street and Seventh Avenue on the night of the Harlem conference. Marshall told him that he knew Becker but did not know Rose and could not say that he saw them speak to one another.

Marshall explained in detail: "Assistant District Attorney Groehl then told me that I could be arrested and held in the House of Detention until it was time for me to testify unless I testified willingly. Having theatrical engagements still unfilled in other cities, I explained that it would be impossible for me to remain in New York until the trial was called.

"The Assistant District Attorney then stated that he would have an attaché of his office accompany me outside of New York, and this man went with me everywhere I went, day and night, and never was I out of his sight a moment. We spoke frequently of the testimony I was to give at the trial."

Marshall said a representative of the D.A.'s office accompanied him from Washington to Richmond, Virginia, then to New York, back to Washington, and finally to New York where he was booked into the Maryland Hotel until he was summoned to testify. He said that he had paid all his own expenses until he returned to New York. Then, the state picked up the tab. As he had given up all his theatrical bookings during that period, he was given three checks, two for seventy dollars each and one for one hundred fifty dollars.

Marshall's statement at the end of the affidavit summed up its importance to the defense. It said: "I never knew Jack Rose and I did not know it was he who is said to have met Becker on the street that night. My only knowledge of Rose came from what Mr. Groehl told me and what I read in the papers."

If the recantation brought new hope to the defense team it did not last very long. The following day, Sunday, Marshall denied having repudiated his original story. He had come to New York at Johnston's request to meet with Manton and amplify the story he had told in Philadelphia the previous day. At the same time, however, there was action on another front. Marshall's stepfather, Marcellus McDaniel, had gone to see Groehl and told him that the young man's mother was concerned that her son might find himself in trouble for having turned the tables on the district attorney's office. Groehl wasted no time. Accompanied by McDaniel, he went to the basement apartment on East Seventy-sixth Street where Marshall's mother resided as the building's janitor. In no time at all, he obtained affidavits from both McDaniel and his wife, swearing that Marshall had told them more than once that the testimony he gave was the truth. With Groehl still there, Marshall phoned from Manton's office. Groehl took the receiver and asked: "Did you make a statement or an affidavit in Philadelphia as the papers this morning say you did?" "No," he replied. At Groehl's request, Marshall came to his mother's apartment and insisted that he had not repudiated his testimony. He said he was drunk when he signed the affidavit in Philadelphia and that his testimony at trial was the truth.

All the same, the denial was now a part of the record. It could be used by the defense in a request for a new trial or in the appeal that was being prepared, but it had lost a good deal of its force. "My opinion is that the Negro's word is not good," Manton said. "I am independently convinced that he did not see Becker talking with Jack Rose at 124th Street and Seventh Avenue, and in admitting this in Philadelphia he told the truth, but I wouldn't count on his sticking to the truth. Nothing he says can be accepted without corroboration."

Manton was working diligently, and virtually pro bono, while preparing Becker's appeal. The Beckers' resources had long been exhausted. By way of payment, Helen had signed over the deed on their Olinville Avenue house to Manton who put it up for rent. Helen moved into an apartment on University Avenue in the University Heights section of the Bronx. Cockran had withdrawn from the case, at least for the time being.

With his brief for appeal almost ready, Manton decided to play a long shot and moved for a new trial before Supreme Court Justice Bartow S. Weeks. The motion was based on the affidavit signed by Marshall and those sworn to by Johnston and the two newspaper reporters who interviewed Marshall in Philadelphia—Joseph Fenerty and P. D. Chiquoine. There was little chance the motion would be granted and Manton knew it. But it was the only means by which Marshall's statement could be gotten into the record for review by the Court of Appeals. As expected, Weeks denied the motion out of hand, without so much as expressing an opinion. He simply wrote "Motion denied" across the papers Manton had submitted. Arguments before the Court of Appeals, on legal points in the trial record, were scheduled for March 24.

On February 27, Assistant District Attorney Robert C. Taylor received from Manton a 450-page brief outlining the argument he would make before the court. The first 415 pages were given to supporting the overall contention that the verdict was against the weight of evidence and that the testimony on which the conviction rested was not adequately corroborated. The brief also contended that the testimony given by Marshall and Plitt was not credible and that the charge to the jury was "unfair, erroneous, and highly prejudicial in many respects." A month later, Manton made his plea before the court. It took the better part of a day; Taylor made his rebuttal the following day. The case was then put in the hands of the seven justices on the Court of Appeals.

It took exactly two months for the court to make its ruling. On May 25, a Tuesday, the court upheld Becker's conviction. The vote, six-to-one, was the same as in the first appeal, but in the opposite direction. Only Judge John W. Hogan dissented from the opinion written by Chief Judge Willard Bartlett. The court's decision turned, in large measure, on its determination that the Harlem conference had indeed taken place and Marshall's testimony was true.

"The evidence concerning the Harlem conference as a whole is much more convincing than it was on the first trial," the ruling said. "The date, which was then uncertain, is now fixed as being the 27th of June. Marshall was certainly present at the raid then made by defendant's squad, and his presence becomes very significant when considered in connection with Vallon's testimony on the first trial. Vallon then said, in narrating the circumstances of the Harlem conference: 'Lieutenant Becker told us he was going to raid a crap game that night, and there was a little colored boy on the other side of the street, and he called him over and spoke to him. We stepped aside, Rose and I, and by the time he got finished talking to this boy, Webber came along.'

"This mention of the colored boy by Vallon seemed then to be only an unimportant incident of the Harlem conference; but in light of subsequent developments it tends strongly to prove that Vallon himself must have been there and therefore could have participated with the others in the alleged murder plot. It is difficult to see how Vallon would or could have mentioned the colored boy's presence then unless he himself had been present."

The court pointed out that its responsibility in reviewing the record did not include a consideration of the facts of the case; that, according to law, was left entirely to the jury. "It is our duty," the decision read, "to affirm if the trial was fair and without legal error and the verdict was not against the weight of evidence"; also, that "there was sufficient evidence within recognized rules of law in support of the verdict; this done, the responsibility for the result rests with the jurors."

The court took extra care to address the issue of the reliability of the state's witnesses. It said: "Doubtless, a very strong argument can be made in favor of the defendant, based upon the inducement of the avowed accomplices to swear falsely, their opportunity to fabricate evidence, and the lack of conclusiveness in the corroboration.

"All this, however, was a question for the jury with whose determination we are not justified in interfering unless we can say that it was plainly wrong—which, as already stated, we cannot say."

By all indications, the defense was unprepared for the decision. They had not expected the court to place that much credence in Marshall's testimony. His successive recantations, they assumed, would have cast a degree of doubt on his original story and have left the Harlem conference in a twilight zone not distinct enough to support a conviction in a capital case. Now, Becker's options were few and tenuous. He could petition the Court of Appeals for a reargument on the ground that the court had overlooked points in Becker's favor when making its original decision; he could apply for a new trial on the basis of newly discovered evidence, providing new evidence was discovered; he could seek a writ of habeas corpus in the federal district court, claiming that his constitutional rights had been violated; on the same ground, he could bypass the district court and request a writ of error from the United States Supreme Court; and finally, his last chance would be a plea for executive clemency from Governor Whitman, who twice had successfully prosecuted him.

Manton elected to exercise the first option, sensing it was best to begin in the court that had the most immediate jurisdiction. He filed an application to re-argue the case, charging that the court had "misapprehended the testimony of several witnesses," most notably Marshall; William Shapiro, driver of the murder car; Deputy Police Commissioner George Dougherty; and

Charles Plitt, Becker's erstwhile press agent. It also was contended that Justice Seabury's charge had been incomplete, that in summarizing the testimony he had failed to include details that would have been favorable to the defense. Manton was bucking the odds. In the past, the New York State Court of Appeals had never agreed to rehear a criminal case, and its record remained intact. Becker's application was rejected without comment.

Time was running short. Becker's execution was scheduled for the week of July 12. On June 23, Manton went to Albany to meet with the governor. They both agreed it was an informal meeting and there was no discussion of executive clemency. Manton had said he intended to ask Whitman to allow the lieutenant governor or an independent third party to hear any pleas in Becker's behalf, as it was unfair for the man who had prosecuted him to serve as the condemned man's last chance for clemency. But Whitman denied that any such request had been formally made. He also removed any doubt about how he would have responded. If such request had been made, he said, "I could not very well have entertained it. The constitution leaves the duty of dealing with matters of this nature with the governor. . . . I have no intention of shirking my duty or responsibility by running away from what I am well aware will be a trying ordeal." Whitman further indicated that so far as he was concerned, his role in the case was just about over. He said he would hear any pleas that were to be made the following week and whatever decision he rendered at that time would be final.

But the defense was by no means ready to quit. Early in July, with the execution date only days away, W. Bourke Cockran reentered the case; so did John F. McIntyre, who had represented Becker during his first trial. Cockran took charge immediately. He announced that he would go directly to the U.S. Supreme Court and ask for a writ of error, arguing that Becker's constitutional rights of due process and equal protection under the Fourteenth Amendment had been violated in the state courts. Whitman responded by postponing the execution date by two weeks, until the week of July 26, to allow time for the defense to make its plea.

As the court was not in session during the summer months, Cockran's appeal would be made to a single justice. He chose Charles Evans Hughes, who a year later would resign from the court to run for president, unsuccessfully, against Woodrow Wilson and who later would serve as chief justice on the high court for more than a decade. Cockran located Hughes at his summer home in Rangeley, Maine. He pled his case there on Friday, July 9. The principal basis for his argument was that the state's immunity agreement with the four informers deprived Becker of due process by allowing them, in effect, to save their own lives by trading for the life of another. If Justice Hughes allowed the appeal, Becker's execution would be postponed until the full court met again in the fall. But there would be no need to wait. The following day, Hughes denied the writ, saying there was no substantial federal question involved. Short of a plea for executive clemency, the only course still open to the defense appeared to be a habeas corpus action, which, if granted, would send the case to the Supreme Court. But Becker instructed his counsel not to make a habeas application. The court's decision, he believed, was preordained, and even if the writ were given, its only effect would be to delay his execution. Becker had not given up, however. He had another strategy in mind.

It turned out that Becker had not been whiling away the hours in his death-house cell. He had spent a great deal of time writing his own version of the events that put him where he was, the entire story, in fact, of his career as a New York City police officer. He had intended the document to be released after his death, but with his chances running out he decided to play his last card and put it in the hands of the governor. Cockran hand-delivered the manuscript—nearly forty pages in Becker's handwriting, together with the attorney's own supplement of about half that length—to Whitman's office on Tuesday, July 20. Becker's narrative would have challenged the imagination of even the most trusting reader, for he came off sounding like a choirboy whose sensibilities would be jarred at the very suggestion of police corruption. It is likely that little attention would have been paid to his screed except that for the first time in the three years since Rosenthal was slain, the name of Big Tim Sullivan was introduced. He was, Becker claimed, a major player in the events that led to the shooting.

Two years after his death, Sullivan still commanded attention. Word of his involvement put the Becker case back on page one of the local papers. It was the lead story in the *World,* occupying the two right-hand columns, and the off-lead in the *Times* where its three left-side columns were balanced evenly with news that President Wilson had warned Germany about respecting the open sea rights of United States ships following the sinking of the *Lusitania* by German U-boats.

Becker began his chronicle with the first meeting he had with the Tammany leader, in January 1912. This was the story as he told it:

Some time in the latter part of January 1912, Sullivan's half-brother, Larry Mulligan, met with Becker in Luchow's and told him that the senator would like to thank him personally for the manner in which he had been enforcing the Sullivan Law, which made it a crime to carry a concealed weapon. They met the following day at Sullivan's office in the Shanley Building. It soon became apparent that the senator's gratitude was not to be the principal subject of conversation. He told Becker that he had a $12,500 interest in Rosenthal's gambling house and that Commissioner Waldo had told him that Rosenthal should be allowed the same opportunity to operate as any other casino in the Tenderloin. "'Now you see how Waldo feels about it,'" he quoted Sullivan as saying.

Becker continued: "He also said he had sent for me to make sure Rosenthal would not be raided by me. I told Sullivan that, if he had Waldo's word, he need not worry about me, as I only raided when and where Waldo ordered me to, and that, if Waldo did not order me to raid Rosenthal, I would not go near him. This seemed to satisfy Tim. He thanked me and I left for home."

As he stepped from the elevator on the main floor, Becker met Rosenthal, who asked if he had been to see Sullivan. When Becker failed to respond, Rosenthal withdrew a paper from his pocket, handed it to him and said, "I'll show you he is my friend." Becker saw it was a note for $12,500 and was signed "T. D. Sullivan." A few days later, Rose told Becker that he was going into partnership with Rosenthal, investing the sum of $1,500, which would be covered in a chattel mortgage of Rosenthal's household goods.

The trouble began in April when Waldo told Becker he wanted Rosenthal's place closed whether Sullivan was backing him or not. Apparently, word of an agreement had begun making the rounds, and whether Waldo was part of that agreement or not, he felt obliged to act. The raid was made. Becker suspected Rosenthal would seek to retaliate, and he was right. The bad blood that existed between him and Rose began to boil over. The policeman who was stationed at Rosenthal's place was the breaking point. Rosenthal began spreading the word that Rose was Becker's stool pigeon. On May 18, Rose told Becker that Big Jack Zelig had been arrested and that Rosenthal was spreading the story that Rose had set him up. Rose felt his life was in danger and asked Becker to try to fix things with Zelig's gunmen, but Becker declined. Rose appeared to be in mortal fear of Rosenthal. He said he expected to be brought home on a shutter some day. A few weeks later, early in June, he told Becker he was going to move his family to Arverne, Long Island, and he would go to Atlantic City for a few weeks until suspicions about his role in Zelig's arrest died down. Becker did not see Rose again until July 8 when they met at the Union Square Hotel and Rose told him he would do no more stooling.

Events turned critical on Sunday, July 13, two days before the murder, when the morning papers published the first story about police corruption and the operation of the System. Becker said he was not surprised at Rosenthal's action nor was he particularly concerned. "The fury displayed by Rosenthal after the raid did not seem to me at all extraordinary. He was known to have boasted that he never failed 'to get' any member of the [police] force who had molested him. Until the publication of the article . . . I never gave his threat the slightest attention. The publication in the *World* I regarded as the culmination of his efforts. I was satisfied that no evidence could be found to support the criminal charges, and of Rosenthal's uncorroborated testimony I had not the slightest apprehension."

Becker obtained permission from the police commissioner to institute a libel suit against the *World* and then he and Helen went to spend the day at Brighton Beach. When they returned home, at about one o'clock in the morning, his private telephone rang. The man on the other end identified himself as Harry Applebaum, Sullivan's private secretary. He said Big Tim had to see him that night. Applebaum picked him up about half an hour later and drove him to Sullivan's office on Sixtieth Street and Broadway. When they got there, Big Tim asked him, "What about this Rosenthal affazir?" "There's nothing to it," Becker said. Sullivan wasn't so sure. "It must not be allowed to go any further," he said. "Rosenthal has gone too far now, he can't be stopped. He must be got away." He told Becker he was prepared to offer Rosenthal five thousand dollars to leave town.

"That," Becker said, "would be the very worst thing could happen to us.

Everybody would say that either you or I had caused his disappearance, and naturally it would seem that if we induced him to leave, it must be because he had something discreditable to reveal. Now, everything he could say has already been said and published. It is absolutely necessary to my position in the department that his statements be faced and disproved."

"Where a fire of this kind is started," Sullivan said, "there is no knowing where it will reach. Rosenthal has already been very close to me politically and personally, and once inquiry starts they reach the election matters. And secret investigations of elections by grand juries have always been sources of great trouble."

Becker was persistent. "As to the political side of it, Senator, I have no opinion at all," he said. "But I am perfectly clear that, so far as I am concerned, his disappearance would be fatal if it would be suspected that I had connived in it." The senator answered, "Well, perhaps you are right, but I have a favor to ask. Whatever happens in this row between you two, I want you to promise me that you will never bring me in this. If you don't, I am all right."

"I made the promise not to do so," Becker wrote, "and I have kept that promise until now."

Becker might have kept the secret longer than he should have. He was revealing it now as "new evidence"—the kind that could warrant a new trial, but in legal terms the evidence was not new. Becker had the same evidence in his possession during both of his trials but chose not to submit it. Perhaps his decision was made out of fealty to Sullivan. More likely, it was kept from the record because Becker's counsel did not choose to risk putting him on the witness stand and, at least during the second trial, he thought they could win without involving Sullivan. But the law does not allow a defendant to harbor a fail-safe position. He cannot keep evidence in reserve, to be produced only if he is convicted, as ground for a new trial. Yet, though not explicitly stated, it appeared that a new trial was precisely what Becker was seeking. In his letter, he clearly rejected a plea for clemency while at the same time asking that the sentence of death be forbidden.

He wrote: "Although it involves the unprecedented (perhaps some would say preposterous) proceedings of asking His Excellency, Charles S. Whitman, Governor of the State, to review, reverse and in some respects condemn the conduct of Hon. Charles S. Whitman, District Attorney of New York County, in prosecuting an indictment for murder against me, nevertheless that my constitutional rights may be at least asserted, I ask your Excellency most respectfully . . . to forbid execution of the capital sentence pronounced on me.

"I ask your Excellency further, in the light of certain facts, now disclosed for the first time, to forbid my execution on the ground that my guilt of this murder is not established so clearly as to justify the taking of a human life by the public executioner." Renouncing a plea for clemency, he continued, " . . . if I were given the choice between dying a felon's death in the electric chair and living a felon's life in a prison cell I should certainly not be inclined to prefer the longer over the shorter agony."

If the objective of Becker's letter was not altogether clear, Whitman's response was immediate and unambiguous. He shrugged it off as providing no new information or evidence. "I have read Becker's statement," he said the same night that it was delivered. "All I care to say regarding it is that it contains little that was not known to me at the time Becker was on trial for the murder of Herman Rosenthal. The statement sheds no light whatever on the killing of Rosenthal." He said that during Becker's trials he was familiar with virtually all the allegations made in his letter and that he would have questioned Becker about them if he had testified in his own defense.

Whitman's remarks were made on Wednesday, July 21. It was exactly seven days before Becker was scheduled to die.

27

Time was Becker's foe now. The defense was scrambling, scraping at the edges in search of any opening that might advance its case. At Sing Sing, prison officials were already making preparations for his execution. Notes of authorization were on the way to those who had been chosen from among the hundreds of applicants who volunteered to witness the event. Warden Thomas Mott Osborne would not be one of them. A confirmed opponent of capital punishment, Osborne made it his business to be out of town whenever an execution took place. In this instance, he had more than one reason to be away. Two other prisoners were condemned to die on the same day as Becker, not an unusual occurrence in those days.

Late Friday, July 23, five days before Becker's date with death, Cockran obtained a court order to show cause why a new trial should not be granted on the ground of newly discovered evidence. The order was returnable Monday morning before Supreme Court Justice John Ford. The Sullivan story was the principal basis for the request. Both Manton and McIntyre submitted affidavits that they had never heard of Sullivan's connection with the case. Affidavits from other new witnesses also were appended to the plea. Joseph Murphy, a convicted murderer serving a life term in Sing Sing, swore he heard Webber, Vallon, and Rose plotting to frame Becker; Louis Harris, a gambler who had been on the Sam Paul excursion and who was now doing time in

State's Prison for stealing, also said he heard Rosenthal's death being planned and that Rose had told him Becker was framed; another gambler, Benjamin Kauffman, said Rosenthal told him on the night of the murder that he was on his way to the Metropole where he would be given fifteen thousand dollars to keep his mouth shut and that he would be taking off for parts unknown in a few days; Edward C. Ginty, a former deputy sheriff of Danbury, Connecticut, said Rose had told him that, according to plan, Rosenthal was not supposed to be murdered, he was to be paid to remain silent and drop out of sight.

With a hearing before Justice Ford scheduled for Monday, July 26, Osborne extended the date of Becker's execution two days, to Friday, July 30. The judge said he would decide the case on the basis of arguments and affidavits alone; he would hear no outside witnesses. In the meantime, corroboration of sorts came from two unexpected sources. Waldo confirmed that he had indeed met with Sullivan regarding his treatment of Rosenthal. But he said he spurned the senator's offer of "political preferment" if he agreed to go easy on Rosenthal. "I told him," Waldo said, "that Rosenthal was going just as soon as I could 'get him,' and that every other gambler in the city was going." Sullivan's secretary, Harry Applebaum, also offered a nugget in Becker's behalf. He corroborated the story that Sullivan intended to pay Rosenthal for his silence if he was willing to leave town until the dust settled. He also said he heard Rose suggest that Rosenthal should be croaked, and Becker responded that that was the worst thing that could happen because he would be the prime suspect.

On Monday, Becker's forty-second birthday, Cockran spent three hours pleading for his client's life. The core of his argument was that the district attorney had suppressed evidence that would have changed the jury's verdict. Cockran contended that the prosecution had been aware of Sullivan's role in the case and kept it out of evidence in what he described as "an outrage on the administration of justice." He also cited the affidavits the defense had produced from a number of witnesses who had not testified at either trial and then proceeded to attack the evidence produced by the state: "There wasn't a single witness who testified for the prosecution who wasn't bribed— bribed by promise of immunity or by money," he said. He concluded his impassioned plea by laying the final responsibility for whether Becker lives or dies squarely on the conscience of the judge. "If Becker is executed now," he said, "he is executed on a technicality. If these things had been presented to the jury, he never would have been convicted. If he goes to his death, it will be because justice is enmeshed in snares."

Assistant District Attorney Taylor, who was head of the office's Appeals Bureau, delivered his argument in the measured tone of a man who sensed that the force of law was on his side and felt assured that the outcome was not in question. He offered his own set of affidavits—from Jack Rose, Bridgey Webber, Mrs. Rosenthal, and ex-A.D.A. Frank Moss, among others—reaffirming that the testimony they had offered at trial was true. He argued that there was not a single statement in any of the affidavits submitted by the defense that would constitute new evidence, and even if the district attorney stipulated to the truth of everything contained in the affidavits, he said, there would not be sufficient grounds to grant a motion for a new trial.

Justice Ford did not underestimate the gravity of the decision he would render. He spent all Monday night, less four hours for sleep, and all day Tuesday in his chambers in the Emigrant Industrial Savings Bank Building poring over the avalanche of briefs, affidavits, citations, and the trial record submitted to him by both defense counsel and the district attorney. At his elbow were twenty-nine law books with markers showing cases cited by the opposing attorneys. The first question he had to consider was under what circumstances the Supreme Court had the right to reopen a case it had already decided and which was ruled on by the Court of Appeals. Was its right inherent or merely statutory? If it was only statutory, Ford had to determine whether the documentation submitted by the defense constituted new evidence and, if so, was it critical enough to have altered the jury's verdict?

To counter the defense's contention that those standards had been met, the district attorney cited eleven cases supporting his position that the court had no power to reopen the case except by statute and that the material provided by the defense did not qualify under the law as new evidence. The affidavits alleging that Becker had been framed, he said, were cumulative—an extension of evidence already introduced at the trial rather than something entirely new—and the Sullivan episode could not be considered newly discovered evidence, since Becker had known of it all along but chose not to reveal it.

On Wednesday night, after nearly forty-eight hours of deliberation, Justice

Ford denied Becker's application for a new trial. He decided against him on every point. The judge ruled that the authority of the Supreme Court to grant a new trial was not inherent but statutory. The statute, in turn, depended entirely on the production of new and relevant evidence which, Ford wrote, "must fulfill all the following requirements: 1) It must be such as will probably change the result if a new trial is granted; 2) It must have been discovered since the trial; 3) It must be such as could not have been discovered before the trial by the exercise of due diligence; 4) It must be material to the issue; 5) It must not be cumulative to the former issue; and, 6) It must not be merely impeaching or contradicting the former evidence." Ford then moved directly to the heart of the issue: "Does the evidence set forth as newly discovered in the affidavits presented on behalf of the defendant meet these requirements of the statute and of the Court of Appeals? That is the question, and the only question before me." The judge proceeded to demonstrate, point by point, that none of the evidence submitted met the established standards. He concluded with a statement that placed his position, and Becker's, in sharp legal perspective:

"This man was placed on trial three years ago. If he is permitted to go on trial repeatedly things would come to a pass where the witnesses would not be available. It would always be possible for Becker to get witnesses to make affidavits on which to ask for a new trial. There is a natural sympathy we feel not to send a man to the electric chair. The safeguard seems to be the pardoning power. I have no right to listen to pleas for clemency."

There was no appeal from Ford's decision. For Becker, it was the last stop on a three-year trip through the twists and turns of the legal machinery. It would end with his execution in less than forty-eight hours. At Sing Sing, Warden Osborne and Deputy Warden Charles Johnson were notified of the judge's decision by telephone at about ten-thirty that night. It was left to Johnson to bring the news to Becker. He walked through the death house and stopped at Becker's cell. He extended his hand and Becker grasped it. "Charley," he said, "I have bad news for you. Your appeal has been denied." It was the kind of news, even when expected, that no one can really prepare for. Becker remained silent for a moment. Then, barely above a whisper, he repeated the word. "Denied," he said. Then he added, "Well, I'll die like a man, anyhow."

A few minutes later, Father Cashin arrived. He remained with the condemned man for about twenty minutes. Becker appeared to be relatively calm. He said he did not wish to discuss the case any further, but he described his sentiments to Father Cashin. "There is no justice here," he said. "I am confident, however, that I will get it in the next world. I know that the truth will come out, and the world will know that Becker told the truth and is not the murderer he is accused of being. I do not fear death, but I feel the stigma which this death attaches to the name Becker, and I feel the distress and sorrow that it will cause my wife."

Helen Becker had spent the afternoon and evening with her husband. She had left about half an hour before news of Justice Ford's decision reached the warden. She was headed for the Ossining station to take the 10:31 train back to the Bronx. The following day, she would bear her husband's last hope to a meeting with Governor Whitman. It was as thin a hope as one could embrace. Since the Court of Appeals had ruled against Becker, Whitman had been besieged by thousands of letters and telegrams urging executive clemency. Hastily conceived organizations sent petitions to Albany, urging the governor to issue a pardon. Pleas to save Becker's life outnumbered those supporting execution by more than ten to one. Many of the letters came from women who pointed to Becker's home life and the enduring devotion of his wife as evidence that he could not be evil; that, even if guilty, he should not be put to death. But Whitman never wavered. He was about to complete a mission he had embarked on three years earlier, and there was little chance he would decide now to switch course. Becker was a doomed man, and he knew it. His execution was set for 5:45 on Friday morning. He had only one day of life left.

Becker awoke Thursday to the last daylight he would ever know. It would be a busy day. At eight o'clock he was bathed and his head was shaved to allow the electrode to make direct contact with his scalp. He was dressed in a black jump suit with a slit up the left leg where another electrode would be placed against his skin. His shoes, which contained steel arches, were replaced with felt slippers. Every other item—such as a comb and brush—that could be used in a suicide attempt was removed from his cell. All that remained were his bed clothing, a photograph of his wife shorn of frame or glass cover, and a small calendar pad from which he had been tearing off a page each day as the date of execution approached.

The state executioner was on his way to Sing Sing to make a final test of the electric chair. A new electric power plant was to be used that would relay signals between the powerhouse and the death chamber. The signal to turn loose the fatal charge of electricity would no longer be relayed from the executioner to the man running the power plant. Modern technology had made the entire procedure less personal. A placard behind the chair explained: "Five bells, get ready; one bell, turn on current; two bells, turn on more current; three bells, turn on less current; one bell, shut off current; six bells, all through." The new technology, it would soon be discovered, was far from perfect.

At around noontime, Becker was served his last lunch. He had to be aware that everything he did now was for the last time. He had less than eighteen hours left to live. He was permitted to see his last visitors—his wife, his two brothers, and his sister—between two and four in the afternoon. His brothers and his sister arrived as scheduled. Helen did not make it that afternoon. She was in frantic pursuit of the governor, desperate to make her last plea for her husband's life, though mindful that any real sense of hope had long since vanished.

Understanding that she had an appointment to meet with Whitman in the governor's executive chamber at two o'clock that afternoon, Mrs. Becker, accompanied by John Johnston, boarded the Empire State Express that morning, bound for Albany. When they arrived they learned that Whitman had left the capital at around ten o'clock and was not expected back until evening. Johnston phoned the governor's office and was told by his secretary, William B. Orr, that Whitman had gone to Fishkill to take part in a military ceremony; he would then be going to Poughkeepsie where he would spend the night in the Nelson House. With her eye on the clock, knowing that she might forfeit the opportunity to see her husband for the last time, Helen waited for several hours until Orr notified Johnston that the governor would see them at the hotel. They took a train to Poughkeepsie and arrived at about five-thirty. Becker's execution was twelve hours away. Helen waited in another room of the suite while Johnston spoke with Whitman. They were together for about an hour and a half. Johnston did not ask for a pardon. He tried to persuade the governor to grant a reprieve and allow a disinterested party, a man of judicial stature and prominence, to hear his client's plea for executive clemency. Whitman refused.

It was seven-fifteen when Whitman entered the room where Helen was waiting. He bowed politely and said, "I am ready now to hear anything new that you have to offer me in this case, Mrs. Becker. I want you to feel free to tell me everything. If there is anything you know that you have not told and you now think would help your husband, you may tell me with the fullest assurance that it will be regarded as absolutely confidential."

But of course there was nothing new to share with the governor, nothing that hadn't been said before, nothing he had not already heard and dismissed. Helen Becker was not there in the interest of justice; she had come to beg for mercy. "My husband was no saint," she told Whitman, "but, oh, he wasn't the awful murderer that they say."

Whitman listened respectfully, but he remained unmoved. "I am sorry," he said. "It is impossible for me to do anything. I am sorry. I can do nothing."

It was nearly eight o'clock when Helen left. It was too late to take a train to Ossining. She made the trip in a taxi. It was nearly midnight when she arrived. Deputy Warden Charles Johnson ushered her to her husband's cell. They spent about an hour together, then parted for the last time. When Mrs. Becker arrived home she was helped to her third-floor apartment by her sister and brother-in-law. She was sobbing and unable to walk without support. It was two-forty on Friday morning. Charles Becker had three hours left to live.

He spent the next hour or so writing farewell letters to friends who had stood by him during the past three years. Warden Osborne visited with him for a while. He asked Becker if he had gotten any sleep. He said he hadn't. At about four o'clock, Father Cashin and Father James B. Curry, Becker's spiritual adviser, joined them. Father Curry administered Holy Communion. When the warden left, Becker asked the two priests to pray with him. He said, "I think the most beautiful prayer in the Catholic faith is the one beginning, 'Hail, Holy Queen, Mother of Mercy, our life, our sweetness, our hope!'" The priests picked it up where he left off. Then Becker turned to Father Cashin and said: "Father, please bear this message to my friends and to the world. I am not guilty by deed or conspiracy, or in any other way, of the death of Herman Rosenthal. I am sacrificed for my friends." "Charley," the priest said, "do you go out of this world bearing malice toward anyone?" "I forgive everyone, Father," Becker said. "Of those I may have wronged, I beg forgiveness."

Shortly after five o'clock, with less than an hour of life remaining, Becker was visited by Frank O'Toole, a death-house guard who slit his right trouser leg from cuff to knee as the left leg had been slit the day before. Becker thanked him for the courtesies he had extended to his wife; O'Toole shook his hand and left without saying a word. Time was drawing near. What was left of Becker's life was now measured in ticks of the clock.

At five-forty, they came for him. The Acting Principal Keeper, Frederick Dorner, motioned for him from outside his cell. Not a word was spoken. With the two priests on either side of him, Becker started down the narrow corridor. They walked slowly. White curtains hung from the front of the cells on left and right to shield Becker from the other prisoners. The door to the death chamber opened at 5:42. Becker entered with the support of the two priests. They were reading the Litany of the Holy Name, and each time they paused, Becker gave the response, "Lord, have mercy on us" and kissed the silver crucifix he was holding. As he approached the chair, his voice began to quaver. His body sagged. Five prison guards helped him into the chair. Father Cashin stood directly in front of him, reciting a litany to which Becker repeatedly responded, "Jesus, Mary, and Joseph, I give you my heart and my soul." The guards worked as quickly as possible. Heavy straps were buckled over his knees, ankles, wrists, elbows, and chest. A leather cap was fixed to his head, and the electrodes were screwed to his temples. A blindfold was placed across his eyes. Father Cashin continued to recite the litany, speaking faster and faster, but Becker was barely able to respond. His voice was breaking; the words were mumbled.

The executioner was ready to throw the switch when one of the guards noticed that something was wrong. The chest girdle had been strapped under rather than over his arms. The guard made the adjustment. They were ready now. Becker rapidly uttered his last words: "Into Thy hands, O Lord, I commend my spirit." At 5:44, the prison physician, Dr. Charles W. Farr, dropped his right arm. The silence was broken by the crunching sound of the wooden lever located behind and to the right of the condemned man. As the lever dropped, 1,850 volts of current were turned loose. Becker's body stiffened and strained against the straps; his head slumped forward. A bright flame burst through his left temple and blazed for a full minute before fizzling out. He had lost consciousness, but there was still life left in him. The guard who had repositioned the chest strap had neglected to buckle it. Dr. Farr tore open

Becker's shirt and applied the stethoscope. His heart was still beating. Within two minutes, another jolt of electricity was sent into Becker's body. The charge was maintained for ten seconds, twice the time ordinarily required to kill a man. Dr. Farr's stethoscope still detected a faint heartbeat. This time the head-piece was removed and readjusted. A third shock was discharged and again the body heaved. This time, it fell completely limp. At 5:53, the doctor pronounced Becker dead.

A bad burn was found at his left temple, which indicated either a malfunction or improper placement of the electrode. It had taken nine minutes to execute him. The procedure was intended to last not much more than a minute. The experts had underestimated the amount of current necessary to kill a man of Becker's size. Bourke Cockran's thesis of twenty-five years earlier had been proven closer to the truth than Thomas Edison's. The amount of current necessary to kill a man varied with the degree of resistance his body would offer. Edison had called Cockran's notion "nonsense." It wasn't.

The hearse carrying Becker's body broke down on the way back to the city when its engine overheated. It was the hottest July 30 in nearly half a century, as stifling as that airless July night three years earlier when Herman "Beansie" Rosenthal was shot dead and Becker's travails began. The hearse arrived in the Bronx at around midday. Becker's body laid in wake in a quartered oak coffin in Helen Becker's apartment at 2291 University Avenue in the Bronx. Hordes of people came by to pay their respects. Flowers arrived in bunches, in floral arrangements, and in wreaths. They were sent by as varied a group as Warden Osborne and his deputy, Mrs. Becker's fifth-grade class, and by the former Police Inspector Alexander "Clubber" Williams, Becker's early-career model and mentor. But what attracted everyone's attention was a silver plate attached to the end of the coffin that read:

CHARLES BECKER
Murdered July 30, 1915
by
GOVERNOR WHITMAN

The inscription on the plate was the inspiration of Mrs. Becker who had pledged that she would prove her husband was innocent, that he was illegally convicted and sacrificed to the political ambitions of the then-district attorney. It was a symbol of Helen's faith and devotion, but there was something she had failed to consider—the statement could be considered criminally libelous. District Attorney Francis Martin believed that it was. He sent Inspector Joseph Faurot, head of the detective bureau, and First Deputy Police Commissioner Leon Godley to the Becker home on Sunday, the day before the funeral. They notified Mrs. Becker that the plate was in violation of libel laws. Faurot unscrewed it and brought it back to police headquarters.

The funeral was held on Monday, August 2, at the Church of St. Nicholas of Tolentine, at the corner of Fordham Road, just a few blocks from Helen's University Avenue apartment. The church's capacity of seven hundred was stretched to accommodate a crowd of about three thousand. Thousands more (estimates ran as high as ten thousand) milled about outside, hoping to squeeze their way in. The heat had not abated; it covered the city like a blanket. An elderly woman passed out and required medical attention after trying to force her way inside. Police assigned to keep order sent for reserves from a nearby precinct. A policeman on horseback rode back and forth across the pavement, creating a passage through which members of the family could enter the church. The service, a low mass, lasted only twenty-five minutes. It was celebrated by one of the church's young assistant priests, Father George Dermody; the pastor of the church, Father Nicholas J. Murphy, was in Philadelphia and did not return in time for the service. Father Dermody said nothing of Becker's life or the manner in which he died. There was no sermon and no music.

A new cluster of floral treatments arrived at the church in time for the procession to Woodlawn Cemetery, where Becker would be buried alongside his infant daughter. The most impressive was a large cross of lilies, asters, and bay leaves bearing the inscription, "Sacrificed for Politics." It was signed, "From a Friend." Another, signed by three friends, read, "To the Martyr; with sympathy." The cemetery, at the northern edge of the Bronx, was a short ride from the church. The hearse leading the procession was drawn by two black horses and followed by five carriages. It arrived shortly after eleven o'clock. At the gates of the cemetery, the procession was halted while the floral designs were inspected. The legend Sacrificed for Politics was judged inappropriate and reduced to a meaningless "S-F-O." The "To the Martyr" tribute was also removed before the cortege was permitted to proceed. A canvas shelter had been erected to shield Mrs. Becker and other members of the family from the heat. There was no ceremony at the grave-side. The casket was lowered into the ground adorned only by a wreath from ex-Inspector and Mrs. Williams. It read: "In sympathy and respect to Charley."

EPILOGUE

Finally, it was over. The story that had seized the imagination of the city in the summer of 1912 and held it fast for three years ended abruptly and, some might say, inevitably, with the burial of Charles Becker. Few cases had occupied the public's attention so fully for so long a time. But memories fade quickly in the rush of new events, and the world seemed to be at the edge of apocalypse in 1915. Becker's execution, which was the lead story in the July 31 edition of the *World,* had been pushed to the opposite side of page one in the *Times.* The three right-hand columns carried the news that the Germans had broken through the Russian lines in the siege of Warsaw. Residents of the city were fleeing as the German army marched east. Poland was ready to fall; Russia was becoming less of a factor; the United States, reluctantly but surely, was being drawn into the conflict.

As for New York, crime and corruption would not disappear with the demise of the System; it would simply take on a new face. Prohibition was on the way and with it would come an underworld machine that was as sophisticated and neatly organized as U.S. Steel or General Motors. Tammany Hall would flex its muscles, and the administration of corruption would take on a bright new look in the 1920s, almost celebratory in nature, with the city's irrepressible mayor, "Gentleman Jimmy" Walker, leading the parade. A succession of new commissions would investigate crime and the police department, and the only police officer ever to be executed for murder would soon be forgotten. History has a way of feeding on itself; remembrance grows dim as the years pass, and there is always something shaped to a more dynamic present that is ready to stake its claim.

There is a story that has been reprised over the years, which may or may not be factual, but which has the same ring of truth as an Aesop fable. It takes place in the early morning hours as Becker awaits execution. Four men are sitting around a table in Jack's café, about a block from the Metropole and still open round the clock. Arnold Rothstein, at thirty-three already the presumptive CEO of big-time gambling, is joined by Nicky Arnstein, his chief of staff; Frank Ward O'Malley, a newspaper reporter; and Tad Dorgan, a cartoonist for the *Journal*. Rothstein's gold pocket watch, its cover flipped open, lies at the center of the table. Word has it that the watch, tick-for-tick, is as precise as its owner. As the hands approach the designated time of execution, all conversation ceases. At exactly 5:45, Rothstein snaps the watch shut, rises from the table, and says, "That's it."

As David Pietrusza tells it in his biography, *Rothstein,* "That was it for Charles Becker, it for the old style of police graft and corruption, it for the old-style gambling houses of Manhattan. Arnold Rothstein would invent floating crap games that would move from hotel to hotel, apartment to apartment, warehouse to warehouse. Now gambling would move out to the suburbs, out to Long Island. Arnold Rothstein already had a new gambling house in the old Holley Arms Hotel out in Hewlitt, with none other than George Considine, Big Tim's partner in the Metropole, as *his* partner. The cops could no longer be trusted to direct the shakedowns. That would be left to the politicians, but the politicians needed a smart man—"a smart Jew," as Big Tim might have put it—to be their go-between with gamblers, the judges, and the police.

"A new world was being born, and Arnold Rothstein meant to make a profit on every continent."

And he did, but most of it was made on the continent of his home out of his headquarters in the old Tenderloin section of Manhattan, with his main office in Lindy's restaurant at Broadway and Forty-ninth Street. Rothstein is best remembered as the man who fixed the 1919 Black Sox World Series, but that was just his most stunning achievement. The Brain, as he was sometimes called, transformed organized crime by bringing to it structure and diversification. Skimming the profits from gambling houses and houses of prostitution was meat and potatoes for small-time politicians and police shakedown artists, but Rothstein understood that there were bigger coffers to tap. If the System had the early look of a corporation, what succeeded it would more closely resemble a conglomerate of diversified profit centers—if one fell below expectations, others would provide the necessary margin. Rothstein knew all the angles and had an instinct for when to play them and how. If men were ready to gamble, why trust to luck when the outcome could be arranged in advance? Chance was for suckers. Like Willie Sutton, who said he robbed banks because that's where the money was, Rothstein knew to go where the money was. He was soon a big player on Wall Street, devising techniques of swindling the uninitiated. He was also involved in labor racketeering, diamond smuggling, and, with the advent of Prohibition, bootlegging. Finally, he moved to a profit center that seemed to have no limit; he became known as the architect of the modern drug trade.

But it was not just a sense of emerging markets that distinguished Rothstein from other impresarios of crime. He was also a master of technique. If, as has often been said, he was the godfather of organized crime in America, he was, as well, its philosopher king. Working in tandem with Tammany boss Charles Murphy, Rothstein transformed Becker's System by changing the way graft was collected. Under Becker, the police were in charge of collection, with politicians standing aside, taking their cut, and manipulating the strings when necessary. But with the advent of Prohibition, the pot was too big and the stakes too high to leave matters to the police. Payoffs would be made directly to the criminals. The police would get their cut, but they were now on the bottom rung of the corporate ladder. The gangsters went to the politicians when a change in procedure was called for, the office-holders would make the needed adjustments, and the police did as they were told.

Rothstein's criminal genius was widely acknowledged, and so was his influence in the proper administration of corruption. In addition to The Brain, he was known variously as The Big Bankroll, Mr. Big, The Man Uptown, and The Fixer; those on the inside often referred to him simply as A. R. It was said that he could fix any illegal activity through his associations with government officials, the police, and, not of least significance, the criminal fraternity. At one time or another, he was the spiritual adviser of such underworld notables as Dutch Schultz, Waxey Gordon, Lucky Luciano, Meyer Lansky, and Frank Costello. He became enough of a legendary figure to serve as the model for Meyer Wolfsheim in F. Scott Fitzgerald's 1925 novel *The Great Gatsby* and some time later the inspiration for the Damon Runyon character Nathan Detroit.

The lucrative crime empire over which he presided did not, however, quench his thirst for gambling. It was his first love and his most abiding compulsion. He could bank a huge sum from a fixed World Series, but that did not deliver the charge that could only be felt by placing the bet on himself in card games that saw tens of thousands of dollars change hands quickly. In 1928, he took part in a spectacular three-day card game, from September 8 to 10 at the Park-Central Hotel in Manhattan. At the end of the marathon, Rothstein was $320,000 in the hole, an enormous figure in the twenties. The Broadway crowd, which followed the game closely, was shocked when Rothstein refused to pay, charging that the game was fixed. It turned out to be a poor decision. Two months later, on November 4, Rothstein was shot dead in a room in the same hotel. He was forty-six years old, just four years older than Becker when he was executed. The identity of the shooter remains unknown. It is still a subject of speculation and occasional discussion, much the same as the question of whether Charles Becker was actually guilty.

Helen Becker, as it turned out, never conducted the investigation that she had promised would prove her husband's innocence. No doubt relieved to be outside the scope of public scrutiny, she continued to live with her family and pursue her career in the New York City school system. She eventually retired in the forties as principal of an elementary school in Manhattan. She never remarried and died at the age of eighty-eight.

Charles Whitman found that fame was a bounty of short duration. In 1916, he was denied the Republican nomination for president. It went to another New Yorker, Associate Justice of the Supreme Court Charles Evans Hughes, who had played a more modest role in the Becker case. Whitman did win a second two-year term as governor, defeating Judge Samuel Seabury, but two years later he lost his bid for reelection to Alfred E. Smith. After spending a few years in private practice, he ran for his old office of district attorney in 1924, but he lost that race too. His last nibble at public life came in 1935 when, at the age of sixty-seven, he was appointed a commissioner of the Port Authority of New York. He died in 1947 in his room at the University Club. His grandson, John Russell Whitman, later married Christine Todd, who served as governor of New Jersey from 1994 to 2001.

The attorneys who represented Becker went on to distinguish themselves, though not always in favorable circumstances. John McIntyre was named to the State Supreme Court bench in 1916. W. Bourke Cockran, already on in years during Becker's trial and appeal, continued to represent unpopular clients in unpopular causes until his death in 1923. His funeral was attended by four U.S. senators, thirteen congressmen, and two governors, including Al Smith, whom he had nominated for president at the Democratic convention in 1920.

Most of the headlines made by Becker-case alumni belonged to Martin Manton. His career took off within a year of Becker's execution, when he was named to the Federal District Court. Less than two years later, he was escalated to the U.S. Court of Appeals for the Second Circuit. Centered in Washington, D.C., it was considered second only to the U.S. Supreme Court in importance. However, things ended badly for Justice Manton. Having become senior member of the court after some twenty years of service, he was accused of corrupting his office by "running a mill for the sale of justice." He resigned from the bench, was convicted of fraud, and served nearly two years in prison. An expose of Manton's fraudulent activities earned S. Burton Heath, of the *New York World-Telegram,* the 1940 Pulitzer Prize for reporting.

Samuel Seabury relinquished his seat on the Court of Appeals to accept the Democratic Party's nomination for governor in 1916. He ran without the support of the Tammany Hall political machine and was defeated by Whitman. Seabury earned a measure of revenge in 1930 when, at the request of the appellate division of the New York court system, he led an investigation into state and city corruption as head of what became known as the Seabury Commission. The inquiry, which dealt a near-fatal blow to Tammany Hall, confirmed charges that Mayor Walker had been accepting bribes from businessmen seeking municipal contracts. Walker resigned, and Seabury joined the administration of Mayor Fiorello LaGuardia, serving as his political adviser.

He died in 1958 at the age of eighty-five. A playground bearing his name is located at the P. S. 198 elementary school on East Ninety-sixth Street in Manhattan.

Herbert Bayard Swope, the *New York World* reporter and self-proclaimed producer and director of the Becker case for the district attorney's office, moved on from there to attain great wealth and national prominence. He was awarded the first Pulitzer Prize for reporting in 1917 for a series of articles entitled "Inside the German Empire." After a brief term as city editor of the *World* he was named its executive editor in 1920. But his most notable achievements came after he left the newspaper. He served as a consultant to the U.S. Secretary of War and a member of the American Atomic Energy Delegation to the United Nations. As a ghost writer for Bernard Baruch, he is credited with having coined the phrase "Cold War."

Three of the four informers lived out their lives in benign obscurity. Bridgey Webber went on working for the Garfield Paper Box Company in Passaic, New Jersey. Sam Schepps gave up his Seventh Avenue jewelry store and moved into the antique furniture business. Harry Vallon, who lived in Brooklyn, managed to drop out of sight entirely. None of them ever again spoke publicly of the Becker-Rosenthal case.

Jack Rose remained at the fringe of public awareness. He eventually abandoned evangelism and the theater, and opened a successful catering business on Long Island. Along the way, he gave his name to a cocktail of his own creation. It consisted of applejack, grenadine, and lime juice; it did not survive Prohibition. Unlike his co-conspirators, Rose maintained something of a presence on Broadway.

Decades later, a steakhouse bearing his name opened at the corner of Eighth Avenue and Forty-seventh Street, just blocks from the old Metropole. With its smooth, dark wood floors and brown leather booths, it evoked the feel of an old-time chop house where large doses of beef and jug-sized drinks were taken in relative leisure, and the sound of one's voice was unmolested by rap rants and the screeching of cell phones. It was redolent of an era long past and mostly forgotten. Now that is gone too. It was replaced by a Bennigan's, a franchised watering hole lit by sizzle and splash where time seems to have no point of reference. On a visit early in 2006, it was clear that all connections to the past had been severed. No one at the bar knew they were trolling through an area once known in infamy as the Tenderloin. Only a few had ever heard of Tammany Hall. And no one, absolutely no one, recognized the names of Bald Jack Rose or Herman "Beansie" Rosenthal or Police Lieutenant Charles Becker.

BIBLIOGRAPHY

BOOKS

Burns, Ric, James Sanders, and Lisa Ades. *New York, An Illustrated History*, New York: Knopf, 1999.

Chase, James. *1912: Wilson, Roosevelt, Taft & Debs—The Election That Changed the Country*, New York: Simon & Schuster, 2004.

Ellis, Edward Robb. *The Epic of New York City*, New York: Coward McCann, 1966.

Guilds' Committee for Federal Writers' Publications, New York: Random House, 1939.

Jackson, Kenneth T., and David S. Dunbar. *Empire City: New York Through the Centuries*, New York: Columbia University Press, 2002.

Kisseloff, Jeff. *You Must Remember This: An Oral History of Manhattan from the 1890's to World War II*, San Diego: Harcourt Brace Jovanovich, 1989.

Kroessler, Jeffrey A. *New York Year by Year: A Chronology of the Great Metropolis*, New York: New York University Press, 2002.

Lardner, James, and Thomas Repetto. *NYPD: A City and Its Police*, New York: Henry Holt & Co., 2000.

Logan, Andy. *Against the Evidence: The Becker-Rosenthal Affair*, New York: The McCall Publishing Company, 1970.

Pietrusza, David. *Rothstein: The Life, Times, and Murder of the Criminal Genius Who Fixed the 1919 World Series*, New York: Carroll & Graf Publishers, 2003.

Root, Thomas. *One Night in July: The True Story of the Rosenthal-Becker Murder Case . . . A Crime That Rocked the City of New York and the Nation*, New York: Coward-McCann, Inc., 1961.

Trager, James. *The People's Chronology*, New York: Henry Holt, 1992.

ARTICLES

" 'Beansy' and Becker." *Court TV's Crime Library;* http://www.crimelibrary. Com/gangsters_outlaws/mob_bosses/rothstein/becker_5.html?sect= . . . , January 4, 2005.

BIBLIOGRAPHY

Lt. Charles Becker & Ron Arons' "Jews of Sing Sing" Lecture, New York Correction History Society: http://www.correctionhistory.org/singsing/ronarons jewsofsingsing/derby.html.

Benfey, Christopher. "The Newsmaker." *Columbia Journalism Review.* January/February 1993, from *The Double Life of Stephen Crane,* by Christopher Benfey, New York: Alfred A. Knopf.

Berger, Meyer. "The Becker Case—View of the System." *New York Times Magazine,* November 11, 1951.

Bovsun, Mara. "To Catch a Crooked Cop." *New York Daily News,* June 27, 2004. http://nydailynews.com/news/crime_file/v-pfriendly/story/ 206462p-178168c.html.

Bryk, William. "The Primitive American," *New York Press,* December 21, 2000. www.nypress.com/print.cfm?content_id=3307.

"Cockran, William Bourke (1854–1923)—Biographical Information." http://bioguide.congress.gov/scripts/biodisplay.pl?index=C000575.

"Condemned." *Court TV's Crime Library—The Electric Chair.* http://crime library.com/notorious_murders/not_guilty/chair/5.html.

"The Cop and the Corpse." *Old And Sold, Antiques Auction & Marketplace.* http://oldand-sold.com/articles01/article 929.shtml.

"Corner of Second Avenue and East 13th Street;http://members.tripod.com/Fighting9th/History13.htm.

Gado, Mark. "Killer Cop: Charles Becker." *Court TV's Crime Library.* www.crimelibrary.com/gangsters_outlaws/cops_others/becker/1.html?sect=18, April 18, 2003.

"Goff, John. Information From Answers.com." www.answers.com.

Grimes, William. "Where to Take Your Gambling Spirit." *New York Times,* Wednesday, August 2, 2000.

"The History of Sing Sing Prison." *Half Moon Press.* www. hudson river.com/halfmoonpress/stories/0500sing.htm.

"The Hit." http://3.ftss.ilstu.edu/cjhistory/casestud/hit.html.

Hunter, Evan. "For Beansie, The Short Goodbye." *New York Times,* January 25, 1998.

"Mitchel, John Purroy." *The Free Dictionary by Farlex;* http://encyclopedia.Thefreedictionary.com/John%20Purroy%20Mitchell.

Mitgang, Herbert. "The Man Who Rode the Tiger: The Life and Times of Judge Samuel Seabury," provided by Fordham University Press through Google Book Search.

"NYC DOC Mini-History: 1860s–1940s." www.correctionhistory.org/html/chronic/1946rpt/1946rpt.html.

"Rothstein, Arnold (1882–1928) Criminal Mastermind." *Seize the Night.* http://www.carpenoctem.tv/mafia/rothstein.html.

"Samuel Seabury Playground." http://www.nycgovparks.org/sub_your_park/historical_signs/hs_historical_sign.php?id=73 . . .

Slezak, Patty (compiler). "Key Figures in Jefferson Market History." Compiled summer 2000. http://wotlan.liu.edu/-amatsuuchi/timeline/key_figures.html.

Thornton, Robert M. "William Jay Gaynor: Libertarian Mayor of New York." *Liberty Haven.* www.libertyhaven.com/theoreticalphilosphicalissues/libertarianism/libertarianma . . .

"The Upper East Side Book." www.thecityreview.com/ues/madison/ lauren.html.

"World Events for 1912." http://us.imdb.com/Sections/Years/1912/world-events.

"Zelig, Big Jack." www.mobsters8m.com/eastmans.

SOURCE NOTES

The Becker-Rosenthal affair, as it was sometimes called, gripped the attention of New York City, and much of America, in 1912 and held it for the better part of three years. During that time it was front-page news in most of the city's dozen-plus daily newspapers. However, the prominence given the story is less a gauge of the significance it was accorded than the extent of the coverage. The two papers that covered it most thoroughly—*The New York Times* and the *New York World*—devoted page after page to its every detail. On some occasions, the Becker story occupied three or four pages of an edition with a total folio of only eighteen to twenty-four pages. By contrast, in the spring of 2006, the conviction of two New York City detectives—the so-called "Mafia Cops"—for eight murders barely made it to page one of the *Times,* and inside coverage amounted to just half a page in an edition with seven separate sections totaling well over one hundred pages.

Over the years, the Becker case has been reprised periodically in books, magazine and newspaper articles, and in recent years on numerous Internet sites, but it has not been fully told in more than thirty years. In fashioning my own interpretation of events, I have tapped into many sources, as indicated by my bibliography. For the chronology of events, I have relied chiefly on the daily accounts in the *Times.* I began by reading both the *World* and the *Times,* but as I proceeded it appeared to me that the *Times* reports were more reliable and far more objective. Both papers editorially expressed the belief that Becker was guilty and supported his execution, but the disposition of the *World* seemed to infiltrate its news coverage while the *Times* reported the day's events independent of the paper's official views of the case.

Inevitably, I noted discrepancies between newspaper reports and accounts in secondary sources, such as books and articles as well as among the secondary sources themselves. There were inconsistencies in the description of the murder that opens the book, and even such basic items as dates and names varied from one source to another. I checked verifiable facts as closely as possible and resolved other differences sometimes by consensus, at other times by adopting the version of events that seemed most felicitous to the context of the story.

I used secondary sources mainly for background and for brief profiles of some of the characters. These details also varied from one account to another, and my description of background events and personalities are usually a composite of sketches taken from several places. I have endeavored to credit every source I made use of chapter-for-chapter. In some instances, however, where I may have used half a dozen or more sources, I list only those from which I directly derived the material I used; to wit, if a source produced no new information from the one I relied on I did not note it specifically. Where there was only a single source for an item, I cited it in the text and attributed it to the author. For the sake of expedience, I have identified each source by author, title, or the name of the website rather than including the entire reference which, in every instance, is listed in the bibliography.

Prologue: For the account of the murder, in addition to the *Times* and the *World,* I used "For Beansie, the Short Goodbye," (Hunter); "Killer Cop," (Gado); *One Night in July* (Root); and *Against the Evidence* (Logan). The profile of Rosenthal was drawn from *NYPD* (Lardner & Repetto), Logan, Root, and "The Hit." The relationship between Swope and Whitman was adapted chiefly from Logan. For the short profile of Becker I relied on the *Times,* Gado, Logan, Root, and "Jews of Sing Sing Lecture," Lt. Charles Becker and Ron Arons.

Chapter 1: For color and history of New York City at the turn of the century, the waves of immigration, its gangs and turf wars, I relied on *New York, an Illustrated History* (Burns, Sanders, and Ades); *The People's Chronology* (Trager);

The Epic of New York City (Ellis); *The Hit;* Gado; Logan; Root; and *The Whyos,* http://www.geocities.com/nycfacts/crime/gangs/html. The material on Tammany Hall came chiefly from USHistory.com. and Ellis. Background on Becker was drawn from the *Times; Rothstein* (Pietrusza); *NYPD* (Lardner and Repetto); Gado, Logan, and Root. Biographical material on Monk Eastman came mainly from *You Must Remember This* (Kisseloff) and "Gangs of New York, www.bklyn-genealogy-info.com/Society/ Gangs.NYC.html. Background on Big Tim Sullivan was derived from *The Tenement Encyclopedia/Tenement Museum,* www.tenement.org/encyclopedia/irish_tammany.htm; the *Times;* Pietrusza; Logan; Root; Lardner & Repetto; and *The Hit.* The Stephen Crane/Dora Clark incident was informed by "Columbia Journalism Review" excerpt from *The Double Life of Stephen Crane* (Benfey) and Logan.

Chapter 2: The early investigations by the Rev. Parkhurst and the Lexow Committee drew from Lardner & Repetto; Logan; and Root. The Helen Becker material was supplied chiefly by Logan. Background information on Gaynor came mainly from Ellis; *William Jay Gaynor: Libertarian Mayor of New York* (Thornton); and *The Primitive American* (Bryk). Waldo's profile was derived from Ellis; Bryk; Logan; Root; and Lardner & Repetto.

Chapter 3: The history of the police commissioner's office was drawn from Lardner & Repetto. Zelig's profile came from the *Times;* http://www.mobsters.8m. com/cgi-bin/ad/inline?page=eastmans.htm; http://members.tripod.com/Fighting 9th/ History13.htm; Root; and Logan. The sketch of Rose is taken from *The Cop and the Corpse;* Logan; Root; the *Times;* Gado; and "List of historical gang members of New York City, www.answers.com/topic/list-of-historical-gang-members-of-new-york-city; Rosenthal's background, his involvement with the Hesper Club, and early activities were provided by the *World;* the *Times;* Bovsun; Gado; *The Hit;* Logan; and Root.

Chapter 4: Rosenthal's affidavit came from the *World* and the *Times.* The Swope biography from Logan; Pietrusza; Root; Wikipedia; and Encyclopedia Britannica Online. Whitman profile from Lardner & Repetto; Ellis; *The Hit;* Logan; Root; and Charles S. Whitman Papers 1868–1947, Rare Book and Manuscript Library, /archives/collections/html.

Chapter 5: The chronology of events comes from the *Times* and the *World*. The description of the station house was drawn largely from Logan. Other background details and descriptions were informed by Root and Lardner & Repetto.

Chapter 6: From this point on, the events described have been culled almost exclusively from the *Times*. Here and there, a few background details were added from sources already mentioned. Information that is derived from a source outside the scope of the daily narrative will be specifically cited.

Chapter 7: The description of the Tombs comes from "NYC DOC Mini-History: 1860a-1940s," http://www.correctionhistory.prg/htm/chronicl/1946rpt.html.

Chapter 8: News events of 1912 come from Trager; Kroessler; and "World Events for 1912," http://us.imdb.com/Sections/Years/1912/world-events.

Chapter 9: The details of Helen Becker's visits to the Tombs was drawn chiefly from Root.

Chapter 10: The background on Judge Goff was informed by "John Goff": Information From Answers.com.

Chapters 11–18: The trial of Becker, which lasted nineteen days, was covered by the *Times* in great detail. Its daily reports sometimes occupied three-to-four pages, including large sections reprinted from the trial transcript. I relied mainly on these to reconstruct the trial. In Chapter 15, details of the shooting of Teddy Roosevelt were gleaned from *1912* (Chase).

Chapter 19: The historical description of Sing Sing Prison comes from "The History of Sing Sing Prison—by the Half Moon Press," http://www.hudsonriver.com/halfmoonpress/stories/0500sing.htm. The material on the electric chair is taken from "The History of the Electric Chair," www.ccadp.org/electricchair.htm.

Chapter 20: The trial of the four gunmen also was covered fully by the *Times,* from which my account is culled.

Chapter 21: The 1913 news events came "World Events for 1913;" Trager; and Kroessler. In addition to the *Times,* Logan, Pietrusza, and Lardner & Repetto provided material on Big Tim Sullivan's illness and death.

Chapter 23: Background information on W. Bourke Cockran is from "Cockran, William Bourke (1854–1923)," http://bioguide.congress.gov/scripts/biodisplay.pl?=COOO575; "William Bourke Cockran," http://homepage.tinet.ie/-jasbourke_cockran.html; and Logan. The execution of William Kemmler and the dispute with Thomas Edison is derived from http://crimelibrary.com/notorious_murders/not_guilty/chair/5.html. Biographical information on Samuel Seabury is drawn from *The Man Who Rode the Tiger: The Life and Times of Judge Samuel Seabury,* by Herbert Mitgang, provided by Fordham University Press through the Google Book Partner Program.

Chapters 24–25: Becker's second trial was covered in almost as much detail as the first; my account was adapted almost exclusively from the daily reports in the *Times.*

Chapter 26: News of the 1914 election was drawn from daily news reports and embellished by bits of information from Logan.

Chapter 27: Part of the account of Helen Becker's visit with Whitman and her trip to Sing Sing were drawn from Root.

Epilogue: The story of Rothstein awaiting Becker's execution is told by Logan, Root, and Pietrusza. Another source of background information on Rothstein, in addition to Piertrusza, was "Seize the Night: Arnold Rothstein (1882–1928) Criminal Mastermind." http://www.carpenoctem.tv/mafia/rothstein.html. Helen Becker's life after the execution was informed chiefly by Logan. The summary of Whitman's future career came from the *Times* and Root. Manton's rise and fall was described in "Murder, Inc.," by Mark Gribben, http://www.

crimelibraary.com/Gangsters_outlaws/gang/inc/7.html and "The Pulitzer Prizes for 1940," http://www.pulitzer.org/cgi-bin/year.pl?523,24. Seabury's professional career was drawn from Mitgang and "Samuel Seabury Playground," http://www.nycgovparks.org/sub_your_park/historical_sings/hs_historical_sign.php?id=73. Swope's subsequent activities came from "The Pulitzer Prizes for 1917;" Logan; and Pietrusza. Rose's future as caterer and the information about the steak house named for him is from "Where To Take Your Gambling Spirit," William Grimes, *The New York Times,* Wednesday, August 2, 2000, and from personal visits.

ACKNOWLEDGMENTS

Writers of nonfiction who do without the luxury of a staff of researchers are grateful for whatever help they are given, and I wish to offer my thanks to those who were generous with their time and effort.

The Internet has transformed the process of research, putting much of the information we need at our fingertips, but it has not replaced the library as a source of background and historical context. The chief asset of the library, of course, are the librarians who seem to know where to find whatever is needed and are ever eager to provide it. Of particular help to me was Sally Pellegrini, of the New City (NY) library, whose thoughtful generosity saved me countless hours of wading through tides of material and guided me directly to the source. The dedicated ladies at my local Tomkins Cove (NY) library were also of great assistance as were the microfilm specialists at the New York City Public Library. Sylvia Falk, though not a librarian, offered significant aid in helping me to navigate my way through the system.

The staff of Carroll & Graf is always a pleasure to work with. Herman Graf helped me to shape the book and set it on the right path. Keith Wallman edited the manuscript with care and discernment and, together with his art staff, performed wonders in locating the photographs that accompany the text. Jay Boggis was scrupulously precise as copyeditor. A nod of gratitude also is owed to my agent, Peter Sawyer, who supported the project from its inception.

ACKNOWLEDGMENTS

A great deal of the hard research—locating specific information on the Internet and running down news stories and editorials in periodicals nearly one hundred years old—was done by my chief research assistant, my wife Betty, ably assisted this time by our granddaughter Jessica.

And I tip my hat, too, to all those who came to the story before me whose insights into the events often proved instructive.

INDEX

ABOUT THE AUTHOR

Stanley Cohen, a veteran award-winning newspaper and magazine journalist, is the author of *The Wrong Men*, *The Man in the Crowd*, *A Magic Summer: The '69 Mets*, and *The Game They Played*, a *Sports Illustrated* Top 100 Sports Book of All Time. He has taught writing, journalism, and philosophy at Hunter College and New York University. He lives in Tomkins Cove, New York.